Hedging Strategies in Indian SMEs and Non-Financial Firms: A Study of Forex Risk Management

Rishabh Patel

ABSTRACT

The volatility in foreign exchange risk is influenced by change in economic performance of various economies in terms of their GDP, inflation rate, fiscal deficit, employment rate, position in world trade etc. The business firms having international operations are directly affected by change in currency exchange rate. The currency risk or Forex risk is understood as possible loss to payment of international transactions due to unfavorable exchange rates. Ideally, companies of all sizes (small, medium and big) are equally affected by Forex rate fluctuations. But there is diversity in this opinion too. Likewise, Yeo and Lai (2004) stated in their research that SMEs having international exposure are more exposed to foreign exchange risk in comparison to large sized firms. While Doidge, Griffin, & Williamson (2002) argued that the Forex risk exposure of SMEs is less in comparison to large firms. The Forex risk exposure may vary from country to country and also vary for specific types of firms, i.e., small, medium and large.

The study by Dolde (1993) stated that the small firms are more concerned about cost of risk management while the approach of large firms for hedging their risk was not similar to small firms. Due to cost of risk management, small firms were found completely ignoring the derivative instruments for hedging purpose. The top 100 Finnish non-financial firms were considered for a survey on interest rate risk management by Hakkarainen et al. (1997). Bondar et al. (1995) contributed a lot on the issue. Their study clearly indicated that there was lack of awareness among firms to use derivatives for hedging strategies.Several studies have employed the questionnaire approach for the analyzing the exchange-rate exposure management in context to non-financial firms (e.g. Bodnar and Gebhardt, 1999; Hakkarainen et al.,

1998; Bodnar et al., 1998; Marshall, 2000; Ceuster et al., 2000; Mallin et al., 2001). The most referred study is Bodnar et al. (1998), which considered publicly traded U.S. firms. Export is an important constituent in determining the exchange rate exposure of a firm has been established by various theoretical (Marston, 2001) and empirical studies (Allayannis and Ofek, 2001). Allayannis and Weston (2001) come across an affirmative relation between the use of foreign exchange derivatives and firm's value. There are numerous theories that recommend why it may be most favorable for a firm to hedge (Stulz, 1984; Smith and Stulz, 1985; Froot*et al.*, 1993; DeMarzo and Duffie, 1995).The past evidences on the related issue have clearly indicated that large corporate having forex risk exposure are proactive to hedge against such an exposure. They have clear guidelines and experienced and trained team to decide the hedging strategy for them. But when it comes to small and medium enterprises and unlisted firms, no such evidences are available deliberating about the forex risk management by these firms across the world in general and specifically in context to India. Envisaging the research gap through literature survey, the study under consideration has intended to achieve three objectives, i.e., (i) to study the Forex Risk Exposure of SMEs and Unlisted Non-Financial Firms in India, (ii) to study the Forex Risk Exposure Management by SMEs and Unlisted Non-Financial Firms in India, and (iii) to study the determinants of Forex Risk Hedging Strategies by SMEs and Unlisted Non-Financial Firms in India. The study under consideration is both exploratory and descriptive in nature. The evidences obtained through current research have shown that the SMEs and unlisted non-financial firms in India are not fully aware about its measurement and management. In addition to this, the findings of the study have also identified several important determinants of a forex risk hedging strategies. It has also recognized various factors to improvise the forex risk hedging strategies by SMEs and unlisted non-financial firms. The findings of the study have both practical and theoretical implications. The SMEs, unlisted non-financial firms, government and regulators and academia etc. are the different stakeholders who can be benefitted by the findings and suggestions of the study. Also, the present study has contributed to the existing literature and theory by suggesting determinants of forex risk hedging strategies, determinants of improvisation of forex risk hedging strategy and criterian for hierarchy of various determinants.

CONTENTS

List of Tables

List of Figures

ABBREVIATIONS

AHP – Analytic Hierarchy Process

ANP – Analytic Network Process

CAGR – Compounder Annual Growth Rate

CGTF – Credit Guarantee Trust Fund Scheme

CLCSS – Credit Linked Capital Subsidy

CPI – Consumer Price Index

CR – Consistency Ratio

DMIC – Domestic Market Macro Indicators

EEFC – Exchange Earners Foreign Currency Account

EFA – Explanatory Factor Analysis

ETC – Exchange the Counter

FCD – Foreign Currency Derivatives

FGEMI – Foreign/Global Economy's Macro Indicators

FMS – Foreign Market Scenario

Forex – Foreign Exchange

FRHS – Foreign Risk Hedging Instruments

FSI – Firm Specific Indicators

GDP – Gross Domestic Product

GLS – Generalized Least Square

GMM – Generalized Method of Moments

HK – Hongkong

KMO – Kaiser-Meyer-Olkin

LPG – Liberalization, Privatization and Globalization

MCA – Ministry of Corporate Affairs

MCDM – Multi Criteria Decision Making

MNC – Multi National Corporation

MSMEs - Micro, Small and Medium Enterprises

OLS – Ordinary Least Squares

OTC – Over the Counter

P&L – Profit & Loss

PV – Priority Vector

R&D – Research & Developments

RGUMY – Rajiv Gandhi Udyami Mitra Yojana

S&P – Standard & Poor

SEC – Securities Exchange Commission

SIDBI – Small Industries and Development Bank of India

SMCs – Small and Medium Sized Companies

SMEs – Small and Medium Enterprises

SPI – Sharpe Performance Index

TSE – Tokyo Stock Exchange

Chapter 1

Introduction and Background of Study

Since the beginning of era of LPG reforms (1990s) in India, there is a continuous increase in the currency risk of companies in India having any foreign operations, both exports and imports. The volatility in foreign exchange risk is influenced by change in economic performance of various economies in terms of their GDP, inflation rate, fiscal deficit, employment rate, position in world trade etc. The business firms having international operations are directly affected by change in currency exchange rate. According to Apte (2006) "Foreign exchange / Currency exposure is the sensitivity of changes in the real domestic currency value of assets, liabilities or operating income to unpredicted/unanticipatedchanges in exchange rates". The currency risk or Forex risk is understood as possible loss to payment of international transactions due to unfavorable exchange rates. Ideally, companies of all sizes (small, medium and big) are equally affected by Forex rate fluctuations. But there is diversity in this opinion too. Likewise, Yeo and Lai (2004) stated in their research that SMEs having international exposure are more exposed to foreign exchange risk in comparison to large sized firms. While Doidge, Griffin, & Williamson (2002) argued that the Forex risk exposure of SMEs is less in comparison to large firms. The Forex risk exposure may vary from country to country and also vary for specific types of firms, i.e., small, medium and large.

In a study based on Indian companies by Yadav & Jain (2000), a sample of forty four companies was taken and these companies were exposed to Forex risk due to international operations. The findings of the study indicated that 30 percent of the companies hedge their exposure and some steps are taken by all companies to manage their international business.

Therefore measuring Forex risk exposure is important to contribute to existing literature. Once the firms came to know about their foreign exchange risk exposure, its management is the next critical part of managers. The management of Forex risk exposure has been dealt with different strategies. Generally managing this Forex risk is called as hedging (Smith & Stulz, 1985; Stulz, 1984). Batten, Mellor & Wan (1993) investigated upon the foreign exchange risk management practices being followed by large number of firms in Australia. The study is based on the sample size of 72 firms operating in Australia considering the physical products such as spot, forwards, options and short-term and long-term physical swaps. Pramborg (2004) made a comparison between the hedging practices exercised in Swedish and Korean non-financial firms. It was identified that companies in both the countries were hedging currency risk for different objectives, the Korean firms mainly focused on reducing cash flow fluctuations, whereas the Swedish firms more commonly aimed at reducing fluctuations of accounting numbers.

In the words of Modigliani & Miller (1958), there will be no effect of hedging on the value of a firm if there are no imperfections. Nevertheless, there are various market imperfections which are being identified by corporate risk-management theory which can make volatility costly. Broadly, these imperfections are categorized under five main headings and these are: (i) Financial Distress Costs (Smith & Stulz, 1985; Myers, 1977); (ii) Cost associated in managing risk aversion (Smith & Stulz, 1985; Stulz, 1984) (iii) Taxes (Leland, 1998; Stulz, 1996; Smith & Stulz, 1985) and (iv) Expensive External Financing (Froot et al., 1993). There is a general consensus among the risk-management theorist that there is increase in the value of a firm with the use of hedging instrument, but there is lack of consensus among them regarding the type of firm, that is, small, medium or large, benefit more or less. The volatility of the cash flows need to be hedged in order to manage the risk associated with the expensive external financing

(Froot et al., 1993). Apart from this, another motive of hedging is the minimization of volatility in the income which is taxable as it can result in the reduction of potential taxes of firms (Smith &Stulz, 1985). Furthermore, with the help of hedging this decreased volatility in cash-flow can also results in higher tax benefits and more debt capacity of the firm (Leland, 1998; Stulz, 1996; Graham & Rogers, 2002).

Theoretical Framework of Risk Management

Risk

There has been a lack of consensus amongst the researchers regarding the definition of risk and it subsequently resulted in various definitions which includes the occurrence of an event different from expected event, dispersion of actual from expected results, uncertainty, and possibility of loss or chance of loss (Vaughan & Vaughan, 2007; Elliott & Vaughan, 1972). When it comes in context of organizational goals then uncertainty in the accomplishment of end objectives is known as risk (McNamee, 1997); whereas in the context of statistics and financial aspect when there is disparities in the expected results over a period of time then it is known as risk (Kallman, 2005). It means that one can measure the magnitude of risk by analyzing its standard deviation or variance. In the words of Slovic& Peters (2006), "Risk can be defined as perceptions of an individual which is enacted as feelings which is further analyzed by individual". The formal part of the definition is related with the intuitive and instinctive responses to a threat whereas the latter part of the definition is associated with the deliberation, reason and logic in respect of decision making and assessment. Hansson (2008) has categorized the risk into five major parts which are:

1. A factual concept in whicha decision is taken up by individual when they know the probabilities of happening of an event under some conditions.

2. A statistical assumed value of an undesirable happening, which may or may not occur.

·3. A probability of an undesirable occurrence, which may or may not happen.

4. A cause of an undesirable incident, which may or may not occur.

5. An undesirable incident which may or may not arise.

Holton (2004) has defined the risk as under:

"Situations may appear disparate, but they share common elements. First people care about the outcomes. If someone has a personal interest in what transpires, that person is exposed. Second, people don't know what will happen. In each situation, the outcome is uncertain. (...) Risk, then, is exposure to a proposition of which one is uncertain" (Holton, 2004, p. 22).

Being thoughtful to above definition, it is important to understand the different categories of risks associated in case of international business before heading towards the main issue of this article. Broadly there are five categories of international business risk.

1. **Product Risk:** The product risk arise due to the commitment of one the partners in the transaction through sales contract. This type of risk is related to the nature of product, viz., and operational quality of product, performance or services related to product or maintenance. As per the conditions mentioned in the contract, either exporter or importer is responsible for such factors. In case of international business, many times the product risk occurs due to difference in the environment of other country, lack of continuous maintenance due to humid weather conditions or rust damage due to climate change etc. Similarly some additional product risk may arise due to direct payment conditions which are correlated to products, viz., and delay in installment time period by the buyer when exporter gets paid for such services, or transportation risk may also add to product risk where the physical delivery of the product plays the most significant role in whole transaction.

2. **Commercial Risk:** The commercial risk is associated with the inability to make payment by the private sector buyer or non-sovereign buyer in their domestic currency due to incidences like default, bankruptcy/ insolvency or inability of buyer to take up the goods which have been sent bestowing to the contract of supply. It may also arise because of insolvency of a private supplier too in case it is connected with pre-financing operations. In nutshell, commercial risk can be because of insolvency of counterpart (failure of delivery of product or payment of product) not fulfilling their contractual duty because of financial reasons even contractual requirement is fulfilled in first case.

3. **Political Risk:** The scope of political risk is quite extensive when we talk about international business. It consists of firm-specific risk, global-specific risks &country specific risks. As name suggests, the firm-specific risk is micro risk and has a corporate level affect or specific to a project. Such type of risk is observable when there is a conflict in the governance practices of an international company or MNC and its host country. The country specific risks are macro in nature which has origin at country level but may affect the corporate level projects too. Generally transfer risk and cultural or institutional risk come under this category. Transfer risk is associated with restrictions on transfer of funds from or into host country and cultural/institution risk is related to factors like, shared ownership, corruption and nepotism in host country, requirement to employ citizens of host country or any other requirement of host country to protect specific industry etc. And the global specific risk factors are more uncertain because these are related to major factors like cyber-attacks, terrorism and war or other environmental concerns etc.

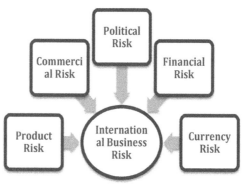

Figure 1: *Types of International Business Risk*

4. **Financial Risk:** Generally the risk factors like the balance of trade, the current account balance, inflation risk and interest rate risk affect the financial risk in international business. These risk factors have an impact on both firm levels, i.e., micro level and global level, i.e., macro level, transactions. It can be easily said that these factors are beyond the control of company/firm as major policy framework for these types of risks is developed by the governments only through monetary policy, fiscal policy or various trade policies

5. **Currency Risk:** And last but know as continuous present category of business risk, i.e., currency risk. It occurs due to volatility of the current exchange rate. The currency exchange risk has great impact on the overall well-being of an economy as it affects the overall composition of output and consumption of a country. It also affects the investing patterns of non-residents of the country. The fluctuations in currency exchange rate might result in profitable or unprofitable transaction since it can reduce the profits if the exchange rate is diverted in the wrong direction.

The present system of settling business transactions in a floating exchange rate system has made currency risk a more significant factor of international business risk. It has become a gamble for the players in international business as exchange rate may appreciate or depreciate. Other risks go hand in hand with currency risk or Forex risk. For example, the market risk is helpful in determining the variation in return on investment therefore it is mandatory to assess the currency risk in a better way to determine the returns on investors in their base currency.

In the midst of all these categories of risk, the currency risk has great economic impact on both large and small firm. It seems to be a global or macro level risk but the impact of currency risk affects the company's business and transaction directly. It has a direct impact on the receivables and payables of the company which affect the financial results. In other words, Forex rate fluctuations affect the settlement of contracts resulting into variation in cash flows of the firm and ultimately the overall valuation is affected. Therefore it is mandatory for the companies having any kind of Forex risk exposure to manage such risk carefully. A company can be affected by currency risk or Forex risk directly or indirectly. When a company is exporting or importing in foreign currencies, any foreign debts or investments or a company has foreign branches or subsidiaries then it is directly exposed to foreign risk. But under some situations, the companies get exposed to Forex risk if the cost structure of their competitor is affected by Forex rate or the price of product in which they are dealing is affected by Forex rate then there is an indirect exposure of Forex risk to such companies. Sometimes the Forex risk or currency risk is directly noticeable while in other cases it is difficult to notice and the impact of risk is noticed at a later stage. Conventionally, the foreign risk exposure or currency risk is categorized on the basis of three factors.

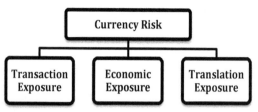

Figure 2: *Types of Currency Risk Exposure*

Transaction exposure is explained as the amount of sensitivity associated with the realization of local currency values of the firm's contractual cash flows denominated in foreign currencies to unexpected exchange rate changes.

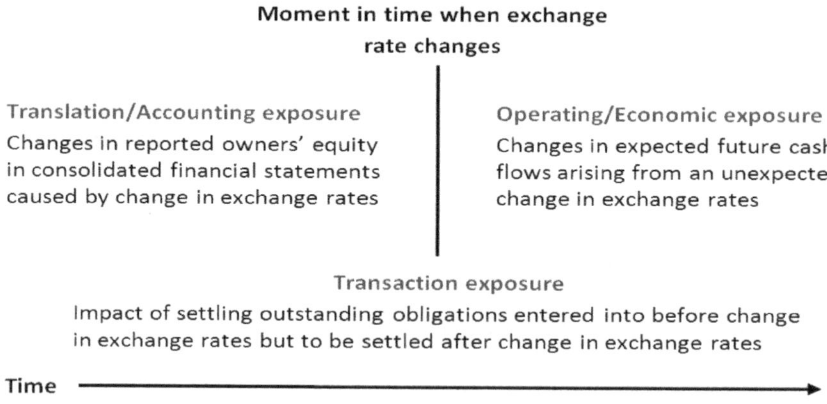

Moment in time when exchange rate changes

Translation/Accounting exposure
Changes in reported owners' equity
in consolidated financial statements
caused by change in exchange rates

Operating/Economic exposure
Changes in expected future cash
flows arising from an unexpected
change in exchange rates

Transaction exposure
Impact of settling outstanding obligations entered into before change
in exchange rates but to be settled after change in exchange rates

Time

Figure 3: *Conceptual comparison of transaction, economic, and translation exposure.*

Source: Etteman, Stonehill and Moffett (2004).

Economic Exposure: It can be understood as operating exposure which measures the variation in the present value of a company consequential to fluctuations in future operating cash flows which is the result of unanticipated alteration in currency exchange rates.

Translation exposure: Itis also called as accounting exposure that impacts the consolidated financial statements. It's a potential risk for ahike or decline in the parent's net worth and reported net income which is causeddue to exchange rate fluctuation since the last translation.

Transaction Exposure: It is concerned with cash flows and influences the items set out in the P&L account, before the alteration in currency exchange rate.

Understanding Forex Risk and Forex Risk Management

Forex Risk

Despite the fact that the perceptions of risk varies from individual to individual, foreign exchange (Forex) risk is the risk of loss that may arise to an entity due to currency exchange fluctuation in which an entity have an exposure. Forex risk, are also known as "currency risk, forex rate risk, or simply exchange risk" which is related with unexpected fluctuations in forex rates (Bartram, Dufey, &Frenkel, 2005). Now that exposure can be either Transaction Exposure due to involvement of different countries' currency denominations or it can be an Economic or Accounting Exposure as per the relevant rules or regulations of Accounting Standards or Regulations applicable in any country. Entity of any country can face both International as well as economic exposure due to the fluctuation in the Domestic Currency which ideally impact competition that an entity is facing.

Foreign Exchange Market

It is the market wherein the firms or individuals or banks engage in buying and selling the foreign currencies or deal in foreign exchange. This market basically facilitates the transfer of PP from one currency to another currency. This is necessary because in case of international trade or transactions it usually involves parties living in different countries would want the trade or transaction to be settled in their own national currency. For e.g. In case of an Indian exporter who is exporting goods to United States would invoice in US Dollars or Indian Rupees or in case of any Indian importer is importing good from United States would require Dollars to settle his payment for importing goods. So in both of the cases Foreign Exchange will happen. Now the question arises what is the need for firms or banks or individuals to exchange one individual currency with another country currency? The answer to this question is demand and supply of the currency due to international trades.

Types of Foreign Exchange Risk

- **Transaction Exposure:** The risk arises due to the fact that companies have entered into financial liability of international trade settlement and currency exchange rates are likely to change in near term.

- **Economic Exposure:** It is perceived as impact on company's cash flows and foreign earnings & investments due to foreign currency exchange rate fluctuation.

- **Translation Exposure:** The risk that companies income, assets & liabilities or equities value may change due to portion of asset, liability, income or equity is denominated in foreign currency.

- **Contingent Exposure:** It is the risk that may arise when firm is bidding for foreign projects or contracts or investments and risk of change in value of such investments/contracts/projects may or may not arise due to change in the currency exchange rates.

- **Value at Risk:** It is the risk of potential impact of exchange rates on the foreign exposure due to change in currency rates during the specific period of time.

ForexRisk Management

Frequent big events in the recent past have increased the foreign exchange fluctuations in the currency and derivatives market. Due to which volatilities in the currency pairs has increased much, which is directly agitating the Financial Interest of an Exporter and Importer as well. Both long term and short term fluctuations in exchange rates make it difficult for the exporters and importers in context to pricing decision and arranging fund flow for their business.

In the words of McNamee (1997), risk can never be managed as the property of risk is

conceptual in nature. That is, it's engaged in anticipating the uncertainties in future. According to

McNamee (1997) "Managing risk is actually managing the organization: planning, organizing,

directing, and controlling organization systems and resources to achieve objectives.

Figure 4: *Risk Management Process*

In order to manage the risk, organizations should bring the change from within and

respond accordingly with the changing environment so that organizations can response to

changed environment in an effective manner. So, organizations should focus on corrective

actions to improve their ability to handle changed environment by incorporating various

characteristics   rather than focusing on kind of risk that could affect the organization, rather

than guessing what kind of risk could affect their company (McNamee, 1997). In the same

manner Finger (1999) comprehends risk-management as "the process of recognizing

&evaluating various type of risk that a society, firm or an individual encounter either due to

environmental factor or due to their own activities which influences the amount of damages and

other kind of results associated with these risks and hence affect the actions which are being

taken by the concern parties in order to mitigate the losses and other consequence associated

with these risk so that these risks could be ministered" (Finger, 1999).There are three steps in the

management of forex risk, which is given by McNamee (1997). The first step is associated with the development of organization's objective related with the hedging, like minimizing the cash flows volatility or reducing some kind of exposure related with forex risk. The second step includes identifying the risk which is associated with the forex risk if there exist any kind of loss due to the change in the foreign exchange. After identifying and measuring the forex risk, the next thing is to prioritize the issues which need to be taken up in order to handle the changes in foreign exchange values. The third step is related with the treatment which needs to be given in order to avoid or diversify the forex risk which can be done by sharing the risk or making plans for contingencies like, investment opportunities, transaction cost, or tax liabilities.

Hedging as a Tool to Manage Forex Risk

Hedging is a preventive strategy, which is mostly utilized either by companies or by individual investors to safeguard their portfolios from the ill effects of price, interest rate, or currency movements. In general, hedging strategy is engaged in minimizing the uncertainty. Therefore, a hedger can be defined as any individual who takes protections in order to avoid any kind of risk (Leland, 1960). In order to examine the manager's choice pertaining to hedging, Smith & Stulz (1985, p. 399) defined hedging as "the attainment of financial assets that minimizes variation of the company's payments". Whereas, hedging ratio is described as percentage of an asset that is hedged by means of derivatives. Hedging is a process through which a company or an investor can counterbalance any loss or profit of initial portfolio by having an opposite position in a derivative. The ultimate aim of any hedging strategy is to have a "Seesaw Effects" wherein one effect, invalidates the another effect. For example, suppose a manufacturing company for which thread is the most vital input cost. Due to the volatility in the prices of thread worldwide, the company assumes that the prices of the raw tread will go high in future days to come. This volatility in the prices of the thread can minimize the company's profit and increase operating cost. So, with a motive to safeguard its-self from this volatility, the company may get into a future contract in thread for eight months. Therefore, if the price of thread increases by 15%, the futures contract will fix in a price with profit that will cancel the loss that company is likely to experience in it daily business operations. The point which a person should note while getting into a hedging is that, if the company goes for such type of hedging then the company is not only protecting itself from any loss (if price of thread rise by 15%), but at the same time the company is also constraining itself from getting any kind of profit (if the price of thread drops by 15%). There are two methods through which a hedger can hedge.

These are either internal hedging or external hedging. When companies do not utilize the financial instruments in order to manage the forex risk then it is known as internal hedging. On the contrary, external hedging is when a company acquires any financial instrument like, currency derivatives, whose value and characteristics are dependent upon the value and characteristics of a currency. Another categorization of hedging is currency movement hedging and interest rate hedging. When a company or individual investors is indulged in substantial borrowings then they can utilize interest rate hedging. The benefit of using this type of hedging is its ability to reduce the expenditure on borrowing by diversifying the risk of any unfavorable or expected movements in the interest rate. On the other hand, international investors or companies, who are having international portfolios, generally practice Currency movement hedging. A hedger who is using currency movement hedging strategy can minimize and manage its threat to exchange rate movement.

As proposed by (McNamee, 1997) "Risk management involve planning, organizing, directing, and controlling organization's resources &functioning in order to accomplish organizational goals". Similarly, Forex risk management can also be defined as "planning, organizing, directing, and controlling" a company's resources &systems toenhancetheir capability to react due to changes in exchange rates. Despite the fact that, the prime motive of using hedging is to get insurance from the ill effects of forex risk volatility, still hedging is also used for managing the forex risk. One another way to manage the forex risk exposure is by doing nothing. So, management of forex risk can also be done by not indulging in hedging. To hedge or not to hedge is just a single stage of forex risk management. So, it is always not advisable to go for hedging as SME's might get profit or no loss from the advantageous movements in the forex rates. There exists disagreement among the researchers regarding the usage of hedging at corporate level. Some of the researchers are in the favor of using the hedging whereas some are not in the favor of using the hedging strategies at corporate level.

For instance, in a case of forex risk hedging made by Dufey & Srinivasulu (1983) specifically for corporate level revealed that there is no need of hedging in a perfect world where "The Uncertainty of Forward Rates & Spot Rates, Hedging of Consumption Bundle, the Efficient Market Hypothesis, the Concept of Self-insurance, Modigliani-Miller (MM) theorem, Capital Asset Pricing Model (CAPM) and Purchasing Power Parity (PPP) theorem all are valid". As we do not live in a world where all these conditions are valid, so companies do indulge in hedging which is also evident from previous literature (Dufey & Srinivasulu, 1983). In support of this notion, various other researchers have suggested the use of hedging strategies for managing the forex risk exposure (Pramborg, 2005; Morey & Simpson, 2001; Moosa, 2004; Marshall, 2000; Loderer&Pichler, 2000; Joseph, 2000; Dhanani, 2003; ; Dash et al., 2008; Brookes et al., 2000). In the words of Brookes et al., (2000), one can manage with little cost and difficulty in case of short-term exchange rate fluctuations but when it comes to long-term exchange rate fluctuations then it is of more concern. Furthermore, Moosa (2004) proposed that when the exchange rate movements are quite adverse then it becomes vital to hedge otherwise it might result greater and infrequent exposures. There exist no such literatures, which depicts that the companies who hedges performs better than the companies who do not hedge. So, companies may or may not indulge in hedging as previously discussed also that hedging and no hedging is just one step in management of forex risk exposure (Allayannis, Brown, & Klapper, 2001). For example, one of the reasons that companies do not go for hedging is the difficulties associated in calculating or estimating the exposure with forex rate as they are not able to measure the firm value and cash flows (Pramborg, 2005; Papaioannou, 2006; Loderer & Pichler, 2000). Another reason for which the companies do not go for hedging can be the cost which is associated in establishing a hedging programme or insignificant exposure of forex (Pramborg, 2005).

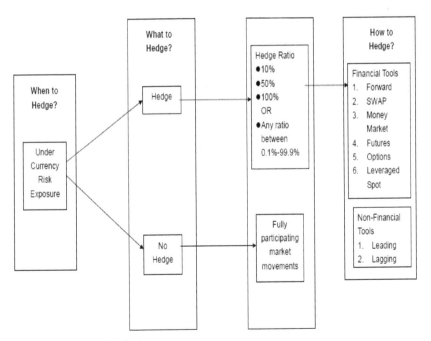

Figure 5: *Decision Tree for Hedging*

Therefore, it is observed that SME's might not go for hedging as compared to large MNC's due to the fact that their involvement in international level is less as compared to MNC's and the cost of setting up a hedging programme is high which is an additional cost for any SME's. So, SME's are less involved in hedging strategies. But if the turnover of SME's is more in foreign currency then the exposure of forex will be quite equal for a SME's as that of a MNC and hence it pose a threat for the SME's foreign exchange and hence they also get indulge in hedging in order to avoid or manage the forex risk exposure.

Concept of Hedging in Over-the-Counter Markets

Fluctuation in the exchange rates, i.e., either appreciation or depreciation can have favorable or unfavorable cash flow impact on an exporter or an importer, and this can be potentially detrimental to his financial position. To insure against such uncertainty of cash flows, the exporter/importer hedges his exposures through forward/options/swaps by entering into contract with counterparties like banks/financial institutions which are authorized to deal and make markets in these products.

Hedging in simple terms is like 'securing a rate or freezing a certain rate for foreign currency receivable/payable'. Fluctuations in exchange rates, post hedging, do not affect the hedged party, as his cash flows are crystallized. However, there might be notional opportunity gain/loss. Table 1 illustrates the same with an example.

Table 1

Exposure of Importer and Exporter

Month	USD/INR	Importers		Exporters		Remarks
		Hedged (Y)	Happy (☺)	Hedged (Y)	Happy (☺)	
		Unhedged (N)	Unhappy ( )	Unhedged (N)	Unhappy ( )	
June 07	45					Reference rate
January 08	39.27	N	☺	N		Note 1
January 08	39.27	Y		Y	☺	Note 1

| August 09 | 52.85 | N | | N | ☺ | Note 2 |
| August 09 | 52.85 | Y | ☺ | Y | | Note 2 |

Source: Financial Derivatives: The Currency & Rates Factor

In the above example, the exposure, i.e., import/export, arose when the prevailing USD/INR exchange rate was 45. Hence, this is termed as the reference rate. Assuming that the exposure was unhedged at that point of time, there could have been two scenarios which are mentioned as follows:

Scenario/Note 1: In case exposure was unhedged, the importer would have been happy since his INR outgo would have reduced per unit of USD, and the exporter would have been unhappy since his INR realization would have reduced per unit of USD and it would have been vice versa in case the exposures were hedged at inception.

Scenario/Note 2: In case exposure was unhedged, the importer would have been unhappy since his INRoutgo would have increased per USD, and the exporter would have been happy since his INR realization would have increased per unit of USD and it would have been vice versa in case the exposures were hedged at inception.

OTC market: OTC stands for 'over-the-counter'. Such markets do not holdany central place for trading and is linked to a network of dealers/traders ,who communicate through phone lines & computer networks . These are customized contracts which are built in on terms of negotiation between the counter-parties. The default risk of one counter party is dependent on the credit worthiness of the other counter party. The forwards which were discussed in the previous chapters are traded in OTC market.

ETC market: ETC stands for 'exchange traded contracts'. Though the economic purpose of ETC is same as OTC, still they differ in certain fundamental ways. ETCs are standardized. In an exchange traded scenario, where the market lot is fixed at a smaller size than the OTC market, all classes of investors, whether large or small, are provided equal opportunities to participate in futures market. Besides this, ETC have greater transparency, efficiency and accessibility.

Hedging Tools and Techniques

Forward Contracts

Future contract is the most used hedging instruments by the hedger and this can be evidenced from the empirical work done by Mathur (1982). The study selected its sample from Fortune 500 companies by adopting random sampling and the results of the study revealed that the companies which were indulged in currency hedging mostly used forward contract for the purpose of hedging. Forward contracts are based on the principal of "buy now but pay and deliver later" agreements. In the modern era of business scenario, forward contracts are also called as "over-the-counter transactions", which generally happens among two or more persons in which both seller and buyer agree on a contract where they will give mentioned sum of currency based on the today's agreed exchange rate. Generally, these types of contracts are not standardized as the maturity of the contract and its size varies. But both the seller and the buyer have to abide according to the contract irrespective of the changed circumstances. It means that, a forward contract are not eligible to be marked or resold in a market as there does not exist secondary market for a forward contract (Hallwood & MacDonald, 2000; Solnik & McLeavey, 2004). Despite having some basic disadvantages, the future contracts are the most widely used instrument for the purpose of hedging and the main reason behind this is that it render huge amount of transactions at lower cost.

Futures Markets

The first successor of forward contracts is the futures contracts. The fundamental basis of a future contract is similar to that of a forward contract but future contracts are standardized contracts in term of its delivery, maturity time, and quantity as well as in quality. The first ever currency futures contract was introduced by Chicago Mercantile Exchange in 1972. Initially, similar to former financial derivatives, the future contracts were intended only for trading related with commodity but with the advancement of commercial trading, it also embraces the floating world currencies. There are many important traits that future contracts carry that of forward contracts, such as it allows for future delivery or buying at a particular price with mentioned date and with given currency amount which is agreed by the buyer and seller (Homaifar, 2004; Hughes & MacDonald, 2002; Hallwood and MacDonald, 2000;Dawson and Rodney, 1994). The future contract is mostly used by hedger and speculators as it not only possess the features of a forward contract but also have some more traits which helps in efficient trading as it provides the price movements advantage to the investors.

Table 2

Differences between Future and Forward Contracts

Forward Contracts	Futures Contracts
Customized contracts in terms of size and delivery dates	Standardized contracts in terms of size and delivery dates
Private contracts between two parties	Standardized contracts between a customer and a clearinghouse
Difficult to reverse a contract	Contract may be freely traded on the market
Profit and loss on a position is realized only on the delivery date	All contracts are marked to market – the profit and loss are realized immediately
No explicit collateral, but standard bank relationship necessary	Collateral (margins) must be maintained to reflect price movements
Delivery or final cash settlement	Contract is usually closed out prior to

Source: Hull (2006, p.6, pp.40-41), Moffett et al. (2006, p.6, p.177) and Solnik and McLeavey(2004)

Options Markets

These types of contracts are quite similar to future markets, where there can be transactions among buyer and seller in an open auction market which is more cost-efficient, orderly designed and organized (Homaifar, 2004). Some of the example of such type of markets is "Australian Stock Exchange (ASX), the New York Mercantile Exchange (NYMEX) and Chicago Mercantile Exchange (CME)".

Table 3

Call Options Rights and Obligations

Buyer (holder)	Seller (writer)
Has the right to buy a futures contract at a predetermined price on or before a defined date.	Grants right to buyer, so has obligation to sell futures at a predetermined price at buyer's sole option.
Expectation: Rising prices	Expectation: Neutral or falling prices

Source: NYMEX (2005).

Table4

Put Options Rights and Obligations

Buyer (holder)	Seller (writer)
Has the right to sell a futures contract at a predetermined price on or before a defined date.	Grants right to buyer, so has obligation to buy futures at a predetermined price at buyer's sole option.
Expectation: Falling prices	Expectation: Neutral or rising prices

Source: NYMEX (2005).

Swaps

Although the emergence of Swap as an instrument was established in early 1980's, still it has gained a lot of acceptance in the financial market throughout the globe (Solnik & McLeavey, 2004; Moffett et al., 2006). This statement is evidenced from the empirical finding of the survey conducted by Australian Bureau of Statistics (ABS) in 2001, which depicts that swaps as tool for hedging is the second most instrument employed by Australian companies. Swaps are the "over-the-counter" transaction not the "exchange-trade" derivatives (Solnik & McLeavey, 2004; Moffett et al., 2006), which is majorly used by investment and commercial banks which have association to "International Swaps and Derivatives Association (ISDA)".

A typical currency swap first requires two firms to borrow funds in the markets and currencies in which they are best known. For example, a Japanese firm would typically borrow yen on a regular basis in its home market. If the Japanese firms were exporting to the United States and earning U.S. dollars, however, it might wish to construct a natural hedge that would allow it to use the U.S. dollar earned to make regular debt service payments on U.S. dollar debt. If the Japanese firm is not well known in the U.S. financial markets, though, it may have no ready access to U.S. dollar debt. Thus, it could participate in a currency swap. The Japanese corporate could swap its yen-denominated debt service payments with another firm that has U.S. dollar debt service payments. The Japanese corporate would then have dollar debt service without actually borrowing U.S. dollar. The swap agreement can be arranged by professional swap dealer who will generally search out matching currency exposures, in terms of currency, amount, and timing. In other words, the swap dealer plays the role of middleman, providing a valuable currency management service for both firms.

Source: Hughes, and MacDonald (2002, p.211) and Moffett, et al. (2006, p.250).

Figure 6: *An Illustration on Currency Swap*

Money Markets

A place where short-term funds are sold or bought is known as money market. Generally, the normal maturity period of these kinds of tools are twelve months. Further, money market can be segregated as: "Eurocurrency markets and local money markets" (Eng et al., 1998). These two types of money market functions on their own interest rate rules, which is mostly based on the prevailing interest rate of that country. Like, "the Eurodollar interest rate inclines to comply with movement of USA interest rate the interest rate".

Table 5

Frequently Used Money Market Instruments

Instruments	Descriptions
Bankers' Acceptance	A draft or bill of exchange accepted by a bank to guarantee payment of the bill.
Certificate of Deposit	A time deposit with a specific maturity date shown on a certificate; large-denomination certificates of deposit can be sold before maturity.
Commercial Paper	An unsecured promissory note with a fixed maturity of one to 270 days; usually it is sold at a discount from face value.
Eurodollar Deposit	Deposits made in US dollars at a bank or bank branch located outside the United States.
Federal Agency Short-term Securities	Short-term securities issued by government sponsored enterprises such as the Farm Credit System, the Federal Home Loan Banks and the Federal National Mortgage Association.
Federal Funds (in the US)	Interest-bearing deposits held by banks and other depository institutions at the Federal Reserve; these are immediately available funds that institutions borrow or lend, usually on an overnight basis. They are lent at the federal funds rate.
Municipal Notes (in the US)	Short-term notes issued by municipalities in anticipation of tax receipts or other revenues.
Repurchase Agreements	Short-term loans, normally for less than two weeks and frequently for one day, arranged by selling securities to an investor with an agreement to repurchase them at a fixed price on a fixed date.
Treasury Bills (T-Bills)	Short-term debt obligations of a national government that are issued to mature in 3 to 12months.

Source: Eng et al., 1998, pp.325-327

The term 'money market' refers to the marketplaceswhere in trading of short term highly liquid financial instruments is done.

Inter-linkage between Money Market and Currency Market

The money market is intimately related to foreign exchange market through the interest arbitrage process wherein the forward premium acts as a link between the foreign & domestic interest rates.

The same has been described below by taking Indian forward market and spot market into consideration. For example, if one-year interest rate of India implied by one year Treasury bill issued by Government of India is 8.25 per cent and one year USD LIBOR is 1 per cent, then ideally forward premium shall be 7.25 per cent and this relation-ship shall hold at any time for any time period. However, the actual forward premium is 6 percent. In such a case, the covered interest arbitrage theory is disturbed, leading to arbitrage opportunities. For example, if a bank which is operating in India has access to USD funding at LIBOR then it can convert its USD into INR and utilize the INR funds for either lending to someone in call money/reverse repo or investing in treasury bill/certificate of deposit/ commercial paper approximately @ 8.25 per cent. Simultaneously, the bank can buy USD at spot rate and pay the forward premium @ 6 per cent. This would lead to arbitrage gain of 2.25 per cent to the bank.

However, in real life, forward premium in countries like India where full capital account convertibility does not exist, does violate covered interest arbitrage theory on account of the following reasons:

1) **Liquidity projections and INR rate view:** This applies to both INR liquidity and USD liquidity.

a) *INR liquidity:* Market participant exercise their view on future liquidity projections through USD/INR forward curve. For example, as on 22 May 2012, three months forward premium is 7.25 per cent but 12 months forward premium is 5.50 per cent. One of the reasons which can be assigned for downward sloping forward curve is the market's expectation of CRR and repo rate cut which would lead to adequate liquidity and lower interest rates in the future. An example of how an interest rate change can impact spot USD/INR exchange rate is as follows. When in a normal market condition, there is sudden repo rate hike by Reserve Bank of India, the first reaction of the market participants would be to sell USD against INR, as market players would look to sell the excess dollars parked with them into INR as the same INR would now earn higher rate of interest.

b) *USD liquidity:* Shortage of USD in the market which can be caused either because of sudden outflow of USD from system or due to central bank intervention, creates demand for USD in the near term. Either of the above causes would lead to market paying higher rate of interest for buying USD and selling INR. Market participants in order to generate more USD, would begin to buy/sell operation in the market, which has historically even lead to forwards entering into negative territory. However, such a situation of forward premium tends to reverse when the USD liquidity in the system improves.

2) **View and action of corporate/Foreign institutional investors/asset liability management desk of banks in spot–** *Corporate*

In case corporate who have export earnings believe that USD/INR outright levels (spot + forward) is attractive to sell, then they would sell USD/INR for value forward date. This would lead to sudden receiving in the market of forward premium and forward premium would come down. Similarly, corporate who have either imports or have borrowed in foreign currency could find USD/INR outright level attractive to buy. This would lead to both spot and forward premiums moving up.

a) *Foreign institutional investors:* In case foreign institutional investors expect an outflow in future and want to protect the value of their portfolio investment, then could begin buying USD/INR for value forward date. This would lead to both forwards and spot USD/INR exchange rate moving higher.

b) *Asset liability management desk:* Banks who have access to USD funding for their balance sheet management may find USD/INR forward levels to be attractive for pay forwards. They can invest the INR generated in the process in certificate of deposit and earn the arbitrage carry.

The wide ranges of participants like banks, primary dealers, financial institutions, mutual funds, trusts, provident funds, etc., deal in money market instruments. In India, the RBI and the SEBI regulate the money market instruments and the participants of money market.

Factors Determining Forex Risk Exposure Hedging Strategies

An enterprise may consider different hedging strategies, which may include full hedging, partial hedging or no hedging. There are various determinants of selecting a particular hedging strategy for Forex risk exposure. A risk averter enterprise would prefer to hedge full Forex risk exposure. Under such a case, the Forex risk manager of the business will have more liberty to take decisions for Forex risk exposure management. Hedging any kind of risk involves cost and next important issue is to select hedging instruments. There are various factors affecting the choice of hedging strategy of a Forex risk manager. Joseph (2000) found sales to market value as an important determinant. Kula (2005) documented that perception towards Forex risk is a significant determinant of Forex risk exposure hedging strategy. González et al (2007) said that the size of Forex risk exposure determine the degree of hedging. Furthermore, market to book value, institutional ownership and size of the firm are important determinants of Forex risk exposure hedging strategy. Pramborg, (2005) and Aabo et al., (2010) said the quantum of export in foreign currency is a key determinant of Forex risk exposure hedging strategy.

The determinants of a Forex risk exposure strategy for one manager may differ from other manager. These include the quantum of risk exposure, the prevailing market conditions, fluctuations in currencies involved in a foreign transaction, the expertise of treasury manager or Forex risk manager, the accessibility of alternative instruments for hedging Forex risk exposure and type of exposure etc. Therefore while managing the Forex risk exposure, the determinants of hedging strategy must be considered.

Significance of Hedging Forex Risk Exposure

There is no disbelief in benefits of hedging the Forex risk exposure. It helps the firms to mitigate their potential losses due to fluctuations in foreign exchange rate. *Etteman, Stonehill and Moffett (2004) gave a conceptual model on impact of hedging on the future cash flows of the business. It showed that the future expected value of a firm is maximum with a hedging strategy rather than remaining unhedged. The following figure has shown this conceptual model.*

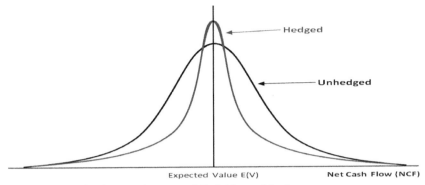

Figure 7: *Impact of hedging on the expected Cash Flows of the firm*

Source: Etteman, Stonehill and Moffett (2004).

Hedging Instruments for Forex Risk Exposure available in India

Akshatha (2013) conducted a study on history and growth of derivatives in Indian markets, perception of investors, how derivatives help in managing risk by hedging and how can capital market increase the use of derivatives. The author has discussed the recommendations of L.C. Gupta committee on derivative market in India. It has been clearly mentioned that there is a change in risk perception of Indian companies regarding Forex risk hedging strategies. The study was concluded with an analysis of factors causing interest of investors in derivative instruments in India. There are various instruments available for hedging Forex risk. Henderson and Callum (2002) did a research on hedging currency risk in Emerging Markets. It considered both the recent developments of hedging instruments in emerging markets and difference between the developed and emerging markets. It was found that while managing currency risk, various characteristics like High Inflation, High Forward Premiums, Options market implications and Lower forward rate biasness were not considered by hedgers. Most of the traditional hedging structures included Plain Vanilla Call, Plain Vanilla Forward, Call Spread, Calendar Spread, Risk Reversal, and Seagull while the enhanced tools include Knock Out, Knock In, Range Binary, Window Option and Fade-In Option. It was identified that management of currency risk cannot be same for every firm and it depends upon the scenario of individual firms. The Forex or currency risk exposure can be prevented by using the internal and external techniques. The Rangarajan committee, Sodhani committee and Tarapore committee gave various recommendations related to foreign exchange market in India and its future perspective. Today the Indian firms have access to various instruments for hedging Forex risk exposure. It includes foreign exchange based forward contracts, future contract, swaps, and options etc. Broadly, in case of India, Exchange Traded derivative instruments, OTC derivative instruments and Exchange Earners Foreign Currency (EEFC) account are the Forex risk exposure instruments available to mitigate the Forex risk exposure. Different markets have assortment of hedging instruments depending on the nature of firms. A study conducted by Bligh (2012) documented that forward contract, money market, futures market, options and currency swaps are popular hedging instruments in American Market. The foreign currency risk managers found option contracts are more expensive than the other hedging instruments available.

The development of OTC derivative markets in India has evolved in a regulated space as compared to financial markets which are developed where derivative markets of OTC is epitomized by financial innovations that are complex and unregulated which have shown extensive growth since last two decades. The foremost components of this regulatory framework incorporate separate responsibilities for the users of all types of OTC derivatives and market makers, nature of participants in the markets and an extensive description of permitted products. Further, in order to have systemic information an effective reporting system is created so that focus could be laid on developing the market infrastructure for settlement and post-trade clearing.

In order to have a complete and efficient exchange trade derivative market, there should be certain guidelines pertaining to policy framework in respect of different markets. Ideally most of the exchange trade market wants to have a market, which is free from frictions with no constraints on having short term, or long-term positions and a unified integration among varied segments encouraged through the free participation by all parties. For a policy maker this is one of the most commonly faced challenges where consideration for financial stability as well as structural and macroeconomicconstraintsrequires some limitations on the underlying markets.

In Indian scenario, though there is a policy which restricts the involvement of economic agents, still there exists a need to have an underlying exposure for exercising forex derivative transaction. The policy intervention in the cash markets is very important in context to the real sector as its tolerance for high volatility in exchange rates and interest rates is limited. Due to the infeasibility in the existence of the exchange traded derivative in this framework, the OTC's market share makes it possible to implement market development in an operational framework considering the constraints. Thus, taking into account above discussions, in view of re-framing the reforms for OTC derivative markets in India, there is need to uplift the OTC market framework instead of concentrating on the binary considerations. (Source: Reserve Bank of India)

Size of OTC Derivative Markets in India

The BIS provides Triennial report based on survey of central banks for their derivative market activities and foreign exchange related activities. In its 2007 report, it has been clearly indicated that the contribution of Indian rupee in total forex market got increased from 0.3% to 0.7%. Likewise, the share of India has also increased from 0.4% to 0.9% in terms of geographical distribution of turnover in foreign exchange market. The scenario of foreign derivative market can also be observed with the help of outstanding position of forex derivatives in the books of banks. As of December 2009, total forex contracts outstanding in the banks' balance sheet amounted to INR 36,142 billion (USD 774.25 billion), of which over 86% were forwards and rest options (Table 6).

Table 6

Showing Outstanding Derivatives of Banks

Statements	December 2009		March 2009		March 2008		March 2007	
	USD Billion	INR Billion	USD Billion	INR Billion	USD Billion	INR Billion	USD Billion	INR Billion
Foreign exchange contracts	774.25	36,142	994.78	50,684	1,377.46	55,057	671.12	29,254
Forward forex contracts	668.17	31,190	876.72	44,669	1,184.89	47,360	565.57	24,653
Currency options purchased	106.08	4,952	118.06	6,015	192.57	7,697	105.55	4,601
Futures	73.84	3,447	68.91	3,511	68.63	2,743	52.53	2,290
Interest rate related contracts	994.73	46,434	879.35	44,803	2,137.35	85,430	962.56	41,958
Single Currency Interest Rate Swaps	987	46,073	870.99	44,377	2,130.57	85,159	954.28	41,597
Total -contracts/ derivatives	1,842.82	86,023	1,943.04	98,998	3,583.44	143,230	1,686.21	73,502

Source: RBI website

Highlights from the latest BIS semiannual survey of over-the-counter (OTC) derivatives markets

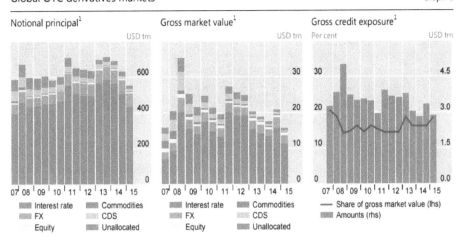

Global OTC derivatives markets — Graph 1

Notional principal[1] · Gross market value[1] · Gross credit exposure[1]

Further information on the BIS derivatives statistics is available at www.bis.org/statistics/derstats.htm.

[1] At half-year end (end-June and end-December). Amounts denominated in currencies other than the US dollar are converted to US dollars at the exchange rate prevailing on the reference date.

Figure 8: *Global OTC derivative market*

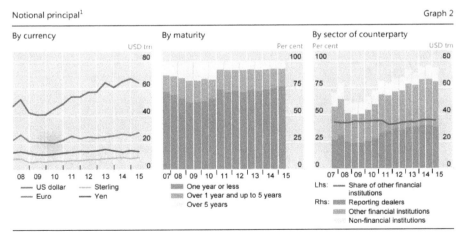

Notional principal[1] — Graph 2

By currency · By maturity · By sector of counterparty

Further information on the BIS derivatives statistics is available at www.bis.org/statistics/derstats.htm.

[1] At half-year end (end-June and end-December). Amounts denominated in currencies other than the US dollar are converted to US dollars at the exchange rate prevailing on the reference date.

Figure 9: *OTC Foreign Exchange Derivatives*

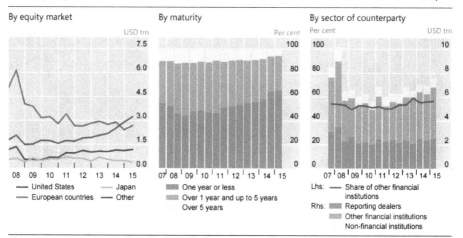

OTC equity-linked derivatives

Notional principal[1]   Graph 4

Further information on the BIS derivatives statistics is available at www.bis.org/statistics/derstats.htm.

[1] At half-year end (end-June and end-December). Amounts denominated in currencies other than the US dollar are converted to US dollars at the exchange rate prevailing on the reference date.

Figure 10: *OTC equity-linked derivatives*

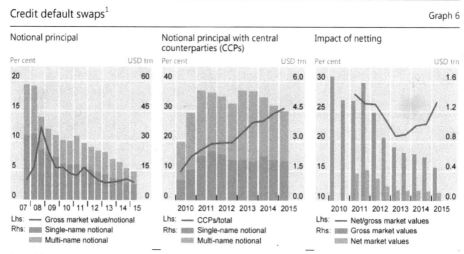

Credit default swaps[1]   Graph 6

Further information on the BIS derivatives statistics is available at www.bis.org/statistics/derstats.htm.

[1] At half-year end (end-June and end-December). Amounts denominated in currencies other than the US dollar are converted to US dollars at the exchange rate prevailing on the reference date.

Figure 11: *Credit Default Swaps*

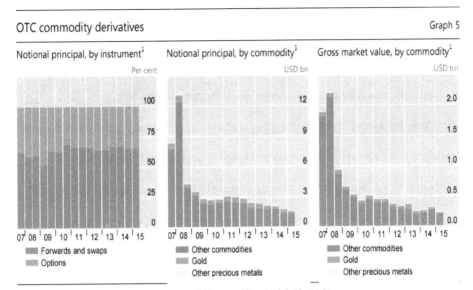

OTC commodity derivatives — Graph 5

Notional principal, by instrument[1] Notional principal, by commodity[1] Gross market value, by commodity[1]

Forwards and swaps / Options

Other commodities / Gold / Other precious metals

Other commodities / Gold / Other precious metals

Further information on the BIS derivatives statistics is available at www.bis.org/statistics/derstats.htm.

[1] At half-year end (end-June and end-December). Amounts denominated in currencies other than the US dollar are converted to US dollars at the exchange rate prevailing on the reference date.

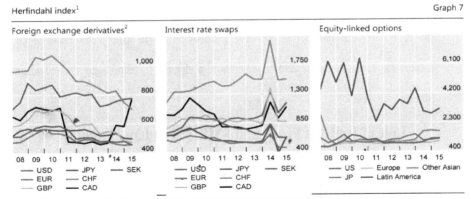

Herfindahl index[1] — Graph 7

Foreign exchange derivatives[2] Interest rate swaps Equity-linked options

USD / JPY / SEK USD / JPY / SEK US / Europe / Other Asian
EUR / CHF EUR / CHF JP / Latin America
GBP / CAD GBP / CAD

Further information on the BIS derivatives statistics is available at www.bis.org/statistics/derstats.htm.

CAD = Canadian dollar; CHF = Swiss franc; EUR = euro; GBP = pound sterling; JPY = Japanese yen; SEK = Swedish krona; USD = US dollar. JP = Japan; US = United States.

[1] The index ranges from 0 to 10,000, where a lower number indicates that there are many dealers with similar market shares (as measured by notional principal) and a higher number indicates that the market is dominated by a few reporting dealers. [2] Foreign exchange forwards, foreign exchange swaps and currency swaps.

Figure 12 *OTC Commodity Derivatives*

1) More stress was laid down on reforming the OTC derivatives markets to reduce systemic risks using Central clearing as a Key element in global regulator. The share of outstanding contracts cleared with the help of central counterparties increased from 29% to 31% in the first half of 2015 in case of Credit default Swaps. Similarly the central clearing is becoming more important in the context of interest rate derivatives markets.

2) There was a rapid decline in the gross market value of outstanding derivative contracts, which is considered as a more reliable measure of amount at risk than the notional amount. Market values decreased from $20.9 trillion to $15.5 trillion between end December 2014 and end-June 2015. The resultant decline is due to the reduction in the notional amount outstanding as well as increase in the long term interest rates.

3) There was a decline in the activities of the global OTC derivative markets during the first half of 2015, the notional amount of the outstanding contracts showed a reduction from $629 trillion at end-December 2014 to $553 trillion at end June 2015. Inspite of changes in the effect of exchange rate movements on positions denominated in currencies other than US Dollar, the notional amount were showing a fall by 10%. The major determinant of the decline was found to be the trade compression, a element for eliminating the redundant contracts.

Role of Unlisted Firms and SME's in Indian Economy

These days, we commonly overhear a buzz word from the marketers that "If India is growing at 7-plus per cent, how come we don't feel it?" One of the main reason that they are not seeing why Indian economy is in real sense growing is the fact that they generally look at the profit and loss and revenue decline in listed companies under Nifty. But, they are ignoring the contribution of millions of small and medium enterprise and unlisted firms that are operating in

India. A report released by RBI depicts that there are more than 45 million of micro, small and medium enterprises (MSME's) and under Ministry of Corporate Affairs (MCA) there are more than fifteen lakh active firms (see annexure) as compared to listed firms in India whose number is around 6000 only. So, from these numbers, we can easily identify the importance of unlisted firms and SMSE's in the contribution of Indian economy and in order to understand the real growth rate the stockbrokers and market commentators also need to look at the contribution by these unlisted firms and SMSE's. But, due to the fragmented nature of these unlisted firms and SMSE's, it is not easy to understand how these unlisted firms and SME's are managing to outpace the listed firms in India. In this direction, an effort has been made by RBI, in which RBI released the financial data of more than 2.3 lakh unlisted firms operating in India. This data does not include the companies who fall under financial industries. Only by looking at the financial database of these 2.3 lakh unlisted firms one can easily make out the importance of the unlisted firms in Indian economy. There are some reasons why unlisted firms have overpowered the listed firms.

1. One of the main reasons is the sale growth rate of unlisted and SME's as compared to listed firms in India. The sales growth rate of unlisted and SME's goes from 13.3 % in the financial year 2013 to 8.7 % in the financial year of 2014 and again went back to 12 % in the financial year 2015. On the contrary, the sales growth rate of listed firms in the last three years has been a constant decline starting from 9.1 % in the financial year 2013 to 4.7 % in financial year 2014 and finally a more dip in the sales growth rate which results in only 1.4 % sales growth rate in the financial year 2015. This is the reason that why the performance of listed firms in antithesis to that of official GDP data. But, the performance of unlisted and SME's are very much in line with the rate of GDP data released by RBI which show that in the past

three years there is continuous increase in the rate of GDP with 5.6 % in 2013 to 6.6% in 2014 and 7.2 % in 2015.

2. Another reason that why unlisted and SME's outperformed the listed firms is the higher profit growth rates by unlisted firms than listed firms in India for past three years. Despite having low profit margins by unlisted firms and SME's in the financial year 2015 (9.1%) than the counterpart which is (13.6%), the unlisted and SME's managed to have higher profit growth rate than listed firms in past three years with a profit growth rate of 16 %, 23.6 % and 12.3 % respectively. Whereas, the profit growth rate of listed firms has seen a shrinking profits with 2 % to 5.1 % to 0.7 % in past three consecutive years.

Therefore, we conclude that Small and Medium Enterprises plays key role in development of Indian markets. Indian Small & Medium Enterprises sector cover more than 6000 products and provides large employment opportunities. It contributes 40% to the exports from the country. Having 8% share in the country's GDP, SME's with its 36 million ancillary units flattering to large industries. SME's with Major export earnings, Location mobility, Technology Orientation with Flexibility in Operations generates 45% of the total manufacturing output. Currently large sector industries are having a limited growth prospects but SME's sector is growing at a CAGR of 4.5% during FY07-11 and has the potential to expand industrial growth across the country. Now a day SME's also investing in R&D to compete in this global economy. Adapting the need of large local manufacturers and Outsourcing from foreign companies has made growth in SME sector.

The census indicates that overall 31.79% of the enterprises are involved in manufacturing activities while rest is engaged in services. Also Unlisted Firms and SME's role in Indian Economy can be explained with the key industries in which SMEs operates.

Table: 7

Investment in Plant and Machinery

Manufacturing Sector Enterprises	Investment in plant & machinery
Micro Enterprises	Rs.25 lakh
Small Enterprises	Rs.5 crore
Medium Enterprises	Rs.10 crore
Service Sector Enterprises	
Micro Enterprises	Rs.10 lakh
Small Enterprises	Rs.2 crore
Medium Enterprises	Rs.5 crore

Source: Ministry of Micro, Small and Medium Enterprises

As per 4th All India Census of MSME conducted by the Ministry of MSME, the number of functional and non-functional registered MSMEs in the country is 15,63,974 and 4,96,355 respectively.The share of MSME products in the exports from the country during last three years is as follows:

Table8

Share of MSMEs products in the Exports

Year	Share of MSMEs Products in the Exports
2013-14	42.42%
2014-15	44.76%
2015-16	49.86%

Source: Ministry of Micro, Small and Medium Enterprises

· Table 9

Key Industries in which Indian SME's Operate

Description	No. of Enterprises(lakh)	% Share
Retail Trade, Except Of Motor Vehicles And Motorcycles; Repair Of Personal And Household Goods.	30.06	15.13
Manufacture Of Wearing Apparel; Dressing And Dyeing Of Fur	29.52	14.85

Manufacture Of Food Products And Beverages	22.89	11.52
Other Service Activities	22.34	11.24
Other Business Activities	12.69	6.38
Sale, Maintenance And Repair Of Motor Vehicles And Motorcycles; Retail Sale Of Automotive Fuel	12.34	6.21
Manufacture Of Furniture; Manufacturing N.E.C.	10.62	5.34
Post And Telecommunications	8.21	4.13
Manufacture Of Textiles	7.36	3.70
Manufacture Of Fabricated Metal Products, Except Machinery And Equipment	7.02	3.53
Total of above ten industry groups	163.06	82.03
Others	35.68	17.97
All	198.74	100

Source: Ministry of Micro, Small and Medium Enterprises

Table 10

Summary Results of Fourth All India Census of MSME

Characteristics	Registered Sector	Unregistered Sector	Economic Census-2005	Total
Per Unit fixed investment (in Lakh)	28.72	1.21	-	-
Total fixed investment (in Lakh)	44913840	24081646	-	68995486
Per unit original value of Plant & Machinery (in Lakh)	6.72	0.48	-	-
Total original value of Plant & Machinery (in Lakh)	10502461	9463960	-	19966421
Per Unit Employment	5.95	2.06	2.06	2.23

Total Employment (in Lakh)	93.09	408.84	303.31	805.24
No. of Women Enterprises (in Lakh)	2.15 (13.72%)	18.06 (9.09%)	6.40 (4.34%)	26.61 (7.36%)
No. of rural units (in Lakh)	7.07 (45.20%)	119.68 (60.22%)	73.43 (49.82%)	200.18 (55.34%)
Size of Sector (in Lakh)	15.64	198.74	147.38	361.76
Total Gross Output (in Lakh)	70751027	36970259	-	107721286

Source: Annual Report 2015-16 of MSME by Government of India

Government has also taken steps for upbringing the sector performance by launching various schemes like Marketing assistance, Promotion of Information and Communication Tools (ICT), Support for Entrepreneurial and Managerial Development of MSMEs through Incubators etc. Some of the schemes can be explained as follows:

1. RGUMY Scheme: Rajiv Gandhi Udyami Mitra Yojana aims to support the newly established entrepreneurs. It helps in developing them their startups by enabling to deal with various technical and legal difficulties.

2. CGTF Scheme: Indian Government jointly with SIDBI launched Credit Guarantee Trust Fund Scheme for small & micro enterprises. It provides the guarantee to the lender that in an event of a failure to pay back the credit free facility availed by MSE unit; Guarantee Trust Fund would protect the 75-80% of the credit facility.

3. CLCSS Scheme: Credit Linked Capital Subsidy scheme is used for technology up-gradation of MSMEs aims to provide 15% capital for the purchase of Plant & Machinery.

4. Other initiatives include MSME Development Institutes, MSME Tool Rooms, MSME Technology development centers and MSME Testing Centers etc.

Performance of Indian MSME Sector is consistent over the period of time. It is projected to

grow over 6% in the coming years.

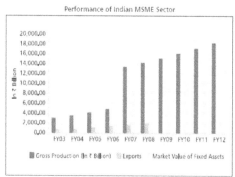

Source. Ministry of Micro, Small, and Medium Enterprises, D&B Research
Export Figures are available only till FY08. Figures for Gross Production and Market Value of Fixed Assets from FY08 to FY 12 are projected
Note. The data for the period up to 2005-06 is only for small-scale industries (SSI). Subsequent to 2005-06, data with reference to micro, small and medium enterprise are being compiled

Figure 13: *Performance of Indian MSME Sector*

Above figures shows Gross production, Exports and Market Value of fixed assets from FY08 to FY 12. This shows the importance of Indian MSME sector towards importance the development of Indian Economy.

Challenges Faced by Unlisted Firms and Small & Medium Enterprises in India

Having good support being provided by the Indian Government to unlisted firms and

SME sector still faces certain challenges in their businesses (Dangayach & Deshmukh, 2005;

Todd & Javalgi, 2007; Coad & Tamvada 2012; Das & Pradhan, 2010). They have concern

towards not getting the required support from the Government departments, Banks, Financial

Institutions and Corporates. Some of the problems are:

- Lower capacity of Production

- Inadequate Capital and Knowledge

- Challenges in getting skilled low cost labor

- Unable to identify new markets

- Follow up issue with Government departments

- Limited capital and knowledge

- Lack of proper Information Technology

Unlisted Firms and SME's Foreign Exchange Risk Exposure

Exchange rates are fluctuating in short period and influence demand and supply forces. Exchange rate of foreign currency Organizations involved in overseas transactions often exposed to currency related risks. There is always time gap between the issue of invoice and receipt/payment of the amount.

As there is more fluctuations in currencies more there will be difference between rate of entering the transaction and actual realization. The demand and supply forces of the market also tend to drive exchange rate movement. Other factors affecting the supply and demand of any currency are:

1. **Macro-economic environment:** Positive economic policies, competitive advantage etc. leads to increase in the demand for a currency. CPI, GDP, Industrial Production also leads to fluctuations in currency exchange rates.

2. **One Price theory:** The price of goods or exchange rate should adjust so that same goods should be sold at same price throughout the world.

3. **Political Influence:** Since politics has influence till the end of the queue, political changes have big influence over the currency market changes.

4. **Interest rate parity:** If the flow in capital becomes free then the rate of exchange can become steady at a point where equality is recognized of real interest rate. The real interest rate refers to the nominal interest rate which is adjusted for the prevailing inflation rate in the country.

Foreign Exchange Risk Management for Unlisted Firms and SME's

Currency fluctuations can adversely impact the Unlisted Firms and SME's. Every organization has to manage the foreign exchange risk. Management of foreign exchange risk can be done with the following steps:

Step1. **Calculation of Risk Exposure**: Foreign exchange risk exposure can be determined with following factors:

- Percentage of Sales or Purchase in foreign currencies.

- Passing on currency losses to customer

- Currency in which we are exposed to

- At what point alteration in exchange rates affects our profitability significantly.

Step 2.**Formation of Risk mitigation strategy**: Foreign Exchange risk can be managed with proper Risk mitigation tool and strategy. Following are some of the strategies-

- **No hedging:** Hedging is not necessary when exposure to foreign currency transaction is insignificant or SME can completely pass on the profit or loss arising from the foreign currency transactions to the customers.

- **Selective hedging:** It implies that SME will hedge only a part of its currency exposure and take profit or loss from the un-hedged portion.

- **Systematic hedging:** More reliance on the foreign exchange cash flow more one should hedge against foreign exchange risk.

Importance of Hedging in Managing Risk & Volatilities

Hedging has its own role in managing the foreign exchange risk management (Brown, 2001). In past decade, hedging had gained at most importance since increase in interdependence of one market over the other (Marshall, 2000; Pramborg, 2005). Emerging Asian economies has gained more importance of hedging due to having international trade with each other. Since India is playing major role in developing the new era of:

1. Reduction in Foreign Exchange Losses: When corporate are involved in overseas transactions, then they are exposed to Foreign exchange risk. One making the use of hedging tools can reduce the expected loss due to Foreign exchange (Hagelin & Pramborg, 2004; Crabb, 2002).

2. Expanding current businesses to different markets: Those corporate who are dealing in one currency regime for their exchange transactions due to having fear of exchange volatility can limit their exchange risk with hedging. This would make them to trade in various overseas markets with different exposure of currencies.

3. Better profitability of stakeholders: Sometimes exposure against the trend of the currency makes huge losses to the corporate. Hedging the exposure protects the profitability and eliminates the risk over the long term. This would help the companies in better representation of their books in front of stakeholders (Allayannis & Weston, 2001; Cartel et al., 2004).

4. Use of new hedging tools: Development in Foreign exchange markets makes the corporate to use different and dynamic tools of risk hedging. New tools of hedging make the companies to hedge specific risk in different manner.

5. Hedging large currency decline: Macro events make the currency markets more volatile. Fall or rise can be easily seen often during the day of Macro events. In the period of events currencies can be protected with different hedging tools. Thus hedging protects the corporatefrom large currency declines.

Concerns over the Use of Hedging Techniques

Although hedging the foreign exchange exposure provide added benefits but every advantage come with the extra charges (Shin & Soenen, 1999). Use of hedging tools by Small and Medium enterprises becomes difficult when financial institute and brokers who provide these services of hedging charges huge sum for it. Following are the some of the concerns with using the hedging techniques:

- It happens that company has taken an exposure and also hedged his position with a hedging tool. But currency moves in the favor of the direction of the exposure and taking the hedge position remain worthless. In that case high cost of hedging parts the profit made from the position i.e. is the potential reward of any investor.

- Cost of hedging: Paying the hedging cost is somehow not possible for every enterprise. Having small exposure in overseas transactions and paying the cost for hedging those transactions is not possible for all. Thus cost of hedging becomes also a hindrance in application of hedging techniques.

Significance of Study

In continuation with elucidations in the previous sections of this chapter, it is easy to understand the mounting significance of measuring the forex risk exposure, its management and hedging it. The past evidences (many such studies have been mentioned in next chapter on Review of Literature) on the related issue have clearly indicated that large corporate having forex risk exposure are proactive to hedge against such an exposure. They have clear guidelines and experienced and trained team to decide the hedging strategy for them. But when it comes to small and medium enterprises and unlisted firms, no such evidences are available deliberating about the forex risk management by these firms across the world in general and specifically in context to India. Some of the major issues related to forex risk of Small and Medium Enterprises and Unlisted Firms are as under.

- ❖ Are SMEs and Unlisted firms really aware about the forex risk exposure?
- ❖ Are these firms measuring their forex risk exposure?
- ❖ Who will take the decision of forex risk management?
- ❖ What type of hedging instruments is available in the market?
- ❖ Which factors can influence the determination of hedging strategy?
- ❖ Do the market practitioners consider the same determinants to make hedging policy guidelines and developing hedging instruments, which are significant for SMEs and Unlisted firms?

So, above are the issues, which were considered before initiating this study so that various stakeholders can be benefitted from the findings of the study. The survey conducted under present study will be of suggestive for SMEs, Unlisted firms, every party involved in forex risk management in SMEs and unlisted firms, viz., managers, CEOs, Owners, Advisors, and BOD etc., industry experts involved in policy formulation and developing hedging instruments, academia and researchers. The findings of the current study will provide sufficient facts and findings to support all these stakeholders in taking decision or continuing research related to forex risk exposure, forex risk management, and determining forex risk hedging strategy.

Above all, there is dearth of research on the issue discussed in the study. Hence, the findings will contribute to the existing body of knowledge and literature on forex risk management.

The next chapter makes an in-depth study of existing literature on the related issue in order to identify the research gap more precisely.

Chapter 2

Review of Literature

Many finance specialists have pondered the benefits of doing hedging. These include classic contribution by Miller and Modigliani in 1958 and then by Smith and Stulz (1985). Smith and Stulz discussed that the managers' risk aversion attitude and their compensation contracts affects the financial risk management in the firm. The earlier studies related to use of derivatives for hedging purpose include, study by Block and Gallaghar (1986) in which the significance of interest rate derivative products were discussed to hedge the interest rate exposure by US companies. The study by Dolde (1993) stated that the small firms are more concerned about cost of risk management while the approach of large firms for hedging their risk was not similar to small firms. Due to cost of risk management, small firms were found completely ignoring the derivative instruments for hedging purpose. The top 100 Finnish non-financial firms were considered for a survey on interest rate risk management by Hakkarainen, A., Kasanen, E. and Puttonen, V (1997). Bodnar, G. M., Hayt, G., Marston, R. and Smithson, C., (1995) contributed a lot on the issue. Their study clearly indicated that there was lack of awareness among firms to use derivatives for hedging strategies. They showed that UK firms were among the highest users of derivative products. The UK based firms were focusing more on their accounting earnings' fluctuations to manage their forex risk exposure. The study by Loderer and Pichler (2000) focused on the risk management by Swiss companies. Their study found that the Swiss companies were not able to describe their risk profile. Similarly many studies based on survey on risk management and hedging practices by the firm were conducted across the world. For example, Bodnar and Gebjardt (1998) focused on European firms. Mallin, C., Ow-Yong, K. and

Reynolds, M.,(2001) focused on UK based nonfinancial firms, Bodnar et al.(2003) considered Netherland based firms, Pramborg (2005) made a comparison among Sweden and South Korean firms, Alkeback and Hagelin (1999) focused on Swedish non-financial firms, Jalivand and Switzer (2000) conducted an extensive survey on risk managers of American, Canadian and European firms.

Several studies have employed the questionnaire approach for the analyzing the exchange-rate exposure management in context to non-financial firms (e.g. Bodnar and Gebhardt, 1999; Hakkarainen, A., Kasanen, E. and Puttonen, V., 1998; Bodnar, G. M., Hayt, G. S. and Marston, R. C., 1998; Marshall, 2000; Ceuster, M.J.K., De Durinck, E.,Laveren, E., Lodewyckx, J., 2000; Mallin, C., Ow-Yong, K. and Reynolds, M., 2001). The most referred study is Bodnar, G. M., Hayt, G. S. and Marston, R. C., 1998;which considered publicly traded U.S. firms. Export is an important constituent in determining the exchange rate exposure of a firm that has been established by various theoretical (Marston, 2001) and empirical studies (Allayannis and Ofek, 2001). Allayannis &Weston (2001) come across an affirmative relation between the use of foreign exchange derivatives and firm's value. However, there are several theories that recommends why it may be most favorable for a firm to hedge its position (Stulz, 1984; Smith & Stulz, 1985; Froot, K. A., Scharfstein, D. S. and Stein, J. C.1993; DeMarzo & Duffie, 1995). The aim of this chapter is to provide a literature review of the current research topic.

Madhusmita and Rath (2017) documented the evidences of determinant of the forex risk exposure by Indian companies. The study took sample firms from manufacturing and service sector for a period of 13 years. The results of their research depicted that service sector in India is more exposed to the foreign exchange rate fluctuation in comparison to manufacturing sector.

Both of these sectors were found negatively related with the exchange rate in terms of their size while exports and market to book ratio of the firms under study were significantly related with the foreign exchange rate. Liriano (2016) presented a paper in conference at International Finance Corporation regarding stylized facts on the use of forex derivatives by exporters and importers from Chile. An extensive dataset of 5,600 firms was used over a sample period from 2000 to 2015. It was identified that Chilean firms were using currency derivative hedging strategies in proportion to their net forex risk exposure. An interesting outcome of this research was that the large number of small size firms was contributing to the larger share in the derivative market. The forex derivative hedging strategies were aligned with the mismatches in currency by various firms. The Chilean exporters were exposed to short positions while the importers were exposed to long positions in the currency derivatives.

Prasad and Suprabha (2016) discussed the benefits of using hedging strategies to cover forex risk. Their study focused on the economic exposure of Indian firms. A two factor model was used to measure the exposure rate of foreign exchange. The results of the study highlighted that twenty percent of the firms were significantly exposed to the forex risk. An interesting outcome of the study was that the firms were significantly affected by forex rate despite using various instruments of hedging like balance sheet hedging, using natural hedging and using derivatives etc. Patnailet al. (2016) discussed the existing rules, regulations related to foreign currency in India. Necessary issues related to policy framework on foreign exchange were discussed in their study. Their study addressed the issues related to portion of forex risk exposure which is not hedged by the firms, complexities and uncertainties in the regulatory environments etc. The researchers highlighted the risk involved in foreign currency borrowings when the markets are incomplete and a large sized companies contributing significant to GDP were not fully hedged for forex risk exposure.

Bhaskaran and Priyan (2015) made at attempt to explore the factors in context of forex risk management. Their study was destined to know the scenario or pattern in the forex risk management strategies of the firm. A sample of 64 cases was taken by the researcher and out of 64 cases, the firms were divided into two groups. The findings of the study indicated that the firms in the study were taking hedging positions for shorter duration only. And in the situation of long-run forex risk exposure by the firms, the firms had to restructure their business or had to change the business model to manage a long-term forex risk exposure. Vasumathy (2015) conducted a study of Indian Export SMEs to know their awareness and understanding regarding foreign risk hedging, risk management practices, attitude of SMEs towards using derivative instruments for the purpose of hedging etc. The author also highlighted the scantiness of the research evidences on the related issue. The researcher adopted a descriptive approach to understand the currency risk management practices by small and medium enterprises. The findings of the research indicated that the small and medium export units in India behaved neutrally when it came to use the derivative instruments for the purpose of managing the currency risk. The firms did not adopt even the alternative methods of hedging the currency risk. But, the SMEs had shown consistency in monitoring the foreign exchange rate fluctuations in the domestic and international markets.

Singhrun and Bal (2014) took a sample of three IT companies of India. The objectives of their research were to study the availability of various hedging instruments in India and to know the implementation mechanism for hedging strategies by sample units. The authors recommended that the future of IT based companies will be more challenging and risky.

Therefore the IT firms need to be more prepared for the adversities of the future. The study also recommended that the Indian firms should increase the use of derivative instruments and strategies for hedging the forex risk. The derivative hedging strategies like bilateral netting, invoice billing, compound options, range foreign exchange agreements etc need to be used by firms to hedge the forex risk.

Raghavendra & Velmurugan (2014) conducted a study on sample size of 100 IT firms in India in order to examine their currency hedging practices. The questionnaire was developed by reviewing the literature on same topics in context to different countries. The outcome of the research concluded that foreign exchange risk was the major financial risk which is faced by the IT Firms & future contracts could be used to minimize such risk. The study suggested that the average time horizons for the use of currency hedging instruments were the contracts maturing in between 6 to 12 months. Further it's concluded that the Indian IT firms are risk averse in practicing currency hedging and they perform analyses for predicting short term exchange rates.

Chong, Chang & Tan (2014) tries to chalk out the factors which generally influence the forex risk management mainly by the non-financial firms. It focuses on financial derivatives for managing the exposure from exchange. The study was conducted through a survey in which the questionnaires were circulated to the Treasurers and Financial Controllers of the firms. Descriptive analysis was employed to assess the profiles status of the respondents. Further, factor analysis was carried out to chalk out the factors which influence the use of financial derivatives. This paper focuses on Malaysia, where trading in derivatives has not been much popular. The study has only taken non-financial firms into consideration because they have option to opt for operational or financial hedging while financial firms also use derivatives for trading, speculation. 250 questionnaires were distributed to non-financial companies operating in

Malaysia, out of which 219 useable questionnaires were used for final analysis. In order to identify the constructs that affects the usage of financial derivatives in the country, explorative factor analysis was performed. EFA resulted in identification of three factors which were named as knowledge and skill, market risk and regulation and final factor named as company assertive level. Results of the study showed that the degree of derivative instrument flexibility and company's assertive level for regulators and market affects the hedging decision of non-financial firms. Furthermore, study also demonstrated that even the Non-financial firms need to hedge against the foreign exchange exposure. But this decision depends upon the perception, skills of firm, market risk, and products available. With the new innovations in financial field, varied kind of financial instruments are available. The resulted outcome of the study indicated that the hedging decision in anon-financial firms is mainly influenced by their assertive level towards the market & regulators and what is level of flexibility for derivative instruments. Besides this hedging decision is also dependent on the intellectual capability that firms acquire to perform hedging strategies Hence, in order to develop derivatives market in Malaysia, people need to be educated.

Hrubošová & Kameníková (2013) conducted a study on hedging practices on forex risk, majorly in small and middle enterprises. It was documented that many companies were facing Forex risk under difficult time of financial crisis. The study concluded that the trend of CZK/EUR in 2012 gives opportunity for using financial derivatives such as forwards, currency options and swaps to protect assets &liabilities against higher exchange fluctuations. In the backdrop of this discussion, it can be stated that understanding of foreign exchange risk exposure and management is important for business firms, the companies providing hedging instruments and for the policy makers to devise strategies to minimize the Forex risk. TuranErol,

AyhanAlgüner, GürayKüçükkocaoğlu,(2013) witnessed the firms in emerging markets have more exposure to forex risk. One important insight by the author was with regard to poorly developed derivative market in emerging market for hedging the forex risk. Their study examined the determinants of forex risk exposure. The research was based on firms in Turkey and identified five major determinants of forex risk exposure. The findings of the study clearly indicated that because of lack of development in derivative market, the firms were not able to hedge their measurable forex risk.

Bodnar, Consolandi, Gabbi & Jaiswal-Dale (2013) examined the derivative usage (both Interest rate and currency) by Italian firms, including the determinants of currency and interest rate derivatives in respect to currency and firm size, ratings, geographical location and industry, access to capital markets and education management. A questionnaire related to the usage of derivatives instruments in risk management and practices associated with risk management was sent through online method to 464 non-financial firms operating in Italy. With 18.5 % of return rate the final useable questionnaires that were used for final analysis was 86 firms only. The risks were composed of the currency and the interest rate risk, 67.4% actively managed the currency risk while 65.1% actively manage the interest rate risk while 79% of the firms (surveyed firms) used either of the interest rate or foreign currency derivative contract. The six firm level characters are Size, Geo, Market, Industry, Rating and Managerial Education. Results of the Logit-Regression revealed that Non-financial firms of Italy are mainly affected by the foreign currency risk. The manufacturing sectors mainly opt for the use of the foreign currency derivatives, while the most usual interest rate derivative is the interest rate Swap. The dominance of the interest rate derivatives and currency derivatives indicates its dominance of the small business and large clusters in the northern region.

Du, Ng & Zhao (2013) tries to give an alternative description of the missing variable bias and exposure puzzle different from the prior research work. They measured the foreign currency of a firm using Quantile Regression which is given by Koenker and Bassett (1978). The data for the present study was collected from 30 industries which were operating in US from a period of 1980 to 2009. The study pin pointed that the currency exposure of the firm is dependent on a large number external factors and by using the standard approach the researchers found only 17% of the Portfolios belonging to US firm have currency exposure. The weakness of the standard method with regression is that it does not take into consideration the non-firm specific events leading to foreign exposure. Results showed that the majority of the firms have sizable currency exposure and the previous methods for calculating the same had methodical errors. The practical aptness of this method should be checked and verified.

Kumar & Malyadri (2013) examined the learning derivatives and types of currency derivatives in order to understand currency futures and its advantages over forward contract. Another objective of this study was to understand how currency futures are used for hedging the currency exposure. Apart from this, the study also examines different types of margins and calculation of mark to market margin in case of futures. The major focus of the study was on use of currency future for hedging the export and import trade remittance and currency future as a speculative and arbitrage tool. How the computation of mark to market margin is done when trading member has open position in currency futures for the period more than one day and to identify the risk containment mechanism created by exchange for currency derivative segment. The study concludes that Currency futures can be effectively used for hedging the currency risk. It further states that forwards contracts are often confused with future contracts. But using Currency futures in place of Forwards provides edge in elimination of risk. Some distinct advantages are Price transparency, Eliminating the counterparty risk, Low cost and Access to larger market. Taking the practical example in the study, author explains how future contract works in case of hedging the Currency exposure. It evaluates that forward contract locked the exchange rate for a particular period of time, foregoing any harm or benefit of a weakening or strengthening the currency. Whereas in hedging is initiated using the future contract, one is not only able to fix its losses but also gives the opportunity of earning maximum profits. The last part of the study explains how every Exchange has to prepare the Risk Management mechanism for currency derivative segment. The exchange follows a Value at Risk (VAR) based margining through SPAN (Standard Portfolio Analysis of Risk) for collection of margin from clearing member. The Clearing member in turn collects the margin from Trading members and their clients.

Worasinchai (2013) focuses on the management attitude towards the currency hedging strategy. Management attitude has been related with the exposure to foreign currency transactions and time period of planning. The major focus of the study to identify the management attitude towards hedging depends upon the company's foreign transaction exposure and the planning horizon for the strategies is impacted by the attitude of management (Risk taker or Risk avoider). Data was collected from three companies operating in Thailand and data was collected through survey questionnaire, semi- structured interview, and document review method. Results of the Simulation of Financial Models and Thematic Analysis revealed that when exposure is high, attitude of the investor will be to avoid risk. In case of low exposure, attitude will be risk taker. Further, Risk taker manager will follow short planning horizon, while risk avoider manager will follow both short and long term planning horizon. The results of this paper can be beneficial for Thai firms, international partners, Thai government, financial institutions involved in hedging. With the developments taking place in Thai region, hedging is becoming an important tool to prevent exposure from highly fluctuating currencies.

Akshatha (2013) investigated the history and growth of derivatives in Indian markets, perception of investors, how derivatives help in managing risk by hedging and how can capital market increase the use of derivatives. In the first place, history regarding evolution of derivatives market has been explained with the help of recommendations of Dr. L. C. Gupta, which explains the change in the perception of risk management from 1980s. Further, hedging strategy using futures and options has been explained in the modern frame of complex and risky businesses and analysis on various factors has been performed to assess the investors interested in derivatives. Results of the study demonstrated that derivatives market have and will further boost the global as well as Indian economy .Therefore, there is need to develop it in the right direction with the support of government, regulators and exchanges by educating investors. Most commonly used derivatives are forward, future and options.

Bligh (2012) reviewed the concepts related with the hedging instruments and examined different types of risk which are involved in the transactions which are future oriented. These concepts were explained in this paper through an example in which a USA company owes a payment to a UK vendor due in three months. Further, this article involves the calculation part of foreign currency hedging techniques which involves hedging using forward contract, money market, futures market, option, currency swap. It can be concluded that options are most expensive in comparison to the other available strategies. Bodnar et al. (2012) documented risk management practices by Italian nonfinancial firms. The research was conducted on a sample size of took the sample-size of 464 nonfinancial firms of which 123 firms were listed. The present study was based on a survey which was conducted to get response of the non-financial firms for their risk management practices. The firm size, rating, access to capital market, geographical location, indulgence of sample firms in international trade and education level of management were the major criterion to see the difference in risk management practices. Broadly currency risk and interest rate risk management were managed by derivative instruments. Majority of the companies were doing hedging due to declining trade with emerging countries. The economic and political scenario of risk aversion was causing poor financial literary, diminishing value of lira and lack of innovation.

Bartram, S., Brown, G., & Conrad, J. (2011) investigated the impact of using derivatives on the risk and value of firm. The study was quite extensive and it took a sample of 6,888 nonfinancial firms from forty seven countries. The authors made an attempt to examine the operational hedging and using derivative methods by the firms to mitigate the risk. The findings of the study concluded that the nonfinancial firms were using derivatives products primarily for hedging purpose rather than for speculation purpose & for risk reduction, nonfinancial firms did not prefer operational hedging in place of derivative hedging. Makar& Huffman (2011) tried to explain the variations in amount of FXD in relation to differences in foreign currency exposure and identify the impact of industry membership on hedging practices. Key aspects of the study explained variations in the notional amounts of FXD in relation to difference in foreign currency exposure. Sample for the present study consisting 64 large US MNCs those were expected to be the major users of FXD, for the 1990-1994 periods. The selection of this sample is based on the following parameters: Large US based Multinational as measured by Forbes list of the 100 largest US MNCs; Company disclosed FXD information in its annual report, in accordance with SFAS number 105; Company operated in a manufacturing industry as reported on S&P Compustat data and Company which did not operate in the petroleum refining or related industries. Results of the study conclude that Foreign exchange derivatives use is positively associated with foreign currency exposure. Sample companies FXD amounts average 10.1% of consolidated assets and company's foreign sales represent 47.8% of consolidated assets. First part concludes that US MNCs increase their use of FXD by 0.68% for each 1% increase in the relative level of foreign sales. Aabo, Tom, Jochen Kuhn, Giovanna Zanotti, (2011) studied the impact of founder family's influence on the risk management by medium-sized manufacturing firms specifically for foreign risk management. The study concluded that the difference in the risk management strategies of firms in which founder of family was taking management decision in comparison to their counterparts was insignificant. Further the firms managed by founder family were found more indulged in speculation in addition to hedging practices.

Savchenko & Makar (2010) investigates whether firms have changed their future use of FXDs which are genuinely exposed for foreign currency exposure. To comprehend the exchange rate exposure puzzle the present study used firm-specific approach. The key aspects that were addressed by the study includes the analysis of changes in the use of future for foreign exchange derivatives using firm specific approach and Usage of firm's accounting data to monitor the use of future in foreign exchange derivatives and analyzing their hedging strategy habits based on their foreign currency exposure. For the present study 89 non-financial MNCs operating in U.S.A with ex ante exposure to varying exchange rates as proxied by the foreign sales ratio were selected. Results of the trade weighted exchange rate index revealed that the firms who are not 100% exposed, that is, partial hedgers in other words, make best use of futures and monitoring the same in case of increase or decline in the value of US Dollar while having significant foreign exchange exposure. Results also showed that there exists a substantial exposure either in terms of broad exchange rate index or firm-specific bilateral exchange rates in those firms which utilizes more FXD's in comparison to its foreign sales. Aabo, T., Høg, E., & Kuhn, J. (2010) took a sample of 215 Danish medium sized firms and information was obtained through an online web-based questionnaire which was sent to target respondents. Findings of the study indicated that the medium-sized manufacturing companies were using import as an important element to manage foreign exchange risk. There were less evidences obtained supporting the making changes in the capital structure of the firms to manage forex risk.

Das &Pradhan (2010) tried to shed some light on the issues faced by the exporting SME of India during the 2008 crisis and to examine the poor performance of same SMEs during the reforms. The major focus of the study was to examine the global crisis that could have a great impact on the exporting- SMEs. Besides this the study aimed to examine the unavailability of the structured credit and the limited credit issue. Inadequate risk management by the firms by concentrating the demand and supply to a particular customer &also the well-being of the enterprise is solely dependent on the owner of the firm. Data for the present study was collected from companies/firms who are indulged in exporting for a period of 1900 to 2006. Results of the analysis showed that the Indian SME involving in the exporting business have faced a lot issues due to a variety of reasons. Although there are long term solutions available for this, the SME haven't shown inclination towards implementing them, all these problems have compounded in the course of global crisis. However, the SMEs which are financially well insulated have become more competitive. One limitation of the present study that the study is only an observation of the author, there is also no involvement of any sophisticated statistical tool.

Yadav and Rastogi (2009) concluded that about two-fifths of the firms were risk averse but did not hedge their full exposure. A major number of the firms were following cost-center approach for managing risk. Ownership has been observed to be a significant determinant of strategy used by firms to reduce risk. While a major number of foreign controlled firms and private sector business group firms were categorized as partial hedgers, while most of the public sector firms belonged to the category of negligible hedgers. They concluded that the adoption of risk management techniques is still in infancy. In a more recent study by Dash et al., (2013) itwas suggested that in case of hedging the cash inflows, the best results are yielded by option hedging using out-of-the-money currency put option& in case of hedging the cash outflows, the best results are yielded by option hedging using out-of-the-currency call option. Further the results of the study highlighted that its very risky to remain unhedged towards foreign exchange fluctuations.

Clark & Judge (2009) evaluated the impact of various foreign currency financial hedging strategies determined by kind of exposure (long or short term) and kind of instrument (foreign currency debt, options, forwards and swaps) on firm value. This study comprises 412 non-financial companies as a sample for the year 1995. The OLS and multivariate logistic regression methodology were applied. The findings evident increase in value of the firm using foreign currency derivatives however, foreign currency debt hedging did not provide any hedging premium except when incorporated with foreign currency derivatives. It was further observed that short term derivatives lagged behind than foreign currency swaps in terms of generating value. Schiozer& Saito (2009) identifies determinants in managing currency risk as well as the magnitude of hedging by Non-Financial firms in Latin America (Mexico, Chile, Brazil and Argentina). The study also tries to assess whether the derivatives can generate cash flows to the tune of objectives of hedging and the impact of growth opportunities, tax benefits, informational asymmetry, financial distress costs and economies of scale on risk management decision. Data was collected from companies which are part of Bank of New York Latin American ADR Index.

Data was collected from 55 firms out of which 26 were operating in Brazil, 14 in Mexico, 12 in Chile and 3 in Argentina. Secondary data was obtained from 20-F files submitted to SEC, data stream and economatica databases and financial Statements. Derivatives contracts were classified into Foreign Exchange, Domestic Interest Rates, International Interest Rates and commodities. Sample was segmented into Users and Non users on the basis of different types of financial derivative. Informational asymmetry does not affect the magnitude of derivative holdings but positively impact the decision to use hedging. Tax incentives do not impact the size of hedging currency exposure while growth opportunities directly impact it. Results of the study found that large amount of foreign debt will also increase the size of currency derivatives. Size of the firm will share direct relation with the use of derivatives and inverse relation with the magnitude of risk management. Financial Distress is a major determinant for risk management while tax benefits do not holds much importance. Furthermore, Brazilian and Chilean firms are more engaged in derivatives in terms of both volume and magnitude in comparison to Argentina and Mexico. Brazil and Chile also have higher cash flow potential from derivatives and hold more FX derivatives than Mexican and Argentinean firms. One of the major limitations of this study was that the sample size was not representative of the whole industry and is limited to certain firms with good standing. Apart from this, managerial risk aversion has not been taken into account while determining the factors for currency risk management.

Clark & Judge (2008) investigated if the association between demands for corporate foreign currency hedging and leverage would be biased by foreign currency debt users using the data of 366 UK firms for the period 1995. The relation between the measures of financial distress and the demand for corporate foreign currency hedging was analyzed as well. The methodology of multinomial Logit regression was used for studying hedging decision. The findings highlighted that the misleading inference could be caused failing to differentiate between foreign currency users and non-users with regards to relevance of financial distress on the need for corporate foreign currency hedging. It was revealed that most prior studies represented the employment of derivatives with hedging however, overlooked the significance of foreign currency debt as a hedging method. The financial distress was represented as financial leverage in most of the prior studies that might not be suggestive of financial health of the company. Further, if the sample of foreign currency hedgers divided into companies that do and do not employ foreign debt then the study showed leverage variables as significantly associated to the foreign currency hedging decision for companies which employ foreign currency debt either in combination with foreign currency derivatives or in separation except for company which only employ foreign currency derivatives.

Sivakumar & Sarkar (2008) tries to examine how various hedging instruments are being used by major Indian Firms across different sector and also to know their perspective towards the risks. Further, to insist the need for rupee futures in India due to high usage of the forward contracts. The study suggested that the usage of derivatives in India is highly regulated because the INR is only partially convertible, the most commonly used products are swaps, forwards and options. The firms dealing with more than one currency face a huge risk due to uninformed changes in the exchange rate; also the type of risk management varies with the type and kind of the risk. This paper explains about how different Indian Companies across different sectors use derivative products for hedging their risks. The study concluded that Indian firms, irrespective of the sector, for the purpose of short term hedging they use options or forward whereas, for the purpose of long-term hedging the Indian firms generally make use of swaps as their preferential instrument. Further it is concluded that there has been more easing of the regulations as a result of which there has been a continuous foreign currency inflow. The forwards and the options are the most recognizable instruments. In the year 2007 the Rupee-Dollar futures was introduced and it could be traded, but this has to be regulated properly.

Sivakumar and Sarkar (2008) studied about various companies from different sectors and it was concluded that forwards and currency options were the most preferred instruments of hedging used by sampled Indian companies for short term and swaps were preferred by these companies during long term. Wang (2008) tries to chalk out the factors which generally influence the Forex risk management process of non-financial firms. It focuses on financial derivatives for managing the exposure from exchange. The major focus of the present study was to examine how multinationals and domestics both are affected by the volatility in the exchange rates. More volatile profits of the firm lead to lesser competition and firm value reduces in comparison to competitors. Thus, hedging becomes an important factor to lead in the competitive market especially if other firms are also engaged in it. Data was collected from 387 US firms which falls under S&P 1500 composite index for a period of 2003 to 2005. All the data has been taken from the 10 K disclosures and it is in terms of million dollars and the data has been divided into 3 parts in accordance with Large, Median and Small cap firms. Collected data was analyzed by using COMPUSTAT, Logit Model and OLS Regression Model. Results of the study demonstrated that Firms which hedge the foreign exchange exposure have higher firm value in comparison to non-Hedgers but value of the firm and market competition do not share any relation provided it has a certain level of foreign sales and industry level hedging. Large firms are more involved in hedging as they can afford the costs and they generally have more exposure to currency risk. Furthermore, larger firms also have higher distress costs in terms of leverage, higher chances of information asymmetry because of complex structure. Competitors hedging strategy plays an important role while deciding to hedge, if required. Apart from this, Different industries have different levels of competition; different levels of competition will result into different levels of hedging. Before taking decision to hedge, one should look for hedging strategies followed among the industry, if no one hedges than there is no edge over others by hedging. The major limitation of the study was that the present research considers only the derivatives as the hedging activity but do not take into consideration the other forms of hedging performed by the firm.

Bartram (2008) evaluated foreign exchange rate exposure of the cash flows of large non-financial firms. The hedging ability of the firm was also tested employing proprietary corporate data comprising of foreign currency debt, cash flows and derivatives. The present study suggested the relevance of taking into account the result of corporate hedging by examining the Forex rate exposure on the basis of cash flows, foreign currency debt, derivatives and capital market data of the large multinational corporation. The findings reported that the operating cash flows of the company which are important for business actions, significantly periled to the exchange rates. Concurrently, insignificant exposure of cash flow was observed as a result of using hedging by the multinational corporations to cut down exposure.

Muller & Verschoor (2007) adopted a sample of 3634 Asian firms to examine whether exchange rate fluctuations influence the equity value of particular Asian active companies followed by ascertaining if the patterns of Asian foreign exchange risk exposure were industry type for the period of 1993 till 2003. Further, if the exchange exposure of the firm is more apparent with the rising time horizons was also probed. The study explored if the exchange rate exposure was ascertained with the help of variables considered as proxies for the hedging impetus of a company. The impact of hedging on long and short term exchange rate risk exposure accompanied by variables used for justifying rationale behind hedging of the firms were inquired. It was found that Asian firms went through the effect of economically significant exposure for 25 and 22.5 percent to the US dollar and the Japanese yen, respectively. The level of exposure of the firm to fluctuation in exchange rate changes with return horizon. Also, short term exposure appears to be hedged better and weak liquidity position of the firm inclined to have lower exposures.

Rajendran (2007) in his study tried to prove that Banks with large deposit bases will be able to gain relatively, by externalizing the practices of Risk Management and to understand the intermediator role of the banks due to the Derivative exposure. The usage of the derivatives solves the dual purpose of generating revenues and also to manage the risk exposure in the volatile markets. Further, banks with higher risk co-efficient have higher credit risk and use unimproved loan assessing and recovery process. Finally, private sector banks having huge risk exposure have externalized the risk management process and also the foreign banks with lower risk exposure have externalized as required. Data for the present study was collected from 83 banks for a period of 2005-2006. Results of the study render that growth of derivatives has a profound impact on the advances growth of the banks with smaller deposit size and also the private sector banks. Therefore, too much of restrictive policies can hamper the growth of the loan rate. The hedging process should also be done according to the requirement of the bank. This paper gives a generalized opinion on usage of the derivatives by the banks, however it does not deeply discuss about the products which are required to be used the banks.

Judge (2006), considered 366 large non-financial U.K. firms in his study and documented that the factors that were important in determining relationship between expected financial distress costs and its decision to hedge against the foreign currency exposure. The results provided strong evidences of a more significant foreign currency hedging decision. The findings of the present paper were found better than what was found in earlier studies based on US data. The present study identified that the possible reason for this could be due large number of studies in U.S. included even the hedging firms in their non-hedging sample, such as firms using non-derivative results against the a priori expectations. Besides this country specific method for currency hedging, which causes biasness in the institutional factor could be one of the reason for higher financial distress in U.K Firms.

Kim, Mathur & Nam (2006) using a sample of 424 companies studied whether operational hedging was a complement or a substitute for financial hedging. It was observed that companies with non-operationally hedged made employment of more financial hedging in comparison to the extent of exposure of foreign currency rate as calculated on the basis of export sales. Whereas, companies had more currency exposure which were operationally hedged but the amount of financial derivatives used by them became smaller as compared to exporting companies. This indicated the reason behind the usage of smaller amount of financial derivatives notwithstanding with the higher extent of exposure of currency risk by the global companies. The results also revealed that firm value could be increased with hedging.

Muller &Verschoor (2006) selected the sample of 935 U.S. multinational firms to assess by what means these firms were influenced by the movement of foreign currency during the period of 1990 until 2001. The conditional variance was incorporated by GARCH $(1, 1)$ model into the system. The findings of the study showed that currency movement significantly influenced 29 percent of the sample with the actual functioning in foreign countries. Further, results indicated that returns of U.S. stock responded asymmetrically to the movements of currency. It was observed that the importance and accuracy of exposure estimates could be increased by inserting non-linearity in foreign currency risk exposure. The results showed that asymmetries were found more prominent for large against small currency variations compared with appreciation and depreciation cycles.

Muller &Verschoor (2006) conducted review of extensive literature pertaining to the conceptual fundamentals of exchange risk exposure followed by current advancement towards assessment design and findings of empirical studies during the last two decades. This study invalidated literal unanimity with respect to the appropriate dimensions affecting currency risk exposure and anticipation for an exceptional model including entire intricacy of the consequence of exchange rate blows on the value of company. The findings also highlighted the relevance of cost and revenue structure of the company, input and output market elasticity for ascertaining sensitivity of the firm as a consequence of variation in exchange rate, their own competitive position and competitive environment. Further, internal feature of exchange risk exposure required to be considered while analyzing the linkage between the exchange rate movements and stock returns. The influence of fluctuations in currency over shareholder value was suggested by the amassed bulk of prior literature.

Bris, A., Koskinen, Y., & Nilsson, M. (2006, 2003) suggested that non-financial companies could gain from expanded capacity to support additional financial leverage and undertake prominent business risk with the decrease exposure of foreign exchange rate and market risk. It was indicated that decrease cost of capital as a consequence of lesser market betas embedded with advantages for firm valuations and corporate investment. The results reported significant growth in investment activity with the launch of Euro. Bartram &Karolyi (2006) examined the effect of introduction of the Euro in 1999 over foreign exchange risk exposure, market risk and the stock return volatility. The study took a sample of 3220 non-financial companies from 18 European countries, Japan and the United States of America for the year of 1992-2001. The methodology of two-sample t-tests, chi-square and nonparametric Wilcoxon test were used for the data analysis. The findings of the study evident increase in volatility of total stock return and market risk exposure was reduced significantly with the introduction of Euro outside and inside of Europe for non-financial firms. It was observed that companies resided in the region of Euro showed decrease in market risk and also evident high portion of assets and foreign sales for non-Euro companies in Europe. The results suggested net absolute reductions in the exposure of foreign exchange rate with the launch of Euro for non-financial firms however, economically and statistically these variations were small.

Hu & Wang (2005) conducted a study in relation to the listed non-financial firms of Hong Kong so as to identify the various determinant of foreign currency hedging activities. The findings of the research study were failed to support the assumption of tax loss reduction, underinvestment &financial distress cost reduction. However, the findings supported the assumption in relation to the foreign currency exposure. The results showed that the firm's policies related to currency exposure was the crucial factor determining a foreign currency hedging decision for non-financial companies in HK. On the contrary, in mainland of China, the Firms with major foreign operations were less likely to hedge foreign currency exposure due to non-floating exchange rate between HK dollar and the mainland RMB.

Saito & Schiozer (2005) confirmed the evidences of using derivatives by Brazilian non-financial firms, using a sample of 74 companies. Dash, M., Kodagi, M., &Babu, N., (2008) made a comparison of performance of different Forex risk management strategies for short term Forex cash flows. The results of the study indicated the currency options strategy yielded the highest mean returns in all sample periods for outflows irrespective of variation in exchange rates while forwards strategy was found better one in case of inflows. Pramborg (2005) made an attempt to compare Korean and Swedish non-financial firm's hedging practices. This study made addition to the existing literature by examining the differences in management practices of foreign exchange risk between the firms. From the two countries, only 163 companies answered to a survey disseminated during the period of 2000 to examine the hedging practices and foreign exchange exposure using derivatives and other methods. The Logit regression was employed to analyze the data. The similarities had been observed between the companies with regard to foreign risk exposure and hedging practices. The employment of derivatives by the sample of Korean firms was significantly lower than in the Swedish firms. Features like liquidity, foreign exposure, leverage and size unable to access this phenomenon. The reason could be higher fixed cost received for initiating derivatives programs by Korean firms. And the Korean derivative markets were not mature enough that could leads to higher cost moreover, heavy regulation of OTC derivative use from the Korean authorities. It was evident that Korean firms largely dependent upon alternative hedging methods as the decision to hedge had not country specific rather impelled by variables like firm size and the extent of foreign exchange exposure. Furthermore, Korean firms were found not so stringent in supervising the status of risk as compared to Swedish firms.

Kim & Sung (2005) evaluated the factors influencing the decision of the firm in handling foreign exchange risk in the market. For this, a sample comprised of 223 non-financial companies was considered from Korea. The study concluded that the size of the firm as the prominent factor for hedging. The size of the firm had stronger informative power, with concomitant findings, for external technique relative to internal technique that showed lesser costs. The export revenue alongside with size of the firm was found to be another significant factor that influences hedging decision of the firms. Public companies were in particular, that required to fulfill the disclosure requirements and hence, found to have a stable net income. Abor (2005) examined how Ghana firms manage their foreign currency exposure risk using Forex Management Techniques. Some of the key aspects that were addressed by the present research werethat the firms were classified based on Industry. Further, classified whether firms have risk management system or not. Classification based on the scale rating given by firms to the eight inbuilt goals in the questionnaire. Classification based on number of firms practicing hedging. Classification based on firms using hedging techniques due to high or low trade intensity. Data was collected from 100 firms operating in Ghana and the inclusion of these 100 companied was based on the basis of fulfillment of two basic criterions. First criterion was that, in the past three years the firm should have been at least for the two times indulged in import and the second criterion was that the first should be registered under "Association of Ghana Industries (AGI)". The questionnaire pertaining to the research was sent to these 100 companies out which 68 companies returned the questionnaire. The result of a descriptive analysis revealed that a large number of firms do not practice hedging or do not use derivatives products, they tend to use them when the intensity of imports increases or if there is any increase in the prices of imports or if local currency depreciates. Firms having exposure in Forex are not managing properly either due to low level of awareness & education and also due to under developed nature of financial markets. It is recommended that Firms should educate themselves about the forex management, should have separate department & experts for managing forex and also banks should provide firms with variety of developed hedging tools & also educate their clients, that is, firms about the same.

Helliar (2004) tries to identify which UK based companies go for swap options and what are the problems which they encounter while using this type of market Apart from this another objective of this study is to find why these companies' uses swap market. Data was collected from 594 companies which were operating in UK. The study stated that the increased usage of the derivatives can be attributed to the success of the OTC and to prevent the misuse of the same, the UK FRs standard had come into play. Further, Swaps have become the favored products across the globe, thus this paper probes the same both from an academician's perspective and also the Treasurers perspective. Result showed that the interest rate swaps are more important than the currency rate swaps also the treasurers of the companies are becoming smarter in the hedging of their risks. Also the swaps offer an advantage in the following areas like, access to funding; helps in the balance sheet management; help in the restructuring of the existing debt; outperform the market imperfection; help in the ease of transaction and provides comparative advantage. The implementation of the accounting standards have made the treasurers muse the swaps in a more accountable manner.

Hagelin & Pramborg (2004) scrutinized the association between hedging activity based on financial instruments and the foreign exchange exposure. Unlike previous literature, this study also considered use of debt dominated in foreign currencies along with currency derivatives. In addition, the effect from translation and hedging transaction exposure on firms were assessed. Data was collected from 160 Swedish firms in first phase which was held in the year 1997, 275 firms in second phase which was conducted in the year 2000 and 261 in the last phase which was conducted in the year 2001. The study was conducted on a sample of 617 Swedish firms to assess the relation between foreign exchange exposure and the hedging practices was established during the period of 1997 till 2001. The difference between cost and revenue value in foreign currency is taken as the measure of exposure related with foreign exchange. In order to measure robust standard errors, the study resorted to the Newey& West (1987) GMM method. The findings reported that exposure of the foreign exchange risk was rising in underlying exposure. However, larger companies demonstrated lower intrinsic exposure because of the capacity to utilize operational hedges. The financial hedges were found efficient in lowering the risk of foreign exchange exposure of the firms. Furthermore, effect of risk reduction evident from translation and transaction exposure hedges. Further, results also showed that with the usage of financial hedging instrument there is reduction in the exposure of foreign exchange. It means that as the firm uses more and more financial hedging instrument along with the denomination of the foreign currency there is reduction in the exposure of foreign exchange of the firms.

Fraser & Pantzalis (2004) evaluated the association between stock prices of US multinational corporations and with the variation in foreign exchange rates based on four different measures. The sample comprised of 310 in total from mining and manufacturing firms. The study applied two factors least squares regression to ascertain the stock return with the changes in foreign exchange rate. It was found that most of the firm's utilizing the firm specific foreign exchange indices demonstrated a significant exposure to foreign exchange rates. Studie's results suggested that many corporations observed to be exposed to significant foreign exchange risk along with specific regions of a firm's geographic network system whether related with any exposure depends on the application of the kind of foreign exchange rate index to measure exposure.

Kothari &Guay (2003) tried to analyze the magnitude of risk exposure for 234 large non-financial firms hedged by financial derivatives for the year of 1995. The comparison of these magnitudes to the magnitudes of firm exposure was also made which according to hedging theory forecast would be possibly expensive. The study adopted descriptive statistics and regression analysis as a methodology. The findings reported the market value sensitivities of financial derivative portfolio and cash flow to inherent assets price fluctuations. It was evident that if commodity price, interest rates and currency exchange rates changes at the same time with the median firm's derivatives portfolio and three standard deviations then firm would at the most yield $31 million in value and $15 million in cash. While in comparison to investing and operating cash flows, firm size and other standards, however, those were evident to humble amount. The employment of corporate derivatives seemed to be a small part of non-financial firm's overall risk profile.

Nguyen & Faff (2003) made an attempt to examine whether foreign currency derivatives lower down the foreign currency exposure of the company if utilizing it as hedge. A sample of 144 Australian firms was considered for the period 1999. The OLS and GMM techniques were applied to measure the long term foreign exchange exposure. The findings suggested that Australian companies had minimum exposure to exchange rate variations in the short-run and the employment of foreign currency derivatives lower down exchange rate exposure in the short-run. Further, the level to which companies were exposed to transaction exposure could only be covered by utilizing short return purview and only a humble number of companies were periled to exchange fluctuations in the short run because transaction exposure could be efficiently hedged through financial hedging. However, in the long run Australian companies found to be exposed to foreign exchange rate because it was difficult to hedge economic exposure. In addition, no effect had been measured with the use of foreign currency derivatives, foreign sales and leverage on exchange rate exposure of different return purview.

Chan et al. (2003) studied the Hedging Effectiveness using utility maximization approach depending upon relative price changes in derivative and spot prices. The study considered the approach that whether Forwards or Over-the-Counter-Options provides the optimum hedging effectiveness to hedge NZD/USD transaction exposure to the exporters in New Zealand. The findings of the study concluded that prior to Asian Crisis 1997, for an ordinary risk averse exporter forwards markets were marginally more effective in comparison to the options synthetic forwards for a hedging contract of 1, 3 or 6 months, but during and after crisis option synthetics were more effective. The research also suggested that a normal exporter facing short term and lesser volatile exposure should use forwards market, however an exporter should use options in case of impulsive fluctuation. Further it was also concluded regardless of which derivative product was used, for a risk averse exporter utility derived from a hedged position was always greater than the unhedged position

Chan, Gan & McGraw (2003) analyzed whether forwards or over the counter options gives optimum hedging effectiveness to hedge NZD/USD transaction exposure to the exporters in New Zealand. The study focused on Hedging Effectiveness using utility maximization approach depending upon the derivative prices and relative price change. The data for the present study is taken from the by DataStream data base for a period between 1st July,1985 to 30th June, 2000 which comprise of average bid-ask spot prices. The study used Black Scholes Model, GARCH Model and Sharpe Ratio model for the analysis of the data. Results of the study depicted that prior to 1997 Asian Crisis 1 or 3 or 6 months ,the forwards markets were marginally more effective than the options synthetic forwards forarisk averse exporter but during and after crisis option synthetics were more effective. Further, a normal exporter with facing short term and lesser volatile exposure should use forwards market; however an exporter should use options in case of impulsive fluctuation. In additional to this, it was also concluded regardless to the derivative product is usage; utility derived from a hedged position was always greater than the unhedged position for a risk averse exporter.

Bradley & Moles (2002) tried to explain how large, publicly listed UK firms use currency risk management along with operational hedging for managing exchange rate risk. The study stated that foreign currency debt is a popular amongst the UK firms as it offers flexibility, in addition to the assets-liability management process it proves to be a hybrid strategy. Further, changing the source of inputs is being done by the utility companies, it is also crucial to predict the future foreign currency cash flow. Exchange rate is taken into consideration in the case of general industrial sector, along with service industries. For the identification of non-financial companies which are operating in UK, the researcher used EXTEL Financial database. On the basis of this, the researchers posted 579 questionnaires to all the listed non-financial firms to avoid low response rate. With a response rate of 68%, researchers received 395 useable questionnaires which were used for final analysis. Results of the descriptive analysis and Chi-square analysis revealed that a sizable portion of the firms in UK are ready to blend the strategic and operational techniques so as to manage the foreign currency exchange rate exposure. Firms with foreign subsidiaries are more open to this; along with this the firms favor a hybrid (financial/operating) technique. However, there are hiccups in fully forming a flexible strategic approach. The variations in the survey conducted by the researchers had quite variation in answers, these aren't explained here, as it would give more insights in the practice by different industries.

Crabb (2002) used a sample of 276 US multinational firms to examine the net effect over stock return of those corporations with the exchange rate movement from the period 1992 until

1996. The panel data regression, generalized Tobit and CAPM model were used to measure the exchange rate exposure. The findings evident the effect of exchange rate changes on multinational corporations. It was suggested that the use of foreign currency derivatives (FCD) could mitigate risk of exchange rate exposure. The results highlighted that the financial hedging activities were the reason behind non-significant exchange rate exposure.

Henderson (2002) focuses on the major concerns regarding hedging currency risk in the emerging markets. Emerging markets include both the recent developments and difference between the developed and emerging markets. The major focus of the present study was that while managing currency risk, following peculiar characteristics of emerging market currencies have to be taken into account:- Structurally High Inflation, High Forward Premiums, Options market implications, Lower forward rate biasness. Further, Traditional hedging structures included Plain Vanilla Call, Call Spread, Plain Vanilla Forward, Calendar Spread, Risk Reversal, Seagull while the enhanced tools include Knock Out, Knock In, Range Binary, Window Option and Fade-In Option. Management of currency cannot be same for every firm, it depends on the individual firm scenario. Passive currency management deals with reducing risk while Active currency management deals with gaining without hedging. Results of the study revealed that emerging markets have more options for hedging in comparison to past. Apart from this, Derivatives used to manage risk have developed over the time in terms of liquidity but few emerging markets do not provide liquidity because control of exchange is present.

Pantzalis et al. (2001) observed reduction in currency exposures with the capacity to make operational hedging for the companies together with pooled sample accompanying negative (net exporters) and positive (net importers) exposures. Cartel et al. (2001) indicated reductions in the exchange rate exposure as a result of employing financial and operational hedges together. These findings corroborated the operational hedging as complementary to financial hedging. Allayannis & Ofek (2001) analyzed the employment of foreign currency derivatives for speculative or hedging purposes on the sample of S&P 500 non-financial firms during the period of 1993. In particular, the influence of currency derivatives over firm exchange-rate exposure was investigated. Followed by the factors that induce the firms to hedge and the extent of hedging was studied. The study used Tobit, binomial Probit and Truncated regression method to derive the results. It was indicated that company employ derivatives for hedging in the foreign exchange market rather to speculate. It was also evident that company's exposure by means of foreign trade and foreign sales impel to hedge and direct the company on extent of hedging.

Brown (2001) attempted to look into the program of foreign exchange risk management of HDG Inc. The present study analyzed the determinants that influence why and how the company handles exposure of foreign exchange with the help of using discussion with managers, internal firm documents and data on transactions of foreign exchange derivatives count as 3110. The results indicated that competitive pricing, informational asymmetric and the assistance of internal contracting seemed to induce the firm for hedging. Furtherance, the hedging of HDG reckoned over derivative market liquidity, exposure volatility, accounting treatment, exchange rate volatility and current hedging results. Mallin, C., Ow-Yong, K. and Reynolds, M. (2001) studied the usage of derivatives instruments in the non-financial listed firms in UK. Results showed that derivative instruments were very popular among larger UK companies and main aim of using derivatives in UK Firms was to manage fluctuations in the accounting earnings. This finding of the study was in contrast of US firms.

Loderer & Pichler (2000) examined the practice in Swiss Industrial Corporation in managing the currency risk for the year 1996. The findings of the study revealed that about half of the firms did not know the currency RP of their cash flow and were also unable to quantify the currency RP of their value. Reason behind this could be companies don't feel such a need due the on-balance sheet instruments employment to defend them prior and post currency rates changes. It was perplexing because making a rough estimate of at least the exposure of cash flows could be helpful &even was not forbidden. Further, companies without estimating aggregate transaction exposure had employed currency derivatives to hedge/ insure individual short-term transactions.

Marshall (2000) studied the practice of foreign exchange risk of the large MNCs such as Asia Pacific, UK and USA. The difference in the practice had been measured in terms of size of the MNCs, different regions, the industry sector and the degree of internationalization. The difference was revealed between the regions with respect to objectives and importance of foreign exchange risk, significantly on economic and translation exposure, the policies used for handling economic exposure and the employment of internal or external hedging methods. The industry sector and size of the MNCs other than overseas business were found significant in terms of the importance of exchange rate risk. Moreover, regional factor evident to be significantly influence to bring in differences in handling foreign exchange risk, the policies in dealing economic exposure and the internal hedging technique. Further, USA and UK multinational companies found to be having similar policies on the other hand Asia Pacific Corporation demonstrated significant variation.

Shin & Soenen (1999) tried to find out if US firms were risked to exchange rate by utilizing a sample of stock returns of 1051 US multinational firms during the period of 1983 till

1994. The pooled regression was employed to assess foreign exchange exposure. The results evident that small firms got benefits with the depreciation of US dollar value at international level. These firms had positive significant exposure of foreign exchange. The hedging activities did not prove efficient in case of large firms to rid of exchange risk. However, primary metal and the electrical equipment industries, in particular, were mostly exposed to foreign exchange risk. Chow & Chen (1998) utilizing a sample comprises of 1110 Japanese firms listed on the Tokyo stock exchange (TSE), evaluated the exposure of exchange rate risk and its factor on the basis of cross-sectional regression methodology for the period 1975 till 1992. The findings suggested that the equity returns of Japanese companies decreases with the depreciation of yen because these were found to be strongly negatively exposed. The reason behind this could be the heavy dependence of Japanese firms on imported raw material and they have learned how to grapple with the adverse effect due to yen appreciation. It was found that Japanese companies in non-traded industries &with higher imports ratio hit adversely with the depreciation of yen on the other hand would be less impacted if the firms fall under the industries with higher export. It was also evident that firms with high cash dividends, low liquidity and high leverage had high exposure. Further, small companies had small exposures for the one month return horizon whereas, smaller exposure had experienced by the larger firms with the longer-return horizons.

He and Ng (1998) conducted a study on foreign risk exposure of 171 Japanese multinationals and it was identified that 25% of the sampled firms experienced noteworthy Foreign Exchange exposure. He and Ng also looked at the relationship between Forex exposures and studied the variables that were tacit to reflect derivatives usage. It was evidenced that firms that were opting some mechanism to predict and hedging strategy were less exposed to Forex risk in comparison to their counterparts. Howton& Perfect (1998) examined the pattern of derivatives and the determinants of the derivatives by the companies. The major focus of the present study was on the proofs, on the level of the types of derivatives contracts that are being used. The theoretical determinants in the derivative usage are external financing, financial distress; tax related costs and the risk exposure. For the present study, two samples have been drawn on the basis of following criterion: "The firm must have an annual report available on either Edgar or the SEC Q files, the firm cannot be a utility or a financial institution and finally the firm cannot have experienced bankruptcy in the previous three year". On the basis of these criterions the researchers were left with 451 Fortune/S&P firms and 461 random firms who were taken from Compustat data base for the year 1994. Data was analyzed with the help of descriptive and Tobit model regression analysis. Results of the analysis depicted that the method of using the derivatives by the large US firms and also the motivating factor to use them. Firms using partially the derivative contracts are just 60% and the firms using derivatives properly only 36%. However in the above samples 90% were interest rate contract swaps, futures and forwards consisted of the 80% currency contract. One exemption was observed that the usage of derivatives by random firms' in the study was not strongly associated with the theoretical determinants.

Grant & Marshall (1997) focused on UK companies. Their study was focused on the extent of derivative used by sample firms, the reasons for choosing those special instruments and the perceived risk associated with such instruments. The survey identified that UK firms were well aware of various derivative instruments like options, forwards, and swaps. And these instruments were used to manage currency risk and interest rate risk. The exotic products were used with caution because of liquidity concerns of the underlying market Berkman, Bradbury &Magan (1997) took a sample of 79 New Zealand companies and a comparison was made in 79

New-Zealand non-financial firms and US non-financial firms. The study concluded that more than 65 percent respondents agreed that their firms are exposed of foreign currency risk mainly with USD followed by Australian Dollar. It was also identified that the firms in New-Zealand were more frequent to put their positions on derivatives to their board of directors in comparison to US firms. But both New-Zealand and US based firms had similarity in using derivatives to hedge their positions and managing the risk.

Mun & Morgan (1997) assessed the cross-hedging performance of five major currency futures for local currency or US dollar exchange rate risk confronted by depository financial institutions within a group made out of emerging Asian countries from 1985 till 1994. A generalized method of moments (GMM) and Sharpe Performance Index (SPI) were used to test the cross-hedge performance. The results of the study revealed that minimal variance cross hedging with a futures portfolio function in a much better way than a minimal variance cross-hedge with one currency futures for Thailand, Singapore and Indonesia, on the contrary, minimal variance cross-hedge with one currency futures surpassed for Malaysia and Korea. It was also found that the German mark futures of Korea would be the best alternative of a future contract for the minimal variance cross hedge whereas, Canadian dollar futures of Malaysia. However, among all composition methods, the joint naïve cross-hedge functions worst. Goetz & Hu (1996) argued that the currency swaps are more cost-effective for hedging foreign debt risk and the forward contracts are cost-effective for hedging foreign operations risk.

Bodnar, Hayt & Marston (1995) started with a sample of 2000 US non-financial firms and finally got usable response from only 530 firms and conducted a survey on usage of derivative products by these firms. The findings of study evidenced that more than three fourth of the sample firms were using foreign currency derivatives. It was documented that foreign derivatives were the most commonly used derivatives among other available derivative products. Further in foreign currency derivatives, the forward contract was the top choice of the sample firms. In addition to forward contracts, OTC options were also among the most preferred choice to manage foreign currency risk. More specifically the result of the study can be summarized as follows:

1.) Out of 530 firms in the survey, 35% were using derivatives. Commodity based industries showed the highest usage, while derivative use was least common in service industry. In interest rate risk management swaps were the most used derivative product. For foreign exchange risk management, forwards dominated the other products.

2.) Firms using derivatives to hedge firm commitments were only 80% whereas only 44% of the firms used derivatives to hedge balance sheet and only 43% of the firms used derivatives to study on the direction of financial price.

3.) In concerns about derivatives like credit risk, accounting treatment, transaction cost and liquidity risk; accounting treatment was the issue of greatest concern. Around 67% of firms assigned "Minimizing fluctuation in cash flows" as their primary objective for hedging.

4.) For Counterparty risk, derivative transactions with 12 months or less, 87% of the responding firms said that they required a rating of A or better. For maturities greater than 12 months, a rating of AA or better for the counterparty rises to 60%.

5.) Swap and option pricing software was utilized by 30 to 35% of large firms but by only 10% to 15% of small firms. Option pricing software was slightly more common than swap pricing software.

6.) In reporting derivative activity to the BOD, most of the firms had centralized activity for risk management policy making. Only in the area of execution of transaction, there was a significant amount of decentralization (15%).

Choi & Prasad (1995) focused on examining the sensitivity of the exchange risk and its factor at the firm and industry level for 409 U.S. multinational corporations from 1978 till 1989. The exchange risk sensitivity coefficient had been received by applying OLS (ordinary least squares) model on firms whereas, GLS (generalized least square) model for industry related data. The findings of the study reported that 60 percent companies gained significantly from exchange risk exposure on the other hand, following decrease in the value of dollar, 40 percent companies lost. It was evident that firm specific operational variables leads to variations in exchange risk sensitivity across cross-sections. Further, inter-temporal and cross-sectional variations in the coefficients of exchange risk were also revealed despite the fact that, when the data combined on the basis of 20 SIC industry groups, limited support found for exchange risk sensitivity.

Bodnar, Hayt, Marston & Smithson (1995) aimed at studying the purpose of creation of a database that would be suitable for the academicians in risk Management. Another objective of the study was to find out the usage of derivatives by US Non-Financial Firms. In last, to identify how the Risk management policies and reporting procedures in context to derivatives are being followed in US Non-Financial firms. Study covers the following key aspects: overall use of derivatives; which derivatives are being used and why?; risk management policies and finally the control and reporting procedures. A Questionnaire, which was based on twelve different aspects, was distributed to 2000 Non-Financial corporations in the United States, out of which 530 useable questionnaires were retained for final analysis. For the selection of non-financial firms from the large population, a procedure was established according to which a random sample of non-financial firms was taken from 1993 S&P Compustat database. Samples were based on following factors like industry, size and capital structure. Results of the study demonstrated that out of the 530 firms in the survey, 35% are using derivatives. Commodity based industries shows the highest usage, whereas derivative use is least common in service industry. In interest rate risk management swaps are the most used derivative product. For managing foreign exchange risk, forwards dominates the other products. Further, 80% of the firms use derivatives to hedge firm commitments whereas only 44% of the use derivatives to hedge balance sheet 43% of the firms use derivatives to take a view on the direction of financial price. In concerns about derivatives like credit risk, accounting treatment, transaction cost and liquidity risk; accounting treatment is the issue of greatest concern. Around 67% of firms assign "Minimizing fluctuation in cash flows" as their primary objective for hedging. For Counterparty risk, derivative transactions with 12 months or less, 87% of the responding firms said that they require a rating of A or better. For maturities greater than 12 months, a rating of AA or better for the counterparty rises to 60%. In addition to this, Swap and option pricing software is utilized by 30 to 35% of large firms but by only 10% to 15% of small firms. Option pricing software is slightly more common than swap pricing software. Finally, in reporting derivative activity to the BOD, most of the firms have centralized activity for risk management policy making. Only in the area of execution of transaction, there was a significant amount of decentralization (15%).

Nance et al. (1993) revealed that companies with high profitability and having prominent liquid assets had less inducement to indulge in hedging process as they were exposed to lesser financial and profitability distress. Batten & Mellor (1993) made an attempt to deal with the broad spectrum of financial risk management practices and events comprising employment of computer technology, the level of supervision of central bank and the internal control systems of the Australian corporate sector using a sample of 72 firms. It was found that many companies trade their foreign exchange exposure rather not brought any limits in internal foreign exchange dealings. The various risk of foreign exchange rate was ascertained with the help of respondents. The employment of both synthetic and physical instruments was supported by the industry for managing foreign exchange risk. Further, size of the firm was found to have significant effect on the practice of risk management of the firm.

Belk & Gulam (1990) did a study on UK multi-corporations to observe how these companies manage their foreign exchange exposure management. Majority of the respondents defined their companies as risk averters and it was indicated that the sample companies were actively managing their accounting exposure for managing currency risk. And transaction exposure was focused heavily to manage foreign currency risk. Batten, Mellor and Wan (1993) conducted a study on management practices in relation to foreign exchange risk management of Australian based firm. The findings indicated that all companies were hedging their foreign currency risk. Majority of the firms were managing through transaction exposure while 8 percent of the firms were managing transaction and translation exposure. Only 17 percent of sample firms were managing all three types of exposures. These firms used both physical and synthetic products in order to offset the cash flows generated through foreign operations. The firms were extensively using synthetic products.

Collier et al. (1990) conducted an initial study on UK and US firms and targeted 27 large MNCs (only 23 replied) to study currency risk management practices by them. Their study focused on both transactions as well as translation risk impact on behavior of British and American. The study also tried to find the degree of risk neutrality approach applied in managing the currency risk. It was documented that different kind of policies adopted due to contrasting philosophy towards the transaction risks, different approaches for Management of translation risk and Level of risk taking ability among US corporations. Their study concluded that (a) In case of transaction risk; generally risk averse firms opted for hedging while the organizations with risk neutrality mindset prefer to actively manage i.e. hedging decision is discretionary. Group of firms following risk averse policy believe that management is performed only as a defense to any significant loss not for earning additional profit. Generally companies with high transaction risk preferred to close out the transactions, (b) overall management of translation risk was not found much popular. Some organizations believed that managing risk causing changes in book value of reserves is of no use. While the other set of organizations felt that reserves are important for long term value to shareholders and thus risk should be managed, (c) UK companies were more open to manage translation risk in comparison to US companies. US companies which managed the risk were quite risk averse in their approach, and (d) Thus, we can find that higher transaction risk generally leads to close out policy. Also, large number of UK companies prefers to manage translation risk.

Collier et al. (1990) extended the previous findings dissecting the practices used by large British and American MNC's for currency risk management. The study focuses on both transactions as well as translation risk impact on behavior of British and American. It also tries to find the degree of risk neutrality approach applied in managing the currency risk. For data 27 large MNC's were approached out of which 23 replied (11 UK firms and 12 comparable US companies). The present study focused on different kind of policies adopted due to contrasting philosophy towards the transaction risks, different approaches for management of translation risk and level of risk taking ability among US corporations. Their study concluded that (a) In case of transaction risk; generally risk averse firms opted for hedging while the organizations with risk neutrality mindset prefer to actively manage i.e. hedging decision is discretionary. Group of

firms following risk averse policy believe that management is performed only as a defense to any

significant loss not for earning additional profit. Generally companies with high transaction risk

preferred to close out the transactions, (b) overall management of translation risk was not found

much popular. Some organizations believed that managing risk causing changes in book value of

reserves is of no use. While the other set of organizations felt that reserves are important for long

term value to shareholders and thus risk should be managed, (c) UK companies were more open

to manage translation risk in comparison to US companies. US companies which managed the

risk were quite risk averse in their approach,   and (d) Thus, we can find that higher transaction

risk generally leads to close out policy. Also, large number of UK companies prefers to manage

translation risk. Block and Gallagher (1986) studied the usage of derivatives instruments for

hedging interest rate exposure in the USA. They conducted this study in post-October 1979,

when the Federal Reserve altered its policy, leading to a boost in the interest rates volatility and

interest rate. The results of the study revealed that about one out of five firms used interest rates

options and futures to hedge the interest rate exposure. Large firms and companies in commodity

oriented industries used these instruments more in comparison of the small firms.

Smith &Stulz (1985) analyzed the effect of hedging policy, contracting costs and taxes on

investment decisions of the firms as information with regard to the broad diversity of hedging

practices so determined. The study emphasized on following modern finance theory and the

existence of inducement to increase the market value of the firm in the contracting process. The

reason behind hedging of value maximizing company suggested as aversion of managerial risk,

taxes and cost of financial distress. Collier & Davis (1985) focused on centralization vs.

decentralization in currency risk management. Their study was based on 114 large companies of

UK. The research was destined to examine, 1) Divergent facets of management of Currency risk by large UK Multinational companies, 2) Identify Structure of organizational control for managing the risk and, 3) Impact of centralization on the risk taking abilities of the company. As per the survey conducted by them, large no. of UK companies was having Centralized structure to manage the foreign currency risk in comparison to the overseas subsidiaries. Centralized control can be compared with active management while decentralization can be compared with the close out policy. High level of risk will give rise to close out policy and low risk will lead to management of risk. Adler & Dumas (1984) tried to accustom with the definition and measurement of currency risk exposure. This study considered foreign exchange risk exposure of the company in accordance to the interest of analysts and stockholders. It was evident that both exchange risk exposure and market risk could be ascertained in the same manner.

Conclusion

The wide-ranging evidences obtained through studies mentioned above have highlighted the relevance of research on the issues related to forex risk exposure, management and hedging. As discussed above, the issue of forex risk exposure and management is addressed mostly by large corporations and small firms and unlisted firms have indicated that there is lack of knowledge and more ignorance to hedge the forex risk. The following table has given a snapshot of major contribution from various journals on the related issue.

Table 11

List of Journals and Authors Having Major Contribution in the Literature on Forex Risk Exposure/Management/Hedging

Journal	Authors/Year	Country	No. of Papers
The Journal of Risk Finance	Abor,(2005)	Ghana	1

Financial Management	Bligh (2012), Howton& Perfect, (1998), Berkman, Bradbury &Magan, (1997), Bodnar, Hayt, Marston & Smithson (1995), Choi & Prasad, (1995), Adler & Dumas, (1984)	US, New Zealand	6
International Journal of Applied Financial Management Perspectives	Akshatha, (2013); Kumar &Malyadri, (2013)	Unknown	2
Journal of International Money and Finance	Allayannis&Ofek, (2001)	U.S& Japan	1
Journal of Banking & Finance	Bartram, (2008)	German, U.S & European countries	1
Journal of Empirical Finance	Bartram &Karolyi, (2006); Muller &Verschoor, (2006); Loderer&Pichler, (2000)	US, Japan and 18 European countries, Swiss	3
Journal of International Business Studies	Pantzalis, Simkins&Laux, (2001); Batten & Mellor, (1993)	Australia &U.S	2
Accounting and Business Research	Belk &Glaum, (1990); Collier, Davis, Coates &Longden, (1990); Collier & Davis, (1985)	UK, U.S	3
European Financial Management	Bodnar, Consolandi, Gabbi&Jaiswal-Dale,(2013); Clark & Judge, (2009); Clark & Judge, (2008); Grant & Marshall, (1997)	UK, Italy	4
Managerial Finance	Chong, Chang, & Tan,(2014); Bradley & Moles, (2002)	UK, Malaysia	2
Review of Finance	Bris, Koskinen& Nilsson, (2006)	European countries	1
Journal of Financial Economics	Brown, (2001); Guay& Kothari, (2003)	U.S	2
Multinational Finance Journal	Judge, (2015); Judge, (2006); Chan, Gan& McGraw, (2003)	New Zealand, UK	3
Pacific-Basin Finance Journal	Pramborg, (2005); Chow & Chen, (1998); Mun& Morgan, (1997);	Japan, Swedish, Korea & Asian countries	3
International Review of Economics and Finance	Crabb, (2003)	US	1
Economics, Management	Das &Pradhan, (2010)	India	1

and Financial Markets			
Review of Quantitative Finance and Accounting	Du, Ng & Zhao, (2013)	US	1
Journal of Multinational Financial Management	Muller, A., &Verschoor, (2006); Fraser&Pantzalis, (2004); Nguyen, & Faff, (2003); Marshall,(2000); Shin &Soenen, (1999)	U.S, UK, Asia pacific, Australia	5
Economics Letters	Goetz & Hu, (1996)	southern US	1
Journal of International Financial Management & Accounting	Hagelin&Pramborg, (2004)	Swedish	1
The Journal of Finance	He & Ng,(1998)	Japan	1
Journal of applied accounting research	Helliar, (2004)	UK	1
Advances in Finance and Accounting,	Hrubošová&Kameníková,(2013)	Czech Republic	1
Asia-Pacific Financial Markets	Hu & Wang,(2005)	Hong-Kong	1
Decision	Jain, Yadav&Rastogi, (2009)	India	1
Emerging Markets Review	Kim & Sung, (2005)	Korea	1
Journal of Corporate Finance	Kim, Mathur& Nam, (2006)	U.S	1
Journal of Applied Business Research	Makar& Huffman, (2011); Savchenko&Makar, (2010)	U.S	2
Journal of the Japanese and International Economies	Muller &Verschoor, (2007)	Asia	1
Journal of Finance	Nance, Smith & Smithson, (1993)	U.S	1
The Journal of Finance	He & Ng, (1998)	Japan	1
Journal of Business and Financial Affairs	Raghavendra&Velmurugan, (2014)	India	1
Academy of Banking Studies Journal	Rajendran, (2007)	India	1
Emerging Markets Finance and Trade	Schiozer& Saito, (2009)	America	1
The Journal of Financial and Quantitative Analysis	Smith &Stulz, (1985)		1
Concordia University	Wang, (2008)	U.S	1
Indian Streams Research Journal	Budheshwar Prasad Singhraul , GnyanaRanjanBal (2014)	India	1
NIPF working paper series,	IlaPatnaik, Ajay Shah, Nirvikar Singh (2016).	India	1
SDMIMD Journal of management	P. BalaBhaskaran and P. K. Priyan (2015)	India	1
Journal o Accounting and Marketng	Prasad K, Suprabha KR (2016).	India	1

The International Trade Journal	SonaliMadhusmitaMohapatra and Badri Narayan Rath (2017).	India	1
Indian Journal of Finance	Vasumathy S. (2015).	India	1
Eighth IFC Conference on "Statistical implications of the new financial landscape" Basel, 8–9 September 2016	Liriano (2016)	Chile	1

Source: Author Compilation

In lieu of evidences obtained from literature survey, the following research gap has been identified.

Research gap/ Need for present Study

1. The mainstream of past evidences on forex risk awareness, forex risk management and determining forex risk hedging are available from countries other than India.

2. In case of Indian context, the focus of past research has been on listed and large-sized companies. Both unlisted companies and SMEs have not at the drawn evenhanded attention by researchers.

3. There is no consensus regarding the significance of Forex risk exposure management for SMEs. A wide-ranging research is required to prop up or discard this question.

4. The past studies are incomplete in the sense these have focused only on one aspect, viz., Forex risk exposure, Forex risk management and determinants of Forex risk hedging strategies etc. considering a small sample of less 100 or less 200 units. A more comprehensive study is required which addresses all these issues related to SMEs and Unlisted firms.

****

Chapter 3

Research Methodology

The purposefulness of current chapter is to discourse the several subjects related to research methodology of the underlying study. It includes the specification or research design, approach to develop research instrument, reliability and validity of research instrument, determination of sample size, methods of data collection and procedure to collect the data. The current chapter has stipulated the framework used for carrying the whole research work. This framework is developed in consideration with the predetermined objectives of the study. To begin with, first of all research questions and objectives of the study have been addressed and thereafter, the research design has been founded.

Research Questions

The following research questions were recognized after finding research gap in literature survey.

1. Are SMEs and Unlisted non-financial firms in India aware about forex risk exposure?

2. How SMEs and Unlisted non-financial firms in India are managing their forex risk exposure?

3. What are the determinants of forex risk hedging strategies of Indian SMEs and unlisted non-financial firms in India?

Objectives of the Study

The following objectives have been recognized after considering the above cited research questions.

1. To study the Forex Risk Exposure of SMEs and Unlisted Non-Financial Firms in India.

2. To study the Forex Risk Exposure Management by SMEs and Unlisted Non-Financial Firms in India.

3. To study the determinants of Forex Risk Hedging Strategies by SMEs and Unlisted Non-Financial Firms in India.

Research Design

Conceptually, the whole research activities are carried on inside the boundaries of a structure called research design. Ideally, the purpose of a research design is to facilitate the researcher to continue the study in a most efficient way in order to yield maximum information in the form of research outcome. Churchill Jr. (2011) has stated that a research design is to be considered as a plan or general framework of the study, which directs the collection of data and analysis of data in a systematic manner. Malhotra (2004) defined research design as the basis for leading the research study as it postulates the elements of processes required for getting essential information desirable for constructing or answering marketing research plans. Further, a well-defined research design confirms that the study will employ economic procedures and it will be relevant for the problem solving method (Churchill Jr., 2001).Broadly, there are three categories of a research design, i.e., causal, descriptive and exploratory. A causal research establishes/examines the cause and effect relationship between the variables. A descriptive research design is more concerned with the depicting the incidences of something already happened and establishing relationship between variables. While an exploratory research design is envisioned for the elucidation of opinions and thoughts regarding the respondent population or to render insights on how to do more causal research or research problem (Nargundkar, 2003).

The study under consideration is both exploratory and descriptive in nature. As discussed in previous chapter, the research questions addressed in the study are not duly addressed by researchers and most of the past studies in the related field focused on a very narrow side of currency/forex risk exposure by SMEs and large companies both. Hence, current study has made an in-depth analysis to explore this new area of research. Also, by using the information obtained through survey and analyzing the gathered data reflects the descriptive (popularly known as *ex post facto research*).In the present study, surveys are conducted on the owners, CEOs, Finance Controller or other managers involved in forex hedging strategy makers.

Sample Design

The study under consideration has used a snowball method of sampling. The snowball sampling design is apposite for the studies where the sampling units are approached by the references of existing subjects. This is the reason that snowball sampling is also called as 'referral' sampling. Commonly this method is used where it is arduous to find the target respondents. As revealed in previous chapters that the current study is destined to know the forex risk exposure related information from the respondents and largely, the firms are not willing to provide the information related to their internal risk management policies. Therefore, a reference of the existing subject of the research can be of great help to obtain data from more respondents. In addition to this, the snowball sampling method reduces the possibility of sampling errors to the minimum because the sample units are selected wisely and these units are experts in their field.

Sampling Frame

Initially a database for 2487 reference points was developed. These were the SMEs and unlisted non-financial firms in India across different states and regions. These reference points were contacted through telephones and emails and were briefly told about the purpose of present study. Since the most important feature of the sampling unit that it must have foreign risk exposure therefore, no specific region was targeted for the purpose of data collection but any SME or unlisted non-financial firm meeting this basic criteria and registered as SME or Unlisted firm was designated as an eligible sample unit to participate in the survey. Out of 2487 firms listed in our own developed database, only 1843 firms were found having foreign risk exposure on a regular basis that was an essential feature to be eligible to participate in survey. The remaining firms were irregularly involved in foreign transactions, which was only once, or twice in one or two years. Next, out of this sample of 1843 firms, 1069 firms agreed to participate in the survey as remaining were either not willing to share the information asked in survey or were reluctant for other reasons like paucity of time, and lack of interest etc. The final questionnaire was administered on a sample of 1069 firms. The survey was conducted through multiple methods, i.e., telephonic interview, personal visits, email, and online questionnaire. Out of 1069 questionnaires administered, only 458 respondents completed the survey and submitted for further analyses. Finally, after cleaning the data for missing information and unengaged respondents, a final sample of 407 was used for the purpose of data analysis. This response rate is 38% of the sample units who agreed to participate (Out of 1069 units) in the survey and 22% of the sample units eligible for participation (out of 1843 firms) in survey. Although, after reviewing the sample size considered in past studies on the related field, initially the study was targeting a sample size of 150 units, which was a rough estimate of average sample size of samples considered in the past studies. But after a methodical analysis of distinctive opinions of researchers regarding determination of sample size, the study under consideration followed a more logical and statistical way of selecting the sample size. The method of sample size determination has been discussed in the following section.

Two enumerators were hired for gathering the data from the target sample units. The database generated through snowball sampling served the purpose of sampling frame. As discussed above the database of 1069 firms and unlisted non-financial firms from different parts of the country formed the sampling frame.

Sampling Unit

Each of the SMEs or unlisted non-financial firm among 1069 firms was the sampling unit.

Target Population and Respondents

The target population for the present study consists of Small & Medium Enterprises and Unlisted non-financial Firms of all sizes. The reasons for the consideration of this target population have already been well determined during literature survey, i.e., in case of India, majority of the research evidences are available for large companies listed on stock exchanges and the evidences available for related research on SMEs and unlisted firms is either narrow in scope or have provided insufficient evidences to contribute to theory and implications related to forex risk exposure, its management and determinants in general and with special reference to Indian context. Furthermore, the financial companies are excluded from the target population. The reason for excluding the financial firms is that these firms are both source and end user of forex hedging products. The research done by Bodnar & Gebhardt (1999) and Hansen (2009) also has supported the exclusion of non-financial firms for such studies. The owners, CEOs, Finance Controller, Member of Board of Directors or other Managers involved in forex hedging strategy makers were the respondents for treasuring the relevant information. The organization structure of the firms may be dissimilar. Therefore, the decision point related to forex risk hedging strategy can also be different. Generally, the owners, CEOs, Finance Controller or other managers are involved in taking the risk management decision of their firm/company.

Sample Size

Determination of sample size is a multifaceted task. Different approaches exist for the determination of appropriate sample size. Largely, there are three most common criterions for the determination of optimum sample size, i.e., the level of confidence, level of precision and degree of variability. Cohran (1963:75) mentioned the following formula to determine the representative sample size for large populations.

$$n_0 = \frac{Z^2 pq}{e^2}$$

Where $n_0 =$ is the sample size, $Z^2 =$is the abscissa of the normal curve that cuts o an area α at the tails (1-α equals the desired confidence level, e.g., 95%), e = is the desired level of precision, p=is the estimated proportion of an attribute that is present in the population, and q =is 1-p. e value for Z is found in statistical tables which contain the area under the normal curve.

The experts have talked about other criterion too to select an optimum sample size. In one of the earlier studies related to sample size determination by Kish (1965) have suggested a sample in the range of 30-200 elements is sufficient when there is 20%-80% attribute is present and the distribution approaches the normal distribution. Sudman (1996) have suggested a minimum sample size of 100 for each major group and in case of a minor group, 20-50 elements are necessary. The existing literature can also provide guidance to determine the sample size on the related field. Generally a sample of 200-500 elements is considered good for studies based on regression analysis. In addition to this, the researchers are required to add 5-10 percent margin in the sample size for inability to contact the sample units and it should be increased by 30% due to possibility of non-response by the respondents. The statistical tables are also used to determine the sample size. Any of the statistical table or formula used to identify the suitable sample size is the total data points the researcher should collect or obtain. It does not include the margin for

inability to contact or non-response by the sample units.

If we go with the formula given by Cohran (1965:73) and want ±5% level of precision,

desire a 95% level of confidence and assume that maximum level of variability is, i.e. p=0.5. The

optimum sample size for the study under consideration turns out to be 365.

$$n_0 = \frac{Z^2 pq}{e^2}$$

$$n_0 = \frac{(1.96)^2 (0.5)(0.5)}{(0.05)^2}$$

n₀= 365

The past studies on related field are based on varying sample sizes. Many studies are

based on extensive case studies having a sample of less than 10. Generally, a large sample of

300-500 has been considered for studies based on listed companies. Majority of the studies based

on SMEs and reviewed in literature review section has taken a sample of 100 or less than 100.

Therefore considering the specialized nature of data requirement for the present study, initially

the study was targeting a sample size of 150 units. But after a deeper analysis of different

opinions of researchers regarding determination of sample size, the study under consideration

followed a more logical and statistical way of selecting the sample size. Apart from this, one

another acceptable criterion of sample size determination was taken up in the present research,

which is being given by Israel (1992). According to this criterion if we require a precision level

of ±5 and our population size is more than 100,000 then we should have a sample size of 400. In

accordance with this, we have a sample size (407), which is more than 400.

Further, after obtaining the results of objective three, i.e., to find the determinants of

forex risk hedging strategy, it was recognized that if an additional analysis can be done to prioritize the various decision criterion then it would intensify the research findings. The reason for this is naive to cognize, as the relative importance of one construct or criterion can be different from another construct or criteria. Such kind of analysis is done with the expert opinion only. Hence, a sample of ten experts was considered to run a model on prioritizing the decision criterion. The details regarding this procedure have been mentioned under the heading **statistical tools** in further section of this chapter. The Analytic Hierarchy Process technique is used for this purpose.

Types of Data Collected

In addition to primary data collected through survey, the present study has also considered secondary data to get facts and figures related to forex market, hedging instruments and international trade. For this, various sources of information like official websites and reports of Reserve Bank of India, Security Exchange Board of India, Ministry of Corporate Affairs of India, Ministry of Micro, Small and Medium Enterprises, and Bank for International Settlement has been used.

Timeline in Administration of Research Instrument and Data Collection

Developing the Database of 2487 SMEs and Non-Financial Unlisted Firms: 3 Months

Contacting all sample units, i.e., in the first round for seeking Approval for participation in Survey: 2 months

Contacting (through telephone, email, online and offline survey) the 1069 sample units for obtaining desired information through structured questionnaire: 8 months

Operational Definitions

Meaning of Small & Medium Enterprise (SME)

The definition of Small & Medium Enterprise is as under.

"Small and Medium Sized Company" (SMC) means, a company-

i.   Whose equity or debt securities are not listed or are not in the process of listing on any stock exchange, whether in India or outside India;

ii.   Which is not a bank, financial institution or an insurance company;

iii. Whose turnover (excluding other income) does not exceed rupees *fifty crore* in the immediately preceding accounting year;

iv.   Which does not have borrowings (including public deposits) in excess of rupees *ten crore* at any time during the immediately preceding accounting year; and

v.   Which is not a holding or subsidiary company of a company which is not a small and medium-sized company?

Companies (Accounting Standards) Rules, 2016

Unlisted Firms

An active public or private company registered in India but which is not listed on any of the stock exchanges in India

Forex Risk Exposure

A Firm/company having regular (multiple times in a year) transactions in foreign currency is known to have foreign risk exposure. A firm having infrequent or occasional exposure with foreign transaction will not be considered for the survey.

Demographic Profile of the Respondents

The following table shows the snapshot of the demographic profile of the respondents to show the representativeness of the population.

Table 12

Sector wise Distribution of Sample Units

Sectors	Frequency	Percent	Valid Percent	Cumulative Percent
Construction	16	4%	4%	4%
Manufacturing	296	72.7%	72.7%	76.7%
Services	33	8%	8.0%	84.7%
Trading	57	14%	14.0%	98.7%
Any Other	5	1.3%	1.3%	100%
Total	407	100%	100%	

Source: Calculations done by Researcher

From the above table it can be inferred that majority of the firms/companied in the sample are indulged in the manufacturing sector, followed by trading, service, construction and any other respectively.

Table 13

Number of Employees Working in Sample Units

	Frequency	Percent	Valid Percent	Cumulative Percent
Less Than 10	33	8%	8%	8 %
10-30	81	20%	20%	28%
30-50	152	37.3%	37.3%	65.3%
50-80	62	15.3%	15.3%	80.7%
Above 80	79	19.3%	19.3%	100%
Total	407	100%	100%	

Source: Calculations done by Researcher

The scrutiny of the above table shows that in terms of number of employees working in different organizations are quite equal with most of the companies (152 companies/firms) having employee range from 30 to 50. Next, there were 79 companies/firms who have employee more

than 80 in number. Apart from this, there were 81 companies/firms who have employee within

the range of 10-30 employees, 62 companies/firms have employees between the ranges of 50-80

employees and there were 33 companies/firms who have employee in the range of less than 10

employees. It shows that in our sample, majority of the companies/firms have more than 30

employees working in their organizations.

Table 14

Annual Turnover (in terms of INR) of the Sampled Units

	Frequency	Percent	Valid Percent	Cumulative Percent
Less Than 5 Crore	38	9.3%	9.3%	9.3%
5-10	54	13.3%	13.3%	22.7%
10-15	41	10%	10%	32.7%
15-20	27	6.7%	6.7%	39.3%
20-25	8	2%	2%	41.3%
25-30	30	7.3%	7.3%	48.7%
30-35	16	4%	4%	52.7%
35-40	8	2%	2%	54.7%
40-45	11	2.7%	2.7%	57.3%
45-50	14	3.3%	3.3%	60.7%
50-100	49	12%	12%	72.7%
Above 100	111	27.3%	27.3%	100%
Total	407	100%	100%	

Source: Calculations done by Researcher

Results of the above table revealed that majority of the companies/firms (27.3%) is

having annual turnover more than Rs. 100 Crore. It means that in our sample size, we not only have companies/firms which are having annual turnover less than Rs. 100 Crore but also we have

companies/firms who are having the annual turnover of Rs. 100 Crore. Next, 13.3 % of the total

sample size comprised of the companies/firms who have annual turnover of Rs. 5-10 Crore,

followed by 41 companies/firms who have annual turnover of Rs. 10-15 Crore, whereas, 49

companies/firms have annual; turnover of Rs. 50-100 Crore. It means that approximately 40 % of

the sample size of the present study have annual turnover more than Rs. 50 Crore, which is a

good turnover. Apart from this, there are 38 companies/firms who have annual turnover less

than Rs. 5 Crore, 7.3% of the companies/firms have annual turnover between the ranges of Rs.

25 to 30 Crore, 27 companies have annual turnover in the range of Rs. 15-20 Crore, 4% of the

companies/firms have annual turnover in the range of Rs. 30-35 Crore, 8 companies/firms have

annual turnover in the range of Rs. 35 to 40 Crore and finally only 3.3% of the total sample size

of the companies/firms have annual turnover in the range of Rs. 45-50 Crore.

Table 15

Life of the Sampled Units in Terms of Year (Domestic operation)

	Frequency	Percent	Valid Percent	Cumulative Percent
1-5 Year	68	16.7%	16.7%	16.7%
5-10	98	24%	24%	40.7%
10-15	87	21.3%	21.3%	62. %
15-20	62	15.3%	15.3%	77.3%
20-25	35	8.7%	8.7%	86%
25-30	24	6%	6%	92%
30-35	14	3.3%	3.3%	95.3%
Above 35	19	4.7%	4.7%	100%
Total	407	100%	100%	

Source: Calculations done by Researcher

Results of the above table demonstrated that around one fourth of the sample companies/firms have been operating in the rage of 5 to 10 years domestically whereas, there are 68 companies/firms in the range of 1 to 5 years of domestic operation of business. Furthermore, 21.3 % (87) companies/firms falls under the range of 10 to 15 years of experience in terms of their business operation domestically. It means that approximately two third of the sample size of the present study falls under the range of 1 to 15 years of experience in terms of their business operation domestically. Apart from this, results also showed that there are 62 companies/firms who falls under the range of 15-20 years of domestic operation experience whereas, only 19 (4.70%) of the companies/firms have domestic business operation which is more than 35 years in terms of experience. Furthermore, 24 companies/firms falls under the range of 25-30 years of experience and 14 (3.3%) of the companies/firms have 30-35 years of experience in terms of their business operation domestically.

Table 16

Life of the Sampled Units in Terms of Year (International operation)

	Frequency	Percent	Valid Percent	Cumulative Percent
1-5 Year	111	27.3%	27.3%	27.3%
5-10	125	30.7%	30.7%	58%
10-15	73	18%	18%	76%
15-20	41	10%	10%	86%
20-25	24	6%	6%	92%
30-35	11	2.7%	2.7%	94.7%
Above 35	22	5.3%	5.3%	100%
Total	407	100%	100%	

Source: Calculations done by Researcher

The scrutiny of the above table revealed that approximately one third of the companies/firms have 5-10 years of business operating experience at international level whereas, there are 111 companies/firms who have an experience of 1 to 5 years in terms of international business operation. Apart from this, 18.00% (73) companies/firms have 10-15 years of international business operating experience. It means that more than three fourth of the sample companies/firms of the present study have international business operation in the range of 1 to 15 years. On observation that came into existence after looking at these tables is that, majority of the sample companies/firms of the present study either operating domestic or international have an experience in the range of 1 to 15 years. Furthermore, there are 41 companies/firms who have an experience of 15 to 20 years of international business operation. There were 24 (6.00%) of the companies/firms who are having 20-25 years of experience in terms of international business operation. Eleven companies/firms have an experience 30-35 years and 22 (5.3%) have international business operation more than 35 years.

Table 17

Mode Through which business is Involved in International Operations

	Frequency	Percent	Valid Percent	Cumulative Percent
Through Export	166	40.7	40.7	40.7
Through Import	130	32	32	72.7
Both Export & Import	111	27.3	27.3	100
Total	407	100	100	

Source: Calculations done by Researcher

Results of the above table depicted that majority of the sample companies/firms 166 (40.7%) of the present study involved in international business through the mode of export business. Apart from this, the share percentage of companies/firms through import or through both export and import is almost similar, that is, there are 130 (32.0%) of the companies/firms who get involved in international business operation through import and there are 27.3% (111) companies/firms who go international in terms of their business operation through the mode of both export and import.

Table 18

Frequency of Exports and Imports by Sample Unit

	Frequency	Percent	Valid Percent	Cumulative Percent
Daily	81	20	20	20
Weekly	106	26	26	46
Monthly	144	35.3	35.3	81.3
Quarterly	41	10	10	91.3
Semi-annually	11	2.7	2.7	94
Annually	8	2	2	96
Rarely	16	4	4	100
Total	407	100	100	

Source: Calculations done by Researcher

The scrutiny of the above table demonstrated that more than one third of the companies/firms 144 (35.3%) indulge in export or import on monthly basis whereas, there are only 16 companies/firms who rarely involved in export or import, otherwise rest of the companies/firms either daily or annually go for import and export. There are 106 (26.0%) of companies/firms who go for import or export on weekly basis whereas, there are 81 (20.0%) of companies/firms who are indulged in either export or import or both on daily basis. Furthermore, results also revealed that there are 41 (10.0%) of the companies/firms who operate on quarterly basis in terms of export or import whereas, 11 (2.7%) of the companies/firms work on semi-annual basis and only 8 (2.0%) of the companies/firms go for export and import on annual basis.

The results of these analysis revealed that the sample size of the present study is quite representative in terms of SME's which are operating in India. And further, Table 19 tells the demographic profile of sample units on the basis of their turnover in foreign currency as a proportion of total turnover. As mentioned in the table, the highest number of sample units lie in the range of 50-60% indicating that out of their total turnover, around 60% turnover happens in terms of some foreign currency.

Table 19

Proportion of Turnover in Foreign Currency

	Frequency	Percent	Valid Percent	Cumulative Percent
Less than 10%	46	11.3	11.3	11.3
10-20%	36	8.8	8.8	20.1
20-30%	38	9.3	9.3	29.5
30-40%	46	11.3	11.3	40.8
40-50%	49	12	12	52.8
50-60%	66	16.2	16.2	69
60-70%	41	10.1	10.1	79.1
70-80%	31	7.6	7.6	86.7
80-90%	33	8.1	8.1	94.8
90-100% (In case you are a 100% export based firm/company)	21	5.2	5.2	100
Total	407	100	100	

Source: Calculations done by Researcher

Procedure for Development of Research Instrument

A 'funnel approach' was followed while designing the research instrument of study. Before developing the final draft of the research instrument, relevant questions were identified from literature survey which required to be studied in Indian context and meeting the objectives of the study. For this, a semi-structured questionnaire was developed which is given hereunder. This semi-structured questionnaire was sent to five experts from industry and three experts from academia for its **Face Validity** and **Content Validity**. The semi-structured questionnaire included the basic questions related to their organizations and their awareness about forex risk exposure, its management and determinants of forex risk hedging strategies. The format of this semi-structured questionnaire is also mentioned in the following sections. The industry experts were the people who were actively managing the forex risk exposure for various firms (both SMEs and unlisted non-financial firms). These experts were having more than 15 years of experience in the respective field and most of them were holding professional degrees like CA, CFA or other certified degree in forex risk management. The experts from industry were actively working on Forex Derivatives, SMEs Risk Management, and Risk Management by listed and unlisted firms, and making forex risk hedging strategies etc. and experts from academia were renounced academicians with more than 15 years of academic and research experience in related field. All these experts were contacted personally and on the basis of response of experts from industry and academia both, the questions of semi-structured questionnaire were revised. The experts from academia also improved the way of asking the questions in a close-ended manner (dichotomous, multiple choice, and summarizing the related questions in a tabular form etc.) and wherever required, questions were also asked on a five point likert scale. The structured questionnaire of the study began with the general questions and ended with more specific question statements.

The following diagram has depicted the process of research instrument development.

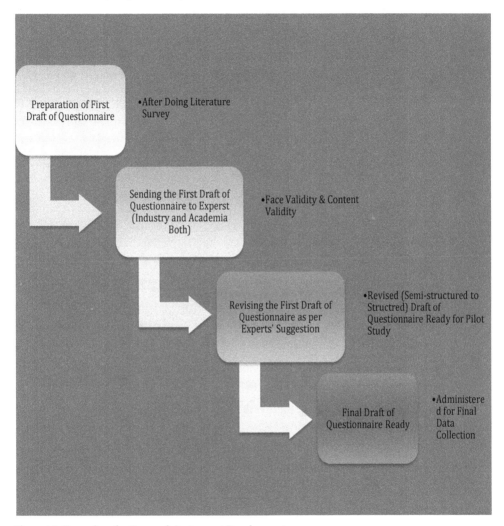

Figure 14: *Procedure for Research Instrument Development*

First Draft of the Questionnaire (Semi-Structured) Administered on 20 SMEs and Unlisted Non-Financial Firms

Survey Regarding Forex Risk Exposure Awareness, its Management and Determinants of Forex Risk Management

Objectives of Survey: *The purpose of this study is to conduct a survey regarding awareness of forex risk exposure, its management and determinants.*

Declaration: *The purpose of this research is academic use only and information provided by you will be kept confidential.*

i. What is the name of your Organization?

ii. To which economic sector the firm/company belongs?

     i. Manufacturing   iv. Services

     ii. Construction   v. Any Other (Please Specify)

     iii. Trading

iii. How many number of employees work in your organization?

     i. Less than 10   iv. 50-80

     ii. 10-30   v. Above 80 (Please Specify)

     iii. 30-50

iv. What is the annual turnover (in terms of Indian Rupee, i.e., INR) of your organization?

v. How the business is involved in international operations?

vi. What is the frequency of Exports and Imports (Please mark √ at appropriate place)

vii. What % of total turnover of your firm/company is in foreign currency?

viii. Who takes the decisions related to forex risk management in your company?

ix. In which of the following currency, your firm/company is exposed to forex risk?

x. Is your firm measuring the Forex Risk exposure?

xi. Are you aware of the concept of forex risk management?

xii. Who defines the foreign Forex risk management policy in your business?

     i. Board of Directors   v. Treasurer

     ii. Company's Management Team   vi. Accountant

     iii. CFO   vii. Finance Controller

     iv. CEO   viii. Any Other (Please Specify)

xiii. What is the purpose of hedging forex risk in your organization?

xiv. What kind of instruments or techniques is your firm/company using for hedging?

xv. What is your criterion of selecting a particular hedging instrument?

xvi. Which factors do you think are important while selecting a hedging strategy for forex risk management for your organization?

xvii. In your opinion, what are the major issues related to awareness regarding forex risk exposure?

xviii. How can you improve forex risk management in your firm/company?

Thanks for your information and participation in survey.

As discussed above, the semi-structured questionnaire was thoroughly revised after testing its **face validity and content validity through experts.** The research instrument was also tested for its **convergent** and **discriminant validity**. The results of convergent and discriminant validity of constructs have been discussed with the results of Exploratory Factor Analysis in the following chapter.

The final questionnaire is divided into four sections.

Section "A" focused on general questions discussing the basic profile of SMEs and Unlisted non-financial firms. There are nine questions in this section.

Section "B" focused on Forex risk exposure of sample units and four questions were asked in order to measure the awareness level regarding Forex risk exposure among the respondents.

Section "C" focused on Forex risk management by sample units. This section consists of 17 questions, which were asked in order to measure the decisions that are being taken for the management of Forex risk.

Finally, Section "D" focused on determinants of Forex risk hedging strategy. This section consists of 10 questions, which were asked on multi-choice format and on five-point likert scale where 1 anchored for "not important" and 5 anchored for "very much important". The concluding draft of the questionnaire was finalized after pilot testing.

Final Draft of Questionnaire

Survey Regarding Forex Risk Exposure Awareness, its Management and Determinants of Forex Risk Management

Objectives of Survey: *The purpose of this study is to conduct a survey regarding awareness of forex risk exposure, its management and determinants.*

Declaration: *The purpose of this research is academic use only and information provided by you will be kept confidential.*

A.   Profile of Firm/Company

A. Name of the Organization (Optional)……………………………………………………………..
B. Address of the Organization (Optional)…………………………………………………………..
C. To which economic sector the firm/company belongs?

vi.	Manufacturing	ix.	Services
vii.	Construction	x.	Any Other (Please Specify)
viii.	Trading		

D. How many number of employees work in your organization?

vi.	Less than 10	ix.	50-80
vii.	10-30	x.	Above 80 (Please Specify)
viii.	30-50		

E. What is the annual turnover (in terms of Indian Rupee, i.e., INR) of your organization?

i.	Less than 5 Crore	vii.	30-35 crore
ii.	5-10 crore	viii.	35-40 crore
iii.	10-15 crore	ix.	40-45 crore
iv.	15-20 crore	x.	45-50 crore
v.	20-25 crore	xi.	Above 50 crore
vi.	25-30 crore	xii.	Above 100 crore

F. For how long the business is in existence? (In terms of Years of Operations)

i. Domestic Operations…………
ii. International Operations

G. How the business is involved in international operations?

i. Through Exports
ii. Through Imports
iii. Both Export and Import

H. What is the frequency of Exports and Imports (Please mark √ at appropriate place)

	Exports	Imports
Daily		
Weekly		
Monthly		
Quarterly		
Semi-annually		
Annually		
Rarely		

I. What % of total turnover of your firm/company is in foreign currency?

i.	Less than 10%	vi.	50-60%
ii.	10-20%	vii.	60-70%
iii.	20-30%	viii.	70-80%
iv.	30-40%	ix.	80-90%
v.	40-50%	x.	90-100% (In case you are a 100% export based firm/company)

B. Forex Risk Exposure Awareness (Please mark √ at appropriate place)

1. What is the percentage of your cost, revenue, assets and debt in terms of foreign currency ,i.e., currency other than INR?

	Less than 10%	10-20%	20-30%	30-40%	40-50%	50-60%	60-70%	70-80%	80-90%	90-100%
Cost										
Revenue										
Assets										
Debt										

2. In which of the following currency, your firm/company is exposed to forex risk? (You can pick more than one.)

i.	U.S. Dollar	vii.	Australian Dollar
ii.	European EURO	viii.	Chinese Yuan
iii.	Swiss Franc	ix.	Hong Kong Dollar
iv.	UK Pound Sterling	x.	Singapore Dollar
v.	Japanese Yen	xi.	Kuwaiti Dinar
vi.	Canadian Dollar	xii.	Any other (Please Specify)

3. Is your firm measuring the Forex Risk exposure?
   i. No (Ignore the following Question)
   ii. Yes

   (a) If yes, how would you define the level of Forex risk exposure by the business? (pick one)

i) Very High	ii) High	iii) Medium	iv) Low	v) Zero

   (b) What is the frequency of measurement of following three types of forex exposures?

	Often	Sometimes	Never
Translation exposure (accounting translation into base currency)			
Transaction exposure (Foreign receivable and payable currency)			
Economic Exposure (Future expected cash flow and competitive position)			

C. Forex Risk Management *

*This section is to be answered by or on behalf of the person taking Forex risk management related decisions. Please mark √ on the option selected.

4. **Are you aware of the concept of forex risk management?**
    i.   Yes, Fully Aware
    ii.   Yes, but Partially aware
    iii. No, Not aware about the concept of forex risk management.

5. **Do you have a forex risk management policy or forex risk hedging policy in your business?**
    i.   Yes
    ii.   No
    iii. No, but currently it is under consideration and soon will be in place.

6. **Who defines the foreign Forex risk management policy in your business?**

ix. Board of Directors	xiii. Treasurer
x. Company's Management Team	xiv. Accountant
xi. CFO	xv. Finance Controller
xii. CEO	xvi. Any Other (Please Specify)

7. **Who implements the policy?**

i. Board of Directors	v. Treasurer
ii. Company's Management Team	vi. Accountant
iii. CFO	vii. Finance Controller
iv. CEO	viii. Any Other (Please Specify)

8. **What is the purpose of hedging forex risk in your organization?** *(You can select more than one option also.)*

	Mark √
To increase profitability	
To hedge against forex rate fluctuation	
To reduce the volatility in earnings	
To reduce the volatility in cash flows	
To use as a risk management tool	
To improvise the financial results of the company	
To increase the market value of firm	
It is essential for the sustainability or survival of business	
To gain from speculation	
Any other, Please specify	

9. **Which of the following method(s) is (are) used to measure the forex risk exposure?** *(You can select more than one option also.)*

	Mark √

Cash flow estimates	
Value at Risk	
Scenario Analysis	
Leading and Lagging	
Matching	
Stress Analysis	
Rough Estimation	
No method is used	
If any other, please specify	

10. How frequently the forex risk exposure is managed (Hedging the risk) in your business?

i. Always	ii. Often	iii. Sometimes	iv. Rarely	v) Never

11. If the answer to Q.10 is never, then what are the reasons for that? Mark √ in appropriate cell.

	Yes	No
Lack of Awareness regarding forex Risk Measurement		
Lack of knowledge regarding estimating the effect of exposure		
Cost of Hedging is more than benefit of hedging		
Lack of trained people to manage forex risk exposure		
Possibility of insufficient loss due to no-management		
Less amount of forex exposure is involved		
Availability of natural hedge		
Insufficient hedging instruments available		
No clear guideline in the business regarding this		
Any other, please specify		

12. What is the average period the company is hedging its foreign exchange rate risk?

i.	Less than 90 days	iv.	360 days
ii.	90 days	v.	2 years
iii.	180 days	vi.	Over 2 years

13. What is the policy of the business regarding hedge ratio in case of forex risk management?

i.	Not specific ratio	iv.	41-60%
ii.	1-20%	v.	61-80%
iii.	21-40%	vi.	81-100%

14. (a) What kind of instruments or techniques is your firm/company using for hedging? *(You can select more than one option also.)*

	Always	Often	Sometimes	Rarely	Never
Cash Flow Matching					
Asset Liability management					
Exchange Traded Futures					
Exchange Traded Options					
Swaps					
OTC Forwards					

OTC Options					
Structured Derivatives					
Hybrid Debts					
Others (Please Specify)					

(b) If you answered "Rarely" or "never" to one of the above questions, Is it because they are (5 point scale).

	Strongly Agree (5)	Agree (4)	Neutral (3)	Disagree (2)	Strongly disagree (1)
Too Complex	1				
Not Allowed					
Causing Accounting Problems					
Not having the desired features					
Cost of using it is more than expected benefits					
Does not have sufficient exposure					
Not offered by my banker					
Does not want to disclose much about Forex risk exposure of business					
Not liquid enough					
Too Risky					
Other (Please Specify)					

(c) For each instrument, what is the average maturity?

	0-90 days	91-180 days	180-360 days	360-days to 2 years	Over 2 years	Not used
Futures						
Forwards						
Options						
Swaps						
OTC Forwards						

OTC Options							
Structured Derivatives							
Hybrid Debts							
Other (Please Specify)							

(d) How do you use these instruments?

	Partial Hedge	Full Hedge	Dynamic Hedge
Futures			
Forwards			
Options			
Swaps			
OTC Forwards			
OTC Options			
Structured Derivatives			
Hybrid Debts			
Other (Please Specify)			

15. For each of the following exposures, which best describes typical hedging horizon?

	Translation	Transaction	Economic
Hedge shorter than the maturity of the exposure			
Hedge the maturity of the exposure			
Hedge longer than the maturity of exposure			

16. What percentage of the exchange rate exposure is the company hedging?

i.	0-20%	iv.	60-80%
ii.	20-40%	v.	80-100%
iii.	40-60%		

17. How often do you readjust the hedge or measure Forex risk?

i.	Daily	iv.	Quarterly
ii.	Weekly	v.	Semi-annually
iii.	Monthly	vi.	Yearly

18. What is the hedging execution strategy of the business

i. There is nothing fixed timeline for execution strategy
ii. At the time of submitting bid
iii. At the time when an order is received from the customer

iv. At the time when revenue is realized from the customer

19. Do you have an Exchange **Earners' Foreign Currency Account?**

i. Yes	ii. No

20. Do you think that an Exchange Earners' Foreign Currency Account (EEFC A/c) can eliminate the forex risk of a business?

i. Yes	ii. No

D. Forex Risk Hedging Determinants

The following set of questions to be answered by the Respondents who take the decision for forex risk management for SMEs/Unlisted Non-Financial Firms.

21. For how many years you are doing forex risk management for company (ies)?

    i. Less than 1 Year   iii. 4-6 Years

    ii. 1-3 Years   iv. More than 6 Years

22. What is your qualification? ………………………………………………………..

23. In which position do you take forex risk management actions for the company?

    i. As an internal team member   ii) As an external consultant

24. If you are an internal team member, then what is your position in the company? _____

25. If you are an external consultant or advisor, then for how many companies do you advise or determine forex risk management strategy?

    i. One   iv. 5-8

    ii. 1-3   v. More than 8 (please specify the number)

    iii. 3-5

26. Hedging forex risk for your organization is

	Strongly Agree (5)	Agree (4)	Neutral (3)	Disagree (2)	Strongly disagree (1)
Very Easy task and does not involve any risk					
Very Complex task and involves high risk					
Moderately complex task and involves moderate risk					
Requires different hedging instruments are required for hedging forex risk for different companies					
A few popular hedging instruments are sufficient for hedging forex risk for all companies					
Only OTC hedging instruments are sufficient to hedge forex risk					

27. Which of the following is applicable while selecting an instrument for forex risk hedging? Essential=5, High Priority=4, Moderate priority=3, low priority=2, Not a priority=1

	5	4	3	2	1
Cost of Contract					
Ease in cancellation and rebooking of contract					

	Legal and Regulatory aspects related to hedging instrument					
	Currency involved in hedging contract					
	Duration of hedging contract					

28. Which of the following factors do you are important while selecting a hedging strategy for forex risk management for your organization?

Very much important=5, Important=4, Moderately important=3, less important=2, Not important=1

		5	4	3	2	1
1	Availability of Forex hedging instruments at Exchange and OTC market					
2	Balance sheet and cash flow position of the firm					
3	Clear Forex Risk Hedging guidelines issued by the firm, viz. use of specific hedging instrument, duration of hedging strategy and time horizon of forex hedging strategy etc					
4	Convertibility of Indian rupee					
5	Demand and Supply Conditions of Foreign Currency					
6	Demand and Supply Conditions of domestic Currency					
7	Development of Banking system					
8	Discovery of New Resources					
9	Ease of using various forex risk hedging instruments like options, futures, synthetic derivatives etc.					
10	Economic condition of the domestic country, i.e., GDP, Inflation Rate, Money Supply, Capital Market Conditions, Balance of Trade Position etc.					
11	Economic condition of the foreign country with whom trade has happened, i.e., GDP, Inflation Rate, Money Supply, Capital Market Conditions, Balance of Trade Position etc.					
12	Experience of Forex Risk Manager in using Forex Risk Hedging Instruments					
13	Fluctuations in Crude oil Prices as it affect the volatility in prices of all major currencies					
14	Fluctuations in US Dollar Prices					
15	Forex Control Mechanism in the foreign country					
16	Forex Risk Exposure of the Business in proportion to total Turnover,					
17	Future Expectations regarding movement in Foreign exchange rate					

18	Government regulations Regarding Forex Market					
19	Identification of new resources					
20	Interest Rate Fluctuations in the Domestic Market					
21	Interest Rate Fluctuations in the International Market					
22	Intervention of Central Bank in Forex Market					
23	Movement in commodity prices related to firms involved in international trade					
24	Nature of the business of Firm, i.e., how much business is dependent upon the export and import					
25	Option of Customization of Various Forex Risk Hedging Instruments					
26	Overall sentiments regarding Forex Market					
27	Past Experience of the firm in hedging Forex Risk					
28	Perception of Forex Risk Manager regarding various hedging instruments					
29	Political conditions of Domestic country					
30	Political conditions of the foreign country with whom trade has happened					
31	Popularity of the forex risk hedging instrument					
32	Speculation (Forex Market, Real Estate, Securities and Uncovered Interest Arbitrage)					
33	Technological advancements in the country					
34	Volatility in Foreign Currency in which payment has to be made or any other currency used for international settlement					
35	Volatility in the value of Domestic Currency					

29. In your opinion, which of the following variables need to be improved for better Forex risk management (Strongly agree=5, Strongly disagree=1)

	5	4	3	2	1
More trained people are required					
More Hedging instruments need to be introduced					
The cost of hedging devices should be less					

The management of business should play more intense role in formation of a forex risk management policy					
The RBI or Government shall make it mandatory to hedge the forex risk					
The management shall motivate for risk management practices					
The top management or decision maker should gain more expertise in forex risk management					
Hedging instruments shall be introduced with some tax benefit schemes					
More awareness shall be done by RBI					
The bank should aware business whenever it approaches the bank for export-import financing					
Clear guidelines should be forwarded by RBI regarding usage of derivative products					
The business associations should provide necessary assistance and support to their members in managing forex risk					
More innovative, customized and low cost hedging instruments should be introduced by regulators					
More certification and educational programs					
Forex risk management policy must be made mandatory for all Small and Medium Enterprises					
Any other, Please specify					

30.   **Please mention a few points which in your opinion play significant role in Forex risk management for SME s and not discussed above.**

    i.   ....

    ii.   ....

    iii.   ....

****

Results of the Pilot Study

Before, executing the extensive survey and starting the data collection, a pilot study was conducted on a sample of 35 units. It was essential to ensure the reliability of research instrument of the study as well as to establish the feasibility of data collection. The snowball method of sampling was used to reach the target-sampling units. For the purpose of pilot study, the final draft of questionnaire as mentioned above was sent to sample units. The required data from these sample units was collected either through telephonic interview or through personal interview. The results of the pilot study are mentioned below. The Results of the pilot study depicted that overall Cronbach's alpha coefficient is 0.897 which is above the acceptable limit of 0.70 (Nunnaly, 1978).

Table 20a

Reliability Statistics

Cronbach's Alpha	N of Items
0.897	35

Source: Calculations done by Researcher

The Cronbach's alpha after deleting individual variable has also been mentioned in the above table. As shown in table, there is no substantial increase in the Cronbach's alpha if any of the individual variables is removed. Hence, the final questionnaire considered all items for the survey on large sample.

Table 20b

Results of Reliability Test after Pilot Study

	Cronbach's Alpha if Item Deleted
Availability of Forex hedging instruments at Exchange and OTC market	0.891
Balance sheet and cash flow position of the firm	0.893
Clear Forex Risk Hedging guidelines issued by the firm, viz. use of specific hedging instrument, duration of hedging strategy and time horizon of forex hedging strategy etc	0.890

Convertibility of Indian rupee	0.893
Demand and Supply Conditions of Foreign Currency	0.890
Demand and Supply Conditions of domestic Currency	0.892
Development of Banking system	0.892
Discovery of New Resources	0.888
Ease of using various forex risk hedging instruments like options, futures, synthetic derivatives etc.	0.894
Economic condition of the domestic country, i.e., GDP, Inflation Rate, Money Supply, Capital Market Conditions, Balance of Trade Position etc.	0.897
Economic condition of the foreign country with whom trade has happened, i.e., GDP, Inflation Rate, Money Supply, Capital Market Conditions, Balance of Trade Position etc.	0.900
Experience of Forex Risk Manager in using Forex Risk Hedging Instruments	0.899
Fluctuations in Crude oil Prices as it affect the volatility in prices of all major currencies	0.900
Fluctuations in US Dollar Prices	0.901
Forex Control Mechanism in the foreign country	0.895
Forex Risk Exposure of the Business in proportion to total Turnover,	0.889
Future Expectations regarding movement in Foreign exchange rate	0.890
Government regulations Regarding Forex Market	0.898
Identification of new resources	0.896
Interest Rate Fluctuations in the Domestic Market	0.899
Interest Rate Fluctuations in the International Market	0.899
Intervention of Central Bank in Forex Market	0.901
Movement in commodity prices related to firms involved in international trade	0.891
Nature of the business of Firm, i.e., how much business is dependent upon the export and import	0.888

Option of Customization of Various Forex Risk Hedging Instruments	0.890
Overall sentiments regarding Forex Market	0.890
Past Experience of the firm in hedging Forex Risk	0.894
Perception of Forex Risk Manager regarding various hedging instruments	0.890
Political conditions of Domestic country	0.891
Political conditions of the foreign country with whom trade has happened	0.887
Popularity of the forex risk hedging instrument	0.891
Speculation (Forex Market, Real Estate, Securities and Uncovered Interest Arbitrage)	0.892
Technological advancements in the country	0.896
Volatility in Foreign Currency in which payment has to be made or any other currency used for international settlement	0.899
Volatility in the value of Domestic Currency	0.901

Source: Calculations done by Researcher

The satisfactory results obtained through pilot study implied that we can further proceed with the remaining data collection procedure and application of appropriate statistical tools in order to achieve the mentioned objectives of the present study. The following sections have discussed the statistical tools used in the present study.

Statistical Techniques Used

The selection of statistical tool was based on the type of questions asked in survey instruments. Considering the nature of different questions under different sections, the following statistical tools were used in the present study.

Section A: Descriptive Statistics and Cross-tabulation was used to analyze the basic characteristics of the SMEs and non-financial unlisted firms participated in the survey.

Section B: This section fulfills the objective one of the study under consideration. The statistical tools like Descriptive statistics, Chi-Square, Phi coefficient, Cramer's V and contingency coefficient.

Section C: This section fulfills the objective two of the study under consideration. The statistical tools like Descriptive statistics Chi-Square, Phi coefficient, Cramer's V and contingency coefficient.

Section D: This section fulfills the objective three of the study under consideration. It has used Exploratory Factor Analysis and AHP, i.e., Analytical Hierarchy Process to identify the determinants of forex risk hedging strategy.

Mean and Variance

For the analysis of the data, we have used mean and variance. Generally a high variability of the statement and higher mean of the statements is at the center point of distribution, the better the statement will perform (Kline, 2005).

Factor Analysis

Factor analysis is a generic name given to a class of multivariate statistical method whose primary purpose is to define the underlying structure in a data matrix (Hair et al., 1998). Factor analysis allows the identification of a relatively small number of factors that can be utilized to represent relations between a set of interrelated variables, such as a set of statements on a measure or a set of instruments (Goodwin, 1999). In the present study, Exploratory Factor Analysis was employed for the purpose of checking unidimensionality of the statements. Since the prime objective of employing factor analysis was summarization of the data, the researcher used principal component analysis with orthogonal rotation by selecting varimax rotation in order to have completely uncorrelated factors.

Reliability

Reliability means consistency in the results over the period of time. In the present study, we measure the reliability of the scale with the help of Cronbach Alpha. The most acceptable criterion of reliability is given by Nunnally (1978), which states that the value of reliability should be more than 0.7 in order to categorize a scale as reliable scale.

Chi-Square Test

In the present study, chi-square test has been applied in order to find that is there any kind of association that exists among different variables under consideration or not.

Phi coefficient, Cramer's V and Contingency coefficient

Phi coefficient, Cramer's V and contingency coefficient are used to measure the strength of association between emotional maturity and performance. Their values should lie between 0-1. The 0 value indicates no association, but as it moves towards 1, establishes a strong association.

The Analytic Hierarchy Process

It was Thomas Saaty (1980) who introduced the *Analytic Hierarchy Process* (AHP) in 1980. The AHP technique is of great use where decision makers have to take complex decisions and have to set priorities. It is based on Pairwise comparisons and afterwards results are synthesized. Under the AHP process, the decision maker considers a set of evaluation criteria and a set of alternative options to select the best among them. This process generates weights for each of the evaluation criterion considered important for decision makers and decision maker makes a Pair wise comparison of the entire criterion. The most important decision criterion is identified with the highest score it generates. Basically, this process of AHP is based on intuitive judgements of the decision makers and consistency in their Pair wise comparisons of various criterions undertaken. In the case of fixed criterion, The Analytic Hierarchy Process also assigns weight to each option according to the decision maker's Pair wise comparisons of the options which is based on respective criterion. Higher the score of the option better is the performance of that option with respect to the decision criterion considered for that. And at the end, the AHP process combines the weights of the criteria and scores of the options and thus, determines the global score for each option. This global score of each option tells the consequent ranking of that option. Skibniewski and Chao (1992) appreciated this method because of its simple way of combining both, tangible and intangible factors in a systematic manner which provides a simple solution to the decision makers. Saaty (1978), Fong (2000) and Dobi et al. (2010) also supported the AHP saying that it provides systematic and simple solutions to decision makers.

Data Collection

The study under consideration took interview of Ten (10) experts who were actively involved and experienced in developing forex risk hedging instruments for different types of users (individuals, firms, export-import houses, Small and Medium Enterprises, listed and unlisted firms having foreign exposure, and financial institutions etc.) of hedging instruments and are also involved in framing policy guidelines related to forex risk hedging strategies to corporate of all sizes and to regulators too. Based on the results of factor analysis, a questionnaire was developed to collect the desired data on Pair wise comparisons among all criterions for decision making. Saaty (2001) mentioned seven pillars of Analytic Hierarchy Process. These include, Ratio scales, proportionality and normalized ratio scales.

I.   Reciprocal paired comparisons.

II.   The sensitivity of the principal right eigenvector.

III. Clustering and using pivots to extend the scale.

IV.   Synthesis to create a one-dimensional ratio scale for representing the overall outcome.

V.   Rank preservation and reversal.

VI.   Integrating group judgments.

The AHP – Step by Step

The AHP provides a means of decomposing the problem into a hierarchy of sub-problems which can more easily be comprehended and subjectively evaluated. The subjective evaluations are converted into numerical values and processed to rank each alternative on a numerical scale. The methodology of the AHP can be explained in following steps:

Step 1: The problem is decomposed into a hierarchy of goal, criteria, sub-criteria and alternatives. This is the most creative and important part of decision-making. Structuring the decision problem as a hierarchy is fundamental to the process of the AHP. Hierarchy indicates a relationship between elements of one level with those of the level immediately below. This relationship percolates down to the lowest levels of the hierarchy and in this manner every element is connected to every other one, at least in an indirect manner. A hierarchy is a more orderly form of a network. An inverted tree structure is similar to a hierarchy. Saaty suggests that a useful way to structure the hierarchy is to work down from the goal as far as one can and then work up from the alternatives until the levels of the two processes are linked in such a way as to make comparisons possible. Figure 15 shows a generic hierarchic structure. At the root of the hierarchy is the goal or objective of the problem being studied and analyzed. The leaf nodes are the alternatives to be compared. In between these two levels are various criteria and sub-criteria. It is important to note that when comparing elements at each level a decision-maker has just to compare with respect to the contribution of the lower-level elements to the upper-level one. This local concentration of the decision-maker on only part of the whole problem is a powerful feature of the AHP.

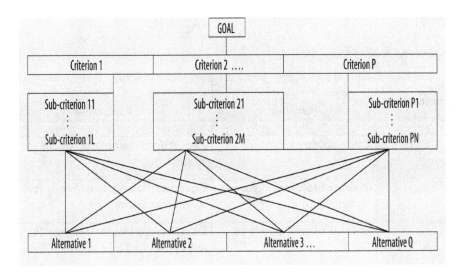

Figure 15:*Generic Hierarchical Structure*

Step 2: Data are collected from experts or decision-makers corresponding to the hierarchic structure, in the Pair wise comparison of alternatives on a qualitative scale as described below. Experts can rate the comparison as equal, marginally strong, strong, very strong, and extremely strong. The opinion can be collected in a specially designed format as shown in Figure 15.

"X" in the column marked "Very strong" indicates that B is very strong compared with A in terms of the criterion on which the comparison is being made. The comparisons are made for each criterion and converted into quantitative numbers as per Table 16.

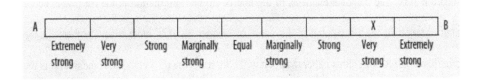

Figure 16 Format *for Pairwise comparison*

Table 21

Fundamental Scale by Saaty

Intensity of Importance on an absolute Scale	Definition	Explanation
1	Equal Importance	Two activities contribute equally to the objective
3	Moderate Importance of one over another	Experience and judgement strongly favor one activity over another
5	Essential or strong importance	Experience and judgement strongly favor one activity over another
7	Very strong importance	An activity is strongly favored and its dominance demonstrated in practive
9	Extreme importance	The evidence favoring one activity over another is of the highest possible order of affirmation
2,4,6,8	Intermediate values between the two adjacent judments	When compromise is needed
Raciprocals	If activity i has one of the above numbers assigned to it when compared with activity j then j has the reciprocal value when compared with i	
Rationals	Ratios arising from the scale	If consistency were to be forced by obtaining n numerical values to span the matrix

Step 3: The Pairwise comparisons of various criteria generated at step 2 are organized into a square matrix. The diagonal elements of the matrix are 1. The criterion in the ith row is better than criterion in the jth column if the value of element (i, j) is more than 1; otherwise the criterion in the jth column is better than that in the ith row. The (j, i) element of the matrix is the reciprocal of the (i, j) element.

Step 4: The principal eigenvalue and the corresponding normalised right eigen-vector of the comparison matrix give the relative importance of the various criteria being compared. The elements of the normalize deigen-vector are termed weights with respect to the criteria or sub-criteria and ratings with respect to the alternatives.

Step 5: The consistency of the matrix of order n is evaluated. Comparisons made by this method are subjective and the AHP tolerates inconsistency through the amount of redundancy in the approach. If this consistency index fails to reach a required level then answers to comparisons may be re-examined. The consistency index, CI, is calculated as

$$CI = (\lambda_{max} - n)/(n - 1)$$

where λ_{max} is the maximum eigen value of the judgment matrix. This CI can be compared with that of a random matrix, RI. The ratio derived, CI/RI, is termed the consistency ratio, CR. Saaty suggests the value of CR should be less than 0.1.

Step 6: The rating of each alternative is multiplied by the weights of the sub-criteria and aggregated to get local ratings with respect to each criterion. The local ratings are then multiplied by the weights of the criteria and aggregated to get global ratings.

The AHP produces weight values for each alternative based on the judged importance of one alternative over another with respect to a common criterion.

Limitations of Study

Every research study has shown its own constraints and limits due to distinctive reasons. The present study is also not unusual on this aspect. The following are the limitations of the study.

The study under consideration was descriptive and exploratory in nature. Hence, there may be a possibility of difference in the view of sample units who finally participated in the survey and sample units who did not participated due to inability to contact them or due to their own precincts for not participating. Consequently, such type of limitation may have influenced the overall findings and generalizations based on data analysis.

Next, as per the nature of study, it was very difficult to access the sample units who fulfilling the criteria for eligible respondents, therefore, the study under consideration focused on any small and medium enterprise or unlisted non-financial firm which was registered in India without making any further analysis of based on their geographical location, viz., region wise, or state wise classification. Hence, the overall sample focused on Indian SMEs and unlisted non-financial firms rather than focusing on SMEs and unlisted non-financial firms established in a specific geographical area.

The target respondents of the present study were very much engaged in their functional areas therefore, in many cases, it required 2-3 follow-up session to get complete information mentioned in survey instrument. Hence, the time, effort and budget constraints were also a limitation to remain strict to a standard sample size of *407*. There were thousands of SMEs and non-financial unlisted firm active in India during the survey period but it was extremely challenging for researcher to approach a sample size bigger than what has been considered in the current study. The Budget or economic cost was a major constraint in increasing the sample size beyond what has been considered in given circumstances.

Organization of the Thesis

The thesis has been developed as under.

Section I	Prefatory Phase
	➤ Title Page
	➤ Declaration
	➤ Acknowledgement
	➤ Index of Contents
	➤ List of Figures
	➤ List of Tables
	➤ Executive Summery
Section II	Main Body of Thesis
	Chapter 1: Introduction/Background of Study
	Chapter 2: Review of Literature
	Chapter 3: Research Methodology
	Chapter 4: Results and Discussion
	Chapter 5: Conclusion, Recommendations and Policy Implications
Bibliography	
Annexure	

Chapter 4

Results and Discussions

The current chapter discusses the results based on data analysis. As discussed in previous chapter that there are basically three objectives of the study and the research instrument was also categorized on the basis of objectives of the study. For example, section A of the research instrument was related to basic profile of the respondents, which has already been discussed in Chapter III. The current chapter focuses on section B, C and D of the research instrument, which are explaining about objective one, two and three of the study. The questions mentioned in these sections have been analyzed with the demographic profile of the respondents. The current chapter has discussed the results in following manner.

A. Measuring the Awareness Level of SMEs and Unlisted non-Financial Firms in India

B. Forex Risk Exposure Management

C. Determinants of Forex Risk Hedging Strategies

A. Measuring the Awareness Level of SMEs and Unlisted non-financial firms in India

The following section deals with the modest analysis depicting the awareness level of Indian SMEs and unlisted non-financial firms for forex risk exposure. The questions given in section B are analyzed with relevant demographic profile of SMEs and Unlisted non-financial firms in India.Table 22 has exhibited the results of cross tabulation of economic sector wise percentage of total cost incurred by the firm in terms of foreign currency. It was observed that 30.8 percent firms in the construction sector had less than 10 percent of total cost and 15.4 percent firmshad 80 to 90 percent of their total cost in terms of foreign currency. Followed by the manufacturing sector, which reported 7.2 percent, firmshaving less than 10 percent of their total cost and 5.9 percent firmswere incurring 90 to 100 percentof their total cost in terms of foreign currency. Similarly, 12.5 percent firms in service sector were having less than 10 percent of their total cost and 9.4 percent firmswere having 90 to 100 percent of their total cost in terms of foreign currency. The firms belonged to Trading sector demonstrated that 15.1 percent firms were having less than 10 percent of their total cost and only 3.8 percent of firms in 90-100 percent cost. In the same manner, 50 percent firms from other sectors reported less than 10 percent of their total cost and 50 percent firms in 80 to 90 percent cost in terms of foreign currency. Hence, it can be concluded that firms in service sector incurred more cost on the contrary, manufacturing sector exhibited less cost in terms of foreign currency.

Table 22

Cross Tabulation of Economic Sector wise Percentage of Total Cost in terms of Foreign Currency

Sector		Cost										Total
		Less than 10%	10-20%	20-30%	30-40%	40-50%	50-60%	60-70%	70-80%	80-90%	90-100%	
Construction	Count	4	0	0	0	0	5	2	0	2	0	13
	% within Sector	30.8	0.0	0.0	0.0	0.0	38.5	15.4	0.0	15.4	0.0	100
Manufacturing	Count	22	22	34	38	44	38	26	38	25	18	305
	% within Sector	7.2	7.2	11.1	12.5	14.4	12.5	8.5	12.5	8.2	5.9	100
Services	Count	4	3	5	3	3	5	3	0	3	3	32
	% within Sector	12.5	9.4	15.6	9.4	9.4	15.6	9.4	0.0	9.4	9.4	100
Trading	Count	8	4	12	3	8	3	5	8	0	2	53
	% within Sector	15.1	7.5	22.6	5.7	15.1	5.7	9.4	15.1	0.0	3.8	100
Any Other	Count	2	0	0	0	0	0	0	0	2	0	4
	% within Sector	50.0	0.0	0.0	0.0	0.0	0.0	0.0	0.0	50.0	0.0	100
Total	Count	40	29	51	44	55	51	36	46	32	23	407
	% within Sector	9.8	7.1	12.5	10.8	13.5	12.5	8.8	11.3	7.9	5.7	100

*Source:*Calculations Done by Researcher

Next, the test of chi-square examines whether the association between categorized variables is statistically significant or not. It helps in ascertaining the systematic association exists between the two variables. The present study has tried to establish whether any association exists between economic sectors and the percentage of total cost spent by them in terms of foreign currency. So, the null hypothesis,Ho, is that there is no association between the variables.

Further, the number of degrees of freedom is a significant feature of the chi-square statistic. The null hypothesis of no associationbetween the economic sectors and the percentage cost of firm in terms of foreign currency will be rejected only when critical value of the chi-square distribution is lesser than the calculated value of test statistic accompanied with the suitable degrees of freedom.Table 23 has reported the results of chi-square test, which examined the association between economic sectors and percentage of total cost of firms in terms of foreign currency.The calculated statistic of chi-square test, at 36 degree of freedom had a value of 65.517, asthis is greater than the critical value and hence, the null hypothesis is rejected depicting thatthe association between the economic sectors and the percentage cost of firm in terms of foreign currency is significant at the 0.05 level. Hence, the alternative hypothesis is accepted.

Table 23

Results of Association between Economic Sector of Firms and Percentage of Total Cost Spent in Foreign Currency

	Value	df	symp. Sig. (2-sided)
Pearson Chi-Square	65.517	36	0.002
Likelihood Ratio	71.034	36	0.000
Linear-by-Linear Association	4.358	1	0.037
N of Valid Cases	407		

Source: Calculations Done by Researcher

In the symmetric measures, the strengthof association between economic sectors and the percentage cost of firm in terms of foreign currency are measured using Phi coefficient, and Cramer's Vcoefficient. The values of Phi coefficient and Cramer's Vcoefficient should restbetween 0-1. The 0 value shows no association, but as it heading towards 1, it

demonstrates astrong association. Table 24 has shown calculated statistics are as follows:

Table 24

Strength of Association between Economic Sectors and percentage of Total Cost Spent in terms of Foreign Currency

		Value	Approx. Sig.
Nominal by Nominal	Phi	0.401	0.002
	Cramer's V	0.201	0.002
N of Valid Cases		407	
a. Not assuming the null hypothesis.			
b. Using the asymptotic standard error assuming the null hypothesis.			

Source: Calculations Done by Researcher

Table 24 has provided the results of symmetric measures between economic sectors

and the percentage of total cost of firm in terms of foreign currency. It was observed that the

values of Phi coefficient and Cramer's V as 0.401 and 0.201respectively. The values

havingsignificance at 0.05 level revealed a significant positive strength of association, but

values less than 0.5 (significance) suggested a medium strength of associationbetween

economic sectors and the percentage cost of firm in terms of foreign currency. It indicated a

medium level of association between these two variables.

Table 25 has presented the results of cross tabulation of economic sector and the

percentage revenue earned by SMEs and unlisted non-financial firms in terms of foreign

currency. It was observed that 30.8 percent firms in the construction sector had reported their

revenues in foreign currency in the ranges of 30 to 40 percent and 80-90 percent each. Next,

in case of manufacturing sector, which showed 2.3 percent firmshaving less than 10 percent

of their revenues in foreign currency and 15.1 percent firms were having their revenue in

foreign currency in the range of 90 to 100 percent. Similarly, 6.2 percent firms in service

sector received the revenue less than 10 percent on the other hand, 6.2 percent firms got the

revenue between 90 to 100 percent. Trading sector indicated7.5 percent firms came under less than 10 percent revenue however, 11.3 percent firms in 90 to 100 percent revenue. In the

similar manner, 50 percent firms from other sectors reported 10 to 20 percent of their

revenues in foreign currency and 50 percent firmswere ranging in 80 to 90 percent. Hence, it

can be determined that firms in manufacturing sector earned more revenue on the contrary,

construction and other sector exhibited less revenue in terms of foreign currency.

Table 25

Cross Tabulation of Economic Sector wise percentage of Total Revenue in terms of Foreign Currency

Sector			Revenue										Total
			Less than 10%	10-20%	20-30%	30-40%	40-50%	50-60%	60-70%	70-80%	80-90%	90-100%	
Construction		Count	0	0	0	4	3	0	2	0	4	0	13
		% within Sector	0.0	0.0	0.0	30.8	23.1	0.0	15.4	0.0	30.8	0.0	100.0
Manufacturing		Count	7	11	7	43	15	42	50	49	35	46	305
		% within Sector	2.3	3.6	2.3	14.1	4.9	13.8	16.4	16.1	11.5	15.1	100.0
Services		Count	2	3	2	6	0	2	0	12	3	2	32
		% within Sector	6.2	9.4	6.2	18.8	0.0	6.2	0.0	37.5	9.4	6.2	100.0
Trading		Count	4	4	8	6	3	3	5	7	7	6	53
		% within Sector	7.5	7.5	15.1	11.3	5.7	5.7	9.4	13.2	13.2	11.3	100.0
Any Other		Count	0	2	0	0	0	0	0	0	2	0	4
		% within Sector	0.0	50.0	0.0	0.0	0.0	0.0	0.0	0.0	50.0	0.0	100.0
Total		Count	13	20	17	59	21	47	57	68	51	54	407
		% within Sector	3.2	4.9	4.2	14.5	5.2	11.5	14.0	16.7	12.5	13.3	100.0

*Source:*Calculations Done by Researcher

Table 26 has depicted the results of chi-square test, which examined the association

between economic sectors and the percentage revenue of firm in terms of foreign currency.

The calculated statistic of chi-square test, at 36 degree of freedom had a value of 95.338, as

this is greater than the critical value and hence, the null hypothesis is not accepted depicting

thatthe association between the economic sectors and the percentage revenue of the firm in terms of foreign currency is significant at the 0.05 level. Thus, the alternative hypothesis is

accepted.

Table 26:

*Results of Association between Economic Sector of Firms and Percentage of Total
Revenues in Foreign Currency*

	Value	df	Asymp. Sig. (2-sided)
Pearson Chi-Square	95.338	36	0.000
Likelihood Ratio	85.287	36	0.000
Linear-by-Linear Association	7.216	1	0.007
N of Valid Cases	407		

Source:Calculations Done by Researcher

Table 27

*Strength of Association between Economic Sectors and percentage of Total Revenues in
terms of Foreign Currency*

		Value	Approx. Sig.
Nominal by Nominal	Phi	0.484	0.000
	Cramer's V	0.242	0.000
N of Valid Cases		407	
a. Not assuming the null hypothesis.			
b. Using the asymptotic standard error assuming the null hypothesis.			

Source: Calculations Done by Researcher

Table 27has exhibited the results of symmetric measures between economic sectors

and the percentage of revenues of SMEs and unlisted non-financial firms in terms of foreign

currency. It was observed that the values of Phi coefficient and Cramer's V as 0.484 and

0.242 respectively. The values havingsignificance at 0.05 level revealedthat a significant

positive medium (the values of coefficients are less than 0.5) strength of associationbetween

economic sectors and the percentage revenue of firm in terms of foreign currency. It implied

a medium level of association between these two variables.

Table 28 has shown the results of cross tabulation of economic sector and the

percentage of firm's assets in terms of foreign currency. It was noticed that in case of firms in

Construction sector, 15.4 percent SMEs and unlisted non-financial firmsbelonged to

construction sector were having less than 10 percent of their assets in foreign currency and

30.8 percent firmswere rested in 80 to 90 percent category. Further, in case of manufacturing sector,6.9 percent firms were holding less than 10 percent of their assets and 12.1 percent sampled firmswere having 90 to 100 percent of their assets in foreign currency. Likewise, 12.5 percent firms in service sector were holding assets less than 10 percent and 18.8 percent firms were holding 90 to 100 percent of their assets in foreign currency. Trading sector revealed 26.4 percent firms comes under less than 10 percent assets however, 3.8 percent firms in 90 to 100 percent assets. Likewise, 50 percent of firms from other sectors reported less than 10 percent of their assets in foreign currency and 50 percent of firms were holding 80 to 90 percent of their assets in foreign currency. In view of this, it can be established that firms in service sector possessed more assets on the other hand, manufacturing sector exhibited less assets in terms of foreign currency.

Table 28

Cross Tabulation of Economic Sector wise percentage of Firm's Total Assets in terms of Foreign Currency

Sector	Asset										Total (in percentage)
	Less than 10%	10-20%	20-30%	30-40%	40-50%	50-60%	60-70%	70-80%	80-90%	90-100%	
Construction	15.4	-	15.4	-	-	38.5	-	-	30.8	-	100
Manufacturing	6.9	3.9	8.9	3.3	12.5	8.9	15.4	16.1	12.1	12.1	100
Services	12.5	-	18.8	6.2	6.2	9.4	-	18.8	9.4	18.8	100
Trading	26.4	3.8	15.1	-	17	11.3	11.3	11.3	-	3.8	100
Any Other	50.0	-	-	-	-	-	-	-	50	-	100
Total	10.6	3.4	10.6	2.9	12	10.1	13	15	11.3	11.1	100

Source: Calculations Done by Researcher

Note: Assets in terms of Foreign Currency means for which payment to acquire the asset was made in foreign currency.

Table 29has shown that calculated statistic of chi-square test, at 36 degree of freedom has a value of 81.890, as this is greater than the critical value, therefore the null hypothesis is rejected suggested thatthe association between the economic sectors and the percentage assets of firm in terms of foreign currency is significant at the 0.05 level. Thus, the alternative hypothesis is accepted.

Table 29

Results of Association between Economic Sector of Firms and Percentage of Total Assets in Foreign Currency

	Value	df	Asymp. Sig. (2-sided)
Pearson Chi-Square	81.890	36	0.000
Likelihood Ratio	90.820	36	0.000
Linear-by-Linear Association	17.278	1	0.000
N of Valid Cases	407		

Source: Calculations Done by Researcher

Table 30 displayed the results of symmetric measures between economic sectors and the percentage of assets of firms in terms of foreign currency. It was observed that the values of Phi coefficient and Cramer's V as 0.449 and 0.224 respectively. Both the coefficients have shown significance at 0.05 levels indicating a significant positive strength of association. But the values of both the coefficients are less than 0.5 and hence, suggested a medium strength of associationbetween economic sectors and the percentage assets of firm in terms of foreign currency. It showed a medium level of association between these two variables.

Table 30

Strength of Association between Economic Sectors and percentage of Total Assets in terms of Foreign Currency

		Value	Approx. Sig.
Nominal by Nominal	**Phi**	0.449	0.000
	Cramer's V	0.224	0.000
N of Valid Cases		407	
a. Not assuming the null hypothesis.			
b. Using the asymptotic standard error assuming the null hypothesis.			

Source: Calculations Done by Researcher

Table 31 depicted the results of cross tabulation of economic sector and the percentage debtof the firm in terms of foreign currency. It was observed that 15.4 percent firms in the construction sector had less than 10 percent debt and 30.8 percent firms were having 80 to 90 percent of their debt in foreign currency. The manufacturing sector has reported 9.5 percent firms having less than 10 percent debt and 6.6 percent SMEs and unlisted non-financial firms were having debt between 90 to 100 percent of their total debt.

Alike, 28.1 percent firms under service sector were having50-60 percent and 21.9 percent firms were having 40 to 50 percent of their total debtin foreign currency. Next, firms under Trading sector confirmed 26.4 percent were having less than 10 percent debt however and 17 percent of firms were having 30-40 percent their total debt in foreign currency. In the same manner, 50 percent firms from other sector reported less than 10 percent debt and 50 percent firms in 70 to 80 percent debt in terms of foreign currency.

Table 31

Strength of Association between Economic Sectors and percentage of Total Assets in terms of Foreign Currency

Sector	Debt										Total
	Less than 10%	10-20%	20-30%	30-40%	40-50%	50-60%	60-70%	70-80%	80-90%	90-100%	
Construction	15.4	-	15.4	-	23.1	-	-	15.4	30.8	-	100
Manufacturing	9.5	1.3	10.2	7.9	9.5	6.9	18.0	15.7	14.4	6.6	100
Services	12.5	-	-	-	21.9	28.1	18.8	-	9.4	9.4	100
Trading	26.4	-	5.7	17	5.7	11.3	15.1	9.4	-	9.4	100
Any Other	50.0	-	-	-	-	-	50	-	-	100
	12.5	1	8.8	8.1	10.3	8.8	17.0	14	12.5	6.9	100

Source: Calculations Done by Researcher

Table 32 has exhibited the results of chi-square test which showed that calculated statistic of chi-square test, at 36 degree of freedom had a value of 81.634, which is greater than the critical value so the null hypothesis is rejected indicating thatthe association between the economic sectors and the percentage debt of firm in terms of foreign currency is significant at the 0.05 level. Therefore, the alternative hypothesis is accepted.

Table 32

Results of Association between Economic Sector of Firms and Percentage of Total of Debt in Foreign Currency

	Value	df	Asymp. Sig. (2-sided)
Pearson Chi-Square	81.634	36	0.000
Likelihood Ratio	93.586	36	0.000
Linear-by-Linear Association	8.578	1	0.003

N of Valid Cases	407		

Source: Calculations Done by Researcher

Table 33

Strength of Association between Economic Sectors and percentage of Total Debt in terms of Foreign Currency

		Value	Approx. Sig.
Nominal by Nominal	Phi	0.448	0.000
	Cramer's V	0.224	0.000
N of Valid Cases		407	
a. Not assuming the null hypothesis.			
b. Using the asymptotic standard error assuming the null hypothesis.			

Source: Calculations Done by Researcher

Table 33has presented the results of symmetric measures between economic sectors and the percentage debt of firms in terms of foreign currency. It was observed that the values of Phi coefficient and Cramer's V as 0.448 and 0.224respectively and found significant at 0.05 level indicating a significant positive strength of association, the value of these two coefficients was found less than 0.5 reflecting a medium strength of associationbetween economic sectors and the percentage of total debt of firms in terms of foreign currency. It indicated a medium level of association between these two variables.

Table 34

Cross Tabulation of Annual Turnover and the percentage of Firm's Cost in terms of Foreign Currency

	Turnover		Cost										Total
			Less than 10%	10-20%	20-30%	30-40%	40-50%	50-60%	60-70%	70-80%	80-90%	90-100%	
Turnover	Less Than 5 Crore	Count	10	4	2	0	3	3	4	0	3	3	32
		% within Turnover	31.2	12.5	6.2	0.0	9.4	9.4	12.5	0.0	9.4	9.4	100
	5-10	Count	5	5	18	6	3	6	0	3	7	0	53
		% within Turnover	9.4	9.4	34.0	11.3	5.7	11.3	0.0	5.7	13.2	0.0	100
	10-15	Count	3	5	6	3	2	3	8	8	3	0	41
		% within Turnover	7.3	12.2	14.6	7.3	4.9	7.3	19.5	19.5	7.3	0.0	100
	15-20	Count	0	12	3	0	3	0	3	3	0	5	29
		% within Turnover	0.0	41.4	10.3	0.0	10.3	0.0	10.3	10.3	0.0	17.2	100

20-25	Count	0	0	0	0	0	5	0	3	0	0	8
	% within Turnover	0.0	0.0	0.0	0.0	0.0	62.5	0.0	37.5	0.0	0.0	100
25-30	Count	0	0	0	3	0	5	6	11	6	0	31
	% within Turnover	0.0	0.0	0.0	9.7	0.0	16.1	19.4	35.5	19.4	0.0	100
30-35	Count	0	0	3	6	3	6	0	0	0	0	18
	% within Turnover	0.0	0.0	16.7	33.3	16.7	33.3	0.0	0.0	0.0	0.0	100
35-40	Count	0	0	0	6	0	3	0	0	0	0	9
	% within Turnover	0.0	0.0	0.0	66.7	0.0	33.3	0.0	0.0	0.0	0.0	100
40-45	Count	0	0	9	0	3	0	0	0	0	0	12
	% within Turnover	0.0	0.0	75.0	0.0	25	0.0	0.0	0.0	0.0	0.0	100
45-50	Count	0	0	0	0	0	3	3	3	3	3	15
	% within Turnover	0.0	0.0	0.0	0.0	0.0	20	20	20	20	20	100
50-100	Count	6	0	3	12	12	6	3	6	0	6	54
	% within Turnover	11.1	0.0	5.6	22.2	22.2	11.1	5.6	11.1	0.0	11.1	100
Above 100	Count	16	3	7	8	26	11	9	9	10	6	105
	% within Turnover	15.2	2.9	6.7	7.6	24.8	10.5	8.6	8.6	9.5	5.7	100
Total	Count	40	29	51	44	55	51	36	46	32	23	407
	% within Turnover	9.8	7.1	12.5	10.8	13.5	12.5	8.8	11.3	7.9	5.7	100

Source: Calculations Done by Researcher

Table 34 has exhibited cross tabulation results of annual turnover and the percentage of total cost incurred by the SMEs and unlisted non-financial firms in terms of foreign currency. It was observed that 31.2 percent of firms with an annual turnover of less than five crore,were having less than 10 percent of their total cost and 9.4 percent firmswere having 90 to 100 percent of their total cost in terms of foreign currency. Next, firms having 5 to 10 crore annual turnover, reported 9.4 percent of firms in this category were having less than 10 percent cost. Similarly, firms with the annual turnover between 10 to 15crore, 7.3 percent of these firms were having less than 10 percent of their total cost in terms of foreign currency. On the other hand, firms havingannual turnover between 15 to 20 crore,17.2 percent of such SMEs and unlisted non-financial firmsshowed 90 to 100 percent of their total cost in terms of foreign currency. Further, firms with the annual turnover between 20 to 25crore reported that 62.5 percent of these firms were having 50 to 60 percent of their total cost in foreign currency. Further, 35.5 percent firms with the annual turnover between 25 to 30crore showed

70 to 80 percent cost. It was found that SMEs and unlisted non-financial firms with annual turnover between 30 to 35crore, 35 to 40crore, 40 to 45crore and 45 to 50 crorewere having more than 20 percent of their total cost in terms of foreign currency **under different classification.** In addition to this 11.1 percent firms with the annual turnover of 50 to 100 crore reported less than 10 percent of their total cost and 90 to 100 percent of their costin foreign currency. Whereas, 15.2 percent firms with the annual turnover above 100 crore depicted less than 10 percent of their total cost and 5.7 percent firmsshowed 90 to 100 percent of their total cost in terms of foreign currency. So, it can be determined that firmswith annual turnover between 45 to 50 crorewere incurring more cost and firms with the less than 5 crore annual turnover were incurring less cost in terms of foreign currency.

Table 35 has reported the results of chi-square test whichexamine the association between annual turnover of the firms and the percentage of their total cost in terms of foreign currency. The calculated statistic of chi-square test, at 99 degree of freedom, is 381.773 that is greater than critical value, therefore null hypothesis is rejected depicting that there issignificantassociation between annual turnover of the firms and the percentage of their total cost in terms of foreign currency at 5 percent level of significance. Consequently, the alternative hypothesis is accepted.

Table 35

Results of Association between Annual Turnover of Firms and Percentage of Total of Cost in Foreign Currency

	Value	df	Asymp. Sig. (2-sided)
Pearson Chi-Square	381.773	99	0.000
Likelihood Ratio	367.331	99	0.000
Linear-by-Linear Association	3.892	1	0.049
N of Valid Cases	407		

Source: Calculations Done by Researcher

Table 36 has presented the results of symmetric measures between annual turnover of the firms and the percentage of their total cost in terms of foreign currency. It was observed that the values of Phi coefficient and Cramer's V as 0.969 and 0.323 respectively and found significant at 0.05 levels indicating a significant positive strength of association. The value of these two coefficients was found more than 0.5 reflecting a significant strength of association between annual turnover of the firms and the percentage of their total cost in terms of foreign currency.

Table 36

Strength of Association between Annual Turnover of Firms and Percentage of Total of Cost in Foreign Currency

		Value	Approx. Sig.
Nominal by Nominal	**Phi**	0.969	0.000
	Cramer's V	0.323	0.000
N of Valid Cases		407	
a. Not assuming the null hypothesis.			
b. Using the asymptotic standard error assuming the null hypothesis.			

Source: Calculations Done by Researcher.

Table 37 has exhibited the cross tabulation results of annual turnover of the SMEs and unlisted non-financial firms and the percentage of their total revenue received in terms of foreign currency. It was observed that 12.5 percent firms with the annual turnover less than five crore had less than 10 percent revenue and 21.9 percent firms received 70 to 80 percent revenue in terms of foreign currency. Next, firms with 5 to 10 crore annual turnover have reported that 18.9 percent firms observed to have 90 to 100 percent revenue. Similarly, firms having their annual turnover in 10-15 crore, 26.8 percent of such firms were having their annual turnover between 80 to 90percent in terms of foreign currency. Further, firms with annual turnover between 15 to 20crore demonstrated less that 31 percent of such firms were having 90 to 100 percent of their total revenues in terms of foreign currency. In the same manner, firms with the annual turnover between 20 to 25 crore, reportedthat their proportion of total revenue was lying in two categories, i.e., 30-40 percent or 90 to 100 percent which was in foreign currency. Added to this, firms with annual turnover in the remaining categories25 to 30, 30 to 35, 35 to 40, 40 to 45, 45 to 50 and 50 to100 crore have shown more than 30 percent of their total revenues in terms of foreign currency. Whereas, 3.8 percent firms with the annual turnover above 100 crore depicted that less than 10 percent of their total revenues and 10.5 percent firms indicated that 90 to 100 percent of their total revenues was in foreign currency. Therefore, it can be identified that firms within the annual turnover of20 to 25 crorewere having comparatively more revenues in foreign currency in comparison to firms having their annual turnover more than 100 crore.

Table 37

Strength of Association between Annual Turnover of Firms and Percentage of Total of Cost in Foreign Currency

Turnover	Revenue										Total
	Less than 10%	10-20%	20-30%	30-40%	40-50%	50-60%	60-70%	70-80%	80-90%	90-100%	
Less Than 5 Crore	12.5	6.2	12.5	15.6	9.4	15.6		21.9		6.2	100
5-10		13.2	11.3	9.4		11.3	9.4	17.0	9.4	18.9	100
10-15	7.3	4.9	4.9	14.6		14.6	19.5	7.3	26.8		100
15-20	6.9	10.3					20.7	20.7	10.3	31.0	100
20-25				62.5						37.5	100
25-30				38.7			19.4	9.7	9.7	22.6	100
30-35				33.3		16.7	33.3			16.7	100
35-40						33.3	33.3	33.3			100
40-45				25.0			25.0	25.0	25.0		100
45-50				20.0				60.0		20.0	100
50-100				5.6	27.8	11.1	22.2	5.6	16.7	11.1	100
Above 100	3.8	5.7	4.8	10.5	2.9	17.1	7.6	21	16.2	10.5	100
Total	3.2	4.9	4.2	14.5	5.2	11.5	14.0	16.7	12.5	13.3	100

Source: Calculations Done by Researcher

Table 38 has shown the results of chi-square test to examine the association between annual turnover of the organization and the percentage revenue of firm in terms of foreign currency. The calculated statistic of chi-square test, at 99 degree of freedom has a value of

284.284, which is greater than the critical value and hence, the null hypothesis is rejected showing the existence of association between annual turnover of the organization and the percentage revenue in terms of foreign currency at 5 percent level of significance. Hence, the alternative hypothesis is accepted.

Table 38

Results of Association between Annual Turnover of Firms and Percentage of Total of Revenues in Foreign Currency

	Value	df	Asymp. Sig. (2-sided)
Pearson Chi-Square	284.284	99	0.000
Likelihood Ratio	300.013	99	0.000
Linear-by-Linear Association	5.008	1	0.025
N of Valid Cases	407		

Source: Calculations Done by Researcher

Table 39

Strength of Association between Annual Turnover of Firms and Percentage of Total of Cost in Foreign Currency

		Value	Approx. Sig.
Nominal by Nominal	Phi	0.836	.000
	Cramer's V	0.279	.000
N of Valid Cases		407	
a. Not assuming the null hypothesis.			
b. Using the asymptotic standard error assuming the null hypothesis.			

Source: Calculations Done by Researcher.

Table 39has given the results of symmetric measures between annual turnover of the organization and the percentage revenue of firm in terms of foreign currency. It was observed that the values of Phi coefficient and Cramer's V as 0.836 and 0.279respectively. As these values are significant at 5 percent level of significance that revealed a significant positive strength of association.

Table 40

Cross Tabulation of Annual Turnover of Organization and the percentage of Firm's Assets in terms of foreign currency

Turnover	Asset										Total
	Less than 10%	10-20%	20-30%	30-40%	40-50%	50-60%	60-70%	70-80%	80-90%	90-100%	
Less Than 5 Crore	37.5	6.2	9.4	12.5	6.2	18.8			9.4		100
5-10	5.7	7.5	11.3		15.1	5.7	20.8	11.3	13.2	9.4	100
10-15	12.2		4.9			19.5		14.6	22.0	26.8	100
15-20	6.9		10.3			10.3	10.3	20.7	10.3	31	100
20-25			25				37.5	37.5			100
25-30			29		6.5	19.4	9.7	19.4	9.7	6.5	100
30-35					50.0	16.7	16.7	16.7			100
35-40							33.3	33.3		33.3	100
40-45	25				25			25		25	100
45-50					20	20	40	20			100
50-100	11.1		16.7	5.6	16.7		16.7	16.7	11.1	5.6	100
Above 100	11.4	7.6	8.6	4.8	12.4	8.6	11.4	12.4	14.3	8.6	100
Total	10.6	3.4	10.6	2.9	12.	10.1	13	15	11.3	11.1	100

Source: *Calculations Done by Researcher.*

Table 40 has indicated the cross tabulation results of annual turnover of the sampled and the percentage of their total assets in terms of foreign currency. As shown in Table 40, firms having less than 5 crore as annual turnover, 37.5% fall under the category of less than 10 percent of their total assets followed by 18.8 percent firms falling in the category of 50-60 percent of their total assets in foreign currency. In case of firms having annual turnover between 5-10 crore, maximum (20.8 percent) were having 60-70 percent of their total assets in foreign currency followed by 15.1 percent firms having 40-50 percent of their assets in foreign currency. Likewise, firms having annual turnover between 10-15 crore were having maximum (26.8 percent) 90-100 percent of their total assets in foreign currency. In case of firms with 15-20 crore annual turnover 31 percent (maximum) firms were having 90-100 percent of their total assets, firms with 20-25 crore annual turnover 37.5 percent (maximum) firms were having 60-70 percent and 70-80 percent of their total assets, firms with 25-30 crore annual turnover 29 percent (maximum) firms were having 20-30 percent of their total

assets, firms with 30-35 crore annual turnover 50 percent (maximum) firms were having 40-

50 percent of their total assets, and firms with 35-40 crore annual turnover 33.3 percent

(maximum) firms were having 60-70 percent, 70-80 percent and 90-100 percent of their total

assets in each of these three categories in terms of foreign currency. Similarly, the additional

results can be observed from Table 40 exhibited below.

Table 41

Results of Association between Annual Turnover of Firms and Percentage of Total of Assets in Foreign Currency

	Value	df	Asymp. Sig. (2-sided)
Pearson Chi-Square	239.987	99	.000
Likelihood Ratio	270.320	99	.000
Linear-by-Linear Association	.024	1	.876
N of Valid Cases	407		

Source: *Calculations Done by Researcher.*

Table 41 reported the results of chi-square test, which examined the association

between annual turnover of the firms and percentage of their total assets in terms of foreign

currency. The calculated value of chi-square test (239.987) is greater than the critical value,

therefore, the null hypothesis is rejected indicating thatthe association between annual

turnover of the sampled firms and the percentage of their total assets in terms of foreign

currency is significant at the 0.05 level. Thus, the alternate hypothesis is accepted.

Table 42

Strength of Association between Annual Turnover of Firms and Percentage of Total of Assets in Foreign Currency

		Value	Approx. Sig.
Nominal by Nominal	Phi	0.768	0.000
	Cramer's V	0.256	0.000
N of Valid Cases		407	
a. Not assuming the null hypothesis.			
b. Using the asymptotic standard error assuming the null hypothesis.			

Source: *Calculations Done by Researcher.*

Table 42 provided the results of symmetric measures between annual turnover of the organization and the percentage assets of firm in terms of foreign currency. It was observed that the values of Phi coefficient and Cramer's V as 0.768 and 0.256respectively. The values havingsignificance at 0.05 levels revealed a significant positive strength of association, but those seeming with less than 0.5 significance suggested a medium strength of associationbetween annual turnover of the organization and the percentage assets of firm in terms of foreign currency. It indicated a medium level of association among these two variables.

Table 43

Table Cross Tabulation of Annual Turnover of Organization and the percentage of Firm's Debt in terms of foreign currency

Turno ver		Debt										Total
		Less than 10%	10-20%	20-30%	30-40%	40-50%	50-60%	60-70%	70-80%	80-90%	90-100%	
Less Than 5 Crore	Count	14	0	2	0	8	3	5	0	0	0	32
	% within Turnover	43.8	0	6.2	0	25	9.4	15.6	0	0	0	100
5-10	Count	5	2	0	13	3	5	6	11	5	3	53
	% within Turnover	9.4	3	0	24.5	5.7	9.4	11.3	20.8	9.4	5.7	100
10-15	Count	5	0	0	0	6	3	6	2	14	5	41
	% within Turnover	12.2	0	0	0	14.6	7.3	14.6	4.9	34.1	12.2	100
15-20	Count	2	0	3	3	3	0	6	9	0	3	29
	% within Turnover	6.9	0	10.3	10.3	10.3	0	20.7	31	0	10.3	100
20-25	Count	0	0	5	0	0	0	3	0	0	0	8
	% within Turnover	0	0	62.5	0	0	0	37.5	0	0	0	100
25-30	Count	0	0	0	3	10	0	3	9	3	3	31
	% within Turnover	0	0	0	9.7	32.3	0	9.7	29	9.7	9.7	100
30-35	Count	0	0	0	0	3	3	3	6	0	3	18
	% within Turnover	0	0	0	0	16.7	16.7	16.7	33.3	0	16.7	100
35-40	Count	0	0	6	0	3	0	0	0	0	0	9
	% within Turnover	0	0	66.7	0	33.3	0	0	0	0	0	100
40-45	Count	3	0	6	0	0	0	0	3	0	0	12
	% within Turnover	25	0	50	0	0	0	0	25	0	0	100
45-50	Count	0	0	3	0	0	0	0	3	6	3	15

	% within Turnover	0	0	20	0	0	0	0	20	40	20	100
50-100	Count	6	0	3	6	0	3	18	6	9	3	54
	% within Turnover	11.1	0	5.6	11.1	0	5.6	33.3	11.1	16.7	5.6	100
Above 100	Count	16	2	8	8	6	19	19	8	14	5	105
	% within Turnover	15.2	1.9	7.6	7.6	5.7	18.1	18.1	7.6	13.3	4.8	100
Total	Count	51	4	36	33	42	36	69	57	51	28	407
	% within Turnover	12.5	1	8.8	8.1	10.3	8.8	17	14	12.5	6.9	100

Source: Calculations Done by Researcher

The above table has shown the proportion of debt in terms of foreign currency in relation to its turnover. As depicted in the table, the smaller the size of the firm, lesser is the exposure of firm/firm for foreign debt. More than 40% of the firms have less than 10% foreign debt in case of firms having turnover lesser than five crore. The firms, having annual turnover more than 100 crore, have shown that their foreign debt is more than 50%of their annual turnover. The larger the size of firm in terms of annual turnover, the higher is the possibility of high amount of foreign debt and hence more exposure to forex risk. This association between more annual turnover of the firm and more is the possibility of high amount of foreign debt has been tested through various tests of association too.

Table 44

Results of Association between Annual Turnover of Organization and the percentage of Firm's Debt in terms of foreign currency

	Value	df	Asymp. Sig. (2-sided)
Pearson Chi-Square	339.318[a]	99	.000
Likelihood Ratio	331.613	99	.000
Linear-by-Linear Association	0.892	1	.345
N of Valid Cases	407		
a. 95 cells (79.2%) have expected count less than 5. The minimum expected count is .08.			

Source: Calculations Done by Researcher

The significant chi-square coefficient has supported the rejection of null hypothesis indicating that there is significant association between annual turnover and foreign debt of the firm. The measures of symmetric relationship between these two parameters have further

supported the association between annual turnover and foreign debt. The phi value near to

one with zero probability indicates a positive and strong association between the parameters

discussed. Similar findings are also reflected through the results of Cramer's V values. The

table given below has exhibited these results.

Table 45

Strength of Association between Annual Turnover of Organization and the percentage of Firm's Debt in terms of foreign currency

		Value	Approx. Sig.
Nominal by Nominal	**Phi**	.913	.000
	Cramer's V	.304	.000
N of Valid Cases		407	
a. Not assuming the null hypothesis.			
b. Using the asymptotic standard error assuming the null hypothesis.			

Source: Calculations Done by Researcher

In further analysis, respondents were asked about exposure of foreign currency risk to

which their firm was exposed. Out of 407 respondents maximum 392 firms were exposed to

forex risk related to U.S. Dollar, followed by European EURO (91firms), Chinese Yuan (23

firms), UK Pound Sterling (20 firms). Only 8 firms each were exposed to the forex risk

related to Australian Dollar and Hong Kong Dollar, 3 firms were exposed to Canadian Dollar

and 2 firms were exposed to Singapore Dollar.

Table 46

In which currency firms were exposed to forex risk

U.S. Dollar	392
European EURO	91
Swiss Franc	0
UK Pound Sterling	20
Japanese Yen	22
Canadian Dollar	3
Australian Dollar	8
Chinese Yuan	23
Hong Kong Dollar	8
Singapore Dollar	2
Kuwaiti Dinar	6

Any other (Please Specify)	2

Source: Calculations Done by Researcher

Results of the Table 46 revealed that majority of the firms/firms, that is, 281 out of 407 (69%) of the firms or firms is not involved in the management of forex risk exposure. It means that only 126 firms or firms are managing their forex risk exposure. In other words, out of our sample size only 30.96% of firms or firms are managing their forex risk exposure. Further, out of this 126 firms/firms, majority of the firms falls under either the category of high of medium level of management in respect of forex risk. So, we can conclude that not very much firms in India is inclined towards the management of forex risk exposure.

Table 47

Showing the level of Forex Risk exposure Measured by Firms

		Frequency	Percent	Valid Percent	Cumulative Percent
Valid	No	281	69	69	69
	Very High	8	2	2	71
	High	53	13	13	84
	Medium	54	13.3	13.3	97.3
	Low	11	2.7	2.7	100
	Total	407	100	100	

Source: Calculations Done by Researcher

Table 48

Cross Tabulation of Annual Turnover of Organization and the Translation exposure (accounting translation into base currency) of the Organization

Turnover	Translation exposure (accounting translation into base currency)			Total
	Often	Sometimes	Never	
Less Than 5 Crore	15.6	71.9	12.5	100
5-10	30.2	52.8	17.0	100
10-15	14.6	65.9	19.5	100
15-20	48.3	41.4	10.3	100
20-25	62.5	37.5	0	100
25-30	45.2	54.8	0	100
30-35	33.3	50	16.7	100
35-40	100	0	0	100
40-45	0	75	25	100
45-50	0	100	0	100

50-100	50	33.3	16.7	100
Above 100	46.7	32.4	21	100
Total	37.1	47.9	15	100

Source: Calculations Done by Researcher

Results of the Table **48,** showed that firms whose annual turnover in term of Indian rupees falls under the category of 35-40 Crore, often manage translation exposure (accounting translation into base currency) followed by firms/firms whose annual turnover in term of Indian rupees falls under the range of 20-25, 15-20, above 100, 25-30, 30-35, 5-10, and 10-15 crore respectively. Overall, 47.9% of the firms/firms sometimes manage for translation exposure (accounting translation into base currency). On the other hand, only 15% of the firms in the sample do not manage for translation exposure (accounting translation into base currency) in the present study which showed that most of the firms either go for often or sometimes options for managing translation exposure (accounting translation into base currency).

Table 49

Results of Association between Annual Turnover of Organization and the Translation exposure (accounting translation into base currency) of the Organization

	Value	df	Asymp. Sig. (2-sided)
Pearson Chi-Square	81.916	22	.000
Likelihood Ratio	102.107	22	.000
Linear-by-Linear Association	3.322	1	.068
N of Valid Cases	407		

Source: Calculations Done by Researcher

Table 49 demonstrated the results of chi-square test which examined the association between annual turnover of organization and the translation exposure (accounting translation into base currency) of the organization. The value of chi-square test statistics, at 22 degree of freedom had a value of 81.916, as this is greater than the critical value the null hypothesis is rejected depicting thatthe association between the annual turnover of organization and the translation exposure (accounting translation into base currency) of the organization is significant at the 0.05 level. Hence, the alternate hypothesis is accepted.

Table 50

Strength of Association between Annual Turnover of Organization and the Translation exposure (accounting translation into base currency) of the Organization

		Value	Approx. Sig.
Nominal by Nominal	Phi	0.449	0.000
	Cramer's V	0.317	0.000
N of Valid Cases		407	
a. Not assuming the null hypothesis.			
b. Using the asymptotic standard error assuming the null hypothesis.			

Source: Calculations Done by Researcher

Table 50 provided the results of symmetric measures between annual turnover of organization and the translation exposure (accounting translation into base currency) of the organization. It was observed that the values of Phi coefficient and Cramer's V as 0.449 and 0.317 respectively. The values havingsignificance at 0.05 level revealed a significant positive strength of association, but those seeming with less than 0.5 significance suggested a medium strength of associationbetween annual turnover of organization and the translation exposure (accounting translation into base currency) of the organization. It indicated a medium level of association among these two variables.

Table 51

Cross Tabulation of Annual Turnover of Organization and the Transaction exposure (Foreign receivable and payable currency) of the Organization

Turnover	Transaction exposure (Foreign receivable and payable currency)			Total
	Often	Sometimes	Never	
Less Than 5 Crore	25.0%	62.5%	12.5%	100%
5-10	22.6%	56.6%	20.8%	100%
10-15	22%	63.4%	14.6%	100%
15-20	37.9%	62.1%	0%	100%
20-25	37.5%	37.5%	25%	100%
25-30	45.2%	48.4%	6.5%	100%
30-35	50.0%	33.3%	16.7%	100%

35-40	33.3%	33.3%	33.3%	100%
40-45	0%	75.0%	25.0%	100%
45-50	20%	40%	40%	100%
50-100	27.8%	44.4%	27.8%	100%
Above 100	63.8%	21.9%	14.3%	100%
Total	37.8%	45%	17.2%	100.0%

Source: Calculations Done by Researcher

Results of the Table 51 demonstrated that overall there are 45% of the firm/firms in the sample of the present study which sometimes go for managing the transaction exposure (Foreign receivable and payable currency) whose annual turnover is in Indian rupees. Results also showed that the firms who often go for managing the transaction exposure (Foreign receivable and payable currency), two third of these firms were those firms whose annual turnover in Indian rupees is more than 100 crore. The firms whose annual turnover is 40-45 crore, these firms mostly (75%) go for some time management of transaction exposure (Foreign receivable and payable currency). Same patter was observed in the firms whose annual turnover falls under the range of less than 5 crore, 5-10, 10-15, 15-20, 25-30, 45-50 and 50-100 crore. That is, all the firms under this range of turnover in Indian rupees mostly go for some times management of transaction exposure (Foreign receivable and payable currency). Another observation from the analysis is that there are very few firms who never go for managing the transaction exposure (Foreign receivable and payable currency).

Table 52

Results of Association between Annual Turnover of Organization and the Transaction exposure (Foreign receivable and payable currency) of the Organization

	Value	df	Asymp. Sig. (2-sided)
Pearson Chi-Square	77.864	22	.000
Likelihood Ratio	85.937	22	.000
Linear-by-Linear Association	5.699	1	.017
N of Valid Cases	407		

Source: Calculations Done by Researcher

Table 52 demonstrated the results of chi-square test which examined the association between turnover of organization and the transaction exposure (foreign receivable and payable currency). The calculated statistic of chi-square test, at 22 degree of freedom had a value of 77.864, as this is greater than the critical value the null hypothesis is rejected depicting thatthe association betweenannual turnover of organization in Indian rupees and the transaction exposure (foreign receivable and payable currency)of the organization is significant at the 0.05 level. Hence, the alternate hypothesis is accepted.

Table 53

Strength of Association between Annual Turnover of Organization and the Transaction exposure (Foreign receivable and payable currency) of the Organization

		Value	Approx. Sig.
Nominal by Nominal	**Phi**	0.437	0.000
	Cramer's V	0.309	0.000
N of Valid Cases		407	
a. Not assuming the null hypothesis.			
b. Using the asymptotic standard error assuming the null hypothesis.			

Source: Calculations Done by Researcher

Table 53 provided the results of symmetric measures between annual turnover of organization in Indian rupees and the transaction exposure (foreign receivable and payable currency). It was observed that the values of Phi coefficient and Cramer's V as 0.437 and 0.309 respectively. The values havingsignificance at 0.05 level revealed a significant positive strength of association, but those seeming with less than 0.5 significance suggested a medium strength of associationbetween annual turnover of organization in Indian rupees and the transaction exposure (foreign receivable and payable currency)of the organization. It indicated a medium level of association among these two variables.

Table 54

Cross Tabulation of Annual Turnover of Organization and the Economic Exposure (Future expected cash flow and competitive position) of the Organization

Turnover	Economic Exposure (Future expected cash flow and competitive position)	Total

	Often	Sometimes	Never	
Less Than 5 Crore	37.5%	40.6%	21.9%	100%
5-10	30.2%	28.3%	41.5%	100%
10-15	46.3%	29.3%	24.4%	100%
15-20	37.9%	41.4%	20.7%	100%
20-25	62.5%	0%	37.5%	100%
25-30	25.8%	35.5%	38.7%	100%
30-35	50.0%	50.0%	0%	100%
35-40	33.3%	33.3%	33.3%	100%
40-45	50.0%	25.0%	25.0%	100%
45-50	20.0%	40.0%	40.0%	100%
50-100	22.2%	44.4%	33.3%	100%
Above 100	47.6%	28.6%	23.8%	100%
Total	37.8%	33.9%	28.3%	100%

Source: Calculations Done by Researcher

Results of the Table 54 revealed that majority of the firms go for managing economic exposure (future expected cash flow and competitive position) whose annual turnover is in Indian rupees. Results also showed that firms whose annual turnover fall under the range of 20-25 crore, they mostly manage economic exposure (future expected cash flow and competitive position). Whereas in case of firms who annual turnover fall under the range of 5-10 and 25-30 crore, they never go for managing economic exposure (future expected cash flow and competitive position). Further, firms whose annual turnover falls under the range of 35-40crore, they have equal proportion for managing economic exposure (future expected cash flow and competitive position). Also firms whose annual turnover falls under the range of 10-15, 30-35, 40-45 and above 100 crore they mostly manage economic exposure (future expected cash flow and competitive position).

Table 55

Results of Association between Annual Turnover of Organization and the Economic Exposure (Future expected cash flow and competitive position) of the Organization

	Value	df	Asymp. Sig. (2-sided)
Pearson Chi-Square	34.728	22	.041
Likelihood Ratio	42.227	22	.006

Linear-by-Linear Association	.359	1	.549
N of Valid Cases	407		

Source: Calculations Done by Researcher

Table 55 demonstrated the results of chi-square test which examined the association between annual turnover of organization in Indian rupees and the economic exposure (future expected cash flow and competitive position). The calculated statistic of chi-square test, at 22 degree of freedom had a value of 34.728, as this is greater than the critical value the null hypothesis is rejected depicting thatthe association betweenannual turnover of organization in Indian rupees and the economic exposure (future expected cash flow and competitive position)of the organization is significant at the 0.05 level. Thus, the alternate hypothesis is accepted.

Table 56

Strength of Association between Annual Turnover of Organization and the Economic Exposure (Future expected cash flow and competitive position) of the Organization

		Value	Approx. Sig.
Nominal by Nominal	Phi	0.292	0.041
	Cramer's V	0.207	0.041
N of Valid Cases		407	
a. Not assuming the null hypothesis.			
b. Using the asymptotic standard error assuming the null hypothesis.			

Source: Calculations Done by Researcher

Table 56 provided the results of symmetric measures between economic sectors and the percentage cost of firm in terms of foreign currency. It was observed that the values of Phi coefficient and Cramer's V as 0.292 and 0.207 respectively. The values havingsignificance at 0.05 level revealed a significant positive strength of association, but those seeming with less than 0.5 significance suggested a low strength of associationbetween annual turnover of organization in Indian rupees and the economic exposure (future expected cash flow and competitive position)of the organization. It indicated a low level of association among these two variables.

B. Forex Risk Exposure Management

The following section converses the outcomes obtained with respect to fulfillment of second objective of the study, i.e., the management of forex risk exposure by SMEs and unlisted non-financial firms.

In lieu of above, the first question asked from target sample units was awareness regarding forex risk management. The results of study revealed (Table 57) that only 15% of the sampled units were fully aware about the forex risk management and 55% of the sampled units were partially aware about forex risk management. A large number, i.e., 122 out of 407 (30%) of the firms were not at all aware regarding the forex risk management.

Table 57

Awareness level of SMEs and Unlisted Non-Financial Firms Regarding Forex Risk Management

	Frequency	Percent	Valid Percent	Cumulative Percent
Yes, Fully Aware	61	15	15	15
Yes, but Partially aware	224	55	55	70
Not aware about the concept of forex risk management	122	30	30	100
Total	407	100	100	

Source: Calculations Done by Researcher

Table 58 has supported the results given in Table 57 and has exhibited that out of 407 firms, only 74 firms were having a specified policy on forex risk management. More than 70 (73.7%) percent of SMEs and unlisted non-financial firms said they were not having any policy document for forex risk exposure management while 7.9% firms admitted that they are in the process of framing such a policy.

Table 58

Number of SMEs and Unlisted Non-Financial Firms Having Forex Risk Exposure Management Policy

	Frequency	Percent	Valid Percent	Cumulative Percent
Yes	75	18.4	18.4	18.4
No	300	73.7	73.7	92.1
No, but currently it is under consideration and soon will be in place	32	7.9	7.9	100
Total	407	100	100	

Source: Calculations Done by Researcher

Table 59 has exhibited that who defines the forex risk management policy in SMEs and unlisted non-financial firms. As depicted in Table 3, in case of 155 out of 407 firms, the management team of the business collectively designs the forex risk management policy followed by Board of Directors and CEOs of the firms. Finance controller and Accountants were also designing the forex risk management policy of their businesses but the number of such firms was very less.

Table 59

Who Defines the Forex Risk Management Policy

	Frequency	Percent	Valid Percent	Cumulative Percent
Board of Directors	100	24.6	24.6	24.6
Company's Management Team	155	38.1	38.1	62.7
CFO	45	11.1	11.1	73.7
CEO	49	12.0	12	85.7
Accountant	17	4.2	4.2	89.9
Finance Controller	13	3.2	3.2	93.1
Any Other	28	6.9	6.9	100
Total	407	100	100	

Source: Calculations Done by Researcher

The implementation of forex risk management policy is also an important concern to manage the forex risk. As shown in Table 60, the management team of the business, CEOs, and Board of Directors were taking the responsibility of effective implementation of the forex

risk management policy of SMEs and unlisted non-financial firms in India.

Table 60

Who Implements the Forex Risk Management Policy in the Firm

	Frequency	Percent	Valid Percent	Cumulative Percent
Board of Directors	47	11.5	11.5	11.5
Company's Management Team	173	42.5	42.5	54.1
CFO	23	5.7	5.7	59.7
CEO	99	24.3	24.3	84
Treasurer	9	2.2	2.2	86.2
Accountant	11	2.7	2.7	88.9
Finance Controller	7	1.7	1.7	90.7
Any Other	38	9.3	9.3	100
Total	407	100	100	

Source: Calculations Done by Researcher

Next significant question asked was related to the purpose of hedging the forex risk.

There can be several purposes of hedging the forex risk by a firm. It can increase the

profitability, reducing the volatility in cash flows or speculation etc. As shown in Table 61,

speculation was also a major reason for hedging the forex risk. Although, the technical

meaning of the term hedging risk itself indicates a specific meaning but finding speculation

(330 out of 407) as a purpose of taking opposite positions in a hedging instrument is an

fascinating outcome of the analysis. In addition to speculation, SMEs and unlisted non-

financial firms also informed that hedging forex risk is essential for the sustainability of their

businesses. 323 out of 407 firms admitted that hedging is indispensable for survival of their

businesses. 326 firms said that they were doing hedging to improve the financial performance

of their businesses, 285 firms said that it reduces the volatility in the earnings of their

business, and 256 firms said that it reduces the volatility in their cash flows etc. The other

purposes of hedging forex risk were related to controlling the risk of fluctuations in foreign currencies, to increase the market value of firm and to increase the profitability of the business. The figures for these have also been mentioned in Table 61.

Table 61

Purpose of Hedging Forex Risk

S. No	Statements	No	Yes
1	To Increase profitability	187	220
2	To Hedge against forex rate fluctuation	210	197
3	To Reduce the volatility in earnings	285	122
4	To Reduce the volatility in cash flows	256	151
5	To Use as a risk management tool	260	147
6	To Improvise the financial results of the company	326	81
7	To Increase the market value of firm	249	158
8	It is Essential for the sustainability or survival of business	323	84
9	To Gain from speculation	330	77
10	Any Other	404	03

Source: Calculations Done by Researcher

Table 62 has shown that the SMEs and unlisted non-financial firms were using multiple methods to measure their forex risk exposure. Among these most popular methods, estimation of cash flows was used most frequently to measure forex risk exposure. The sampled firms were also using rough estimates to forecast their forex risk exposure. Value at Risk, Scenario Analysis and Matching approach were also among other methods adopted by firms to measure forex risk exposure. Although, 78 respondents said that they were not using any kind of methods for this purpose.

Table 62

Methods used to Measure the Forex Risk Exposure

S. No	Statements	No	Yes
1	Cash flow estimates	267	140
2	Value at Risk	290	117
3	Scenario Analysis	340	67
4	Leading and Lagging	361	46
5	Matching	346	61
6	Stress Analysis	372	35

7	Rough Estimation	284	123
8	No method is used	329	78
9	If any other, please specify	399	8

Source: Calculations Done by Researcher

Table 63 has exhibited the tendency of managing the forex risk exposure by the firms. 15.2% of firms said that they always manage their forex risk exposure. It means, whenever there is an exposure of forex risk due to any business transaction, these firms were taking a hedging strategy to manage the forex exposure risk. While 26.3% of the firms said that they often take hedging position for their forex risk exposure. 11.3% and 10.6%of the firms said never or rarely meaning thereby, these firms were not taking any concrete action to manage their forex risk exposure. In any case, the firms falling under last two categories are at a high-risk point due to fluctuations in forex rates.

Table 63

Frequency of Forex Risk Exposure Management

		Frequency	Percent	Valid Percent	Cumulative Percent
Valid	Always	62	15.2	15.2	15.2
	Often	107	26.3	26.3	41.5
	Sometimes	149	36.6	36.6	78.1
	Rarely	43	10.6	10.6	88.7
	Never	46	11.3	11.3	100
	Total	407	100	100	

Source: Calculations Done by Researcher

Table 64 has depicted the reasons by the firms for never managing their forex risk exposure. As mentioned in previous question, 11.3% of SMEs and unlisted non-financial firms said that they never manage their forex risk exposure then these firms were asked to state the reasons for such type of behavior. The results obtained in this context indicated that lack of awareness about measuring forex risk and cost convoluted in hedging the forex risk were two major reasons for never managing the forex risk exposure. In addition to this, possibility of insufficient loss due to no-management, less quantum of forex exposure and availability of natural hedge were among the other reasons mentioned by these firms.

Table 64

Reason for Not Managing Forex Risk Exposure
(Applicable to those who said Never in Previous Question)

S. No		No	Yes	NA	Total
1	Lack of Awareness regarding forex Risk Measurement	15	31	361	407
2	Lack of knowledge regarding estimating the effect of exposure	26	20	361	407
3	Cost of Hedging is more than benefit of hedging	15	31	361	407
4	Lack of trained people to manage forex risk exposure	24	22	361	407
5	Possibility of insufficient loss due to no-management	17	29	361	407
6	Less amount of forex exposure is involved	22	24	361	407
7	Availability of natural hedge	22	24	361	407
8	Insufficient hedging instruments available	38	8	361	407
9	No clear guideline in the business regarding this	23	23	361	407
10	Any other, please specify	43	3	361	407

Source: Calculations Done by Researcher

Results mentioned in Table 65 are indicating that 45.7 % (186) of SMEs and unlisted non-financial firms were taking their hedging position for an average period of 90 days. And 98 firms out of 407 forms were taking hedging positions for an average period of 180 days. Only 7 firms were doing hedging for a complete year, i.e., 360 days. The variation in hedging period can be because of the quantum of forex risk exposure of the respective firms too. But, it is good if the firms having forex risk exposure are having hedging for a period matching with their risk exposure.

Table 65

Average Period of Hedging Forex Risk

		Frequency	Percent	Valid Percent	Cumulative Percent
Valid	Less than 90 Days	116	28.5	28.5	28.5
	90 Days	186	45.7	45.7	74.2
	180 Days	98	24.1	24.1	98.3
	360 Days	7	1.7	1.7	100
	Total	407	100	100	

Source: Calculations Done by Researcher

Hedge ratio is an important aspect of determining the forex risk exposure management. Table 66 has shown that 49.9% of the firms (203) were following no specific hedge ratio for the management of forex risk exposure whereas, 88 (21.6%) firms (highest) were using 41-60% as hedge ratio to manage their forex risk exposure management. Further, 14 % (57) firms were having 21-40% as hedge ratio for the purpose of managing forex risk exposure. Out of 407, 37 firms were having a practice of 1-20% ratio as their hedge ratio policy to manage forex risk exposure. Finally, there were only 7 (1.7%) firms who were having highest hedge ratio, i.e., 81-100% to manage forex risk exposure. The findings has indicated that majority of the SMEs and unlisted non-financial firms in the study were having moderate hedge ratio as a policy to manage forex risk exposure.

Table 66

Policy Regarding Hedge Ratio

		Frequency	Percent	Valid Percent	Cumulative Percent
	Not specific ratio	203	49.9	49.9	49.9
	1-20%	37	9.1	9.1	59
	21-40%	57	14	14	73
Valid	41-60%	88	21.6	21.6	94.6
	61-80%	15	3.7	3.7	98.3
	81-100%	7	1.7	1.7	100
	Total	407	100	100	

Source: Calculations Done by Researcher

There are various instruments provided by financial institutions, which are used for hedging the forex risk. In addition to these instruments, the practitioners also use various techniques like cash flow matching and asset-liability management etc. to hedge the forex risk. Table 67 has exhibited the details about such instruments and techniques used by SMEs and unlisted non-financial firms in India. As depicted in Table 67, cash flow matching technique has been preferred than asset liability management for hedging forex risk. Out of 407 firms, 87 firms said that they always use cash flow matching, and 74 firms said that they often use cash flow matching technique to hedge forex risk. More than 100 firms said that they use asset-liability management to hedge forex risk. As shown in Table 67, structured derivatives is the least used instrument by various firms (247) followed by Hybrid Debt in order to hedge forex risk exposure followed by exchange traded options, swaps, hybrid debts, asset liability management and OTC options respectively. Exchange Traded Futures, OTC traded Options and Exchange Traded Options were also found comparatively popular instruments of hedging forex risk by SMEs and unlisted non-financial firms in India.

Table 67

Types of Instruments or Techniques used for Hedging

S. No	Statements	Always	Often	Sometimes	Rarely	Never	Total
1	Cash Flow Matching	87	74	49	34	163	407
2	Asset Liability management	55	48	58	31	215	407
3	Exchange Traded Futures	38	90	63	53	163	407
4	Exchange Traded Options	43	64	27	36	237	407
5	Swaps	37	44	23	75	228	407
6	OTC Forwards	48	186	62	31	80	407
7	OTC Options	45	77	58	23	204	407
8	Structured Derivatives	39	32	26	63	247	407
9	Hybrid Debts	44	60	11	76	216	407
10	Others (Please Specify)	-	-	5	28	374	407

Source: Calculations Done by Researcher

There are multiple options available in selecting the instrument or technique to hedge the forex risk. But the SMEs and unlisted firms were not using all such instruments and techniques with same frequency. When they were asked that why they were not considering any specific instrument or technique for the purpose of hedging forex risk then there these firms stated many reasons for not using or rarely using specified type of instrument or technique. As depicted in Table 68, such reasons can be that the instrument or technique is too complex, causing problem in accounting treatment, not allowed in some markets, high cost involved or too complex etc. There were 285 firms (70%) who were either agreed or strongly agreed that complexities involved in the hedging instrument was the major reason for not considering a specific instrument for hedging purpose. The next prominent reason was

related to accounting problems (364), followed by higher cost than expected benefits (356),

insufficient exposure (353), not having the desired features (333), not having sufficient

exposure of market instruments (253), and lack of willingness to disclose much about forex

risk exposure of business (230) respectively. The least important reason that was affecting the

firms' decision regarding not choosing of a specific hedging instrument or technique "Not

liquid enough" (304). Whereas 207 respondents believed that these hedging instruments are

too risky to use for managing forex risk exposure. In nutshell, there are many reasons which

are causing firms' decision to not to use various instruments and techniques of hedging the

forex risk exposure.

Table 68

Reasons for 'Never' or 'Rarely' Using Hedging Instruments or Techniques

S. N		Strongly Disagree	Disagree	Neutral	Agree	Strongly Agree	Total
1	Too Complex	0	5	17	194	191	407
2	Not Allowed	0	161	222	17	7	407
3	Causing Accounting Problems	2	5	36	210	154	407
4	Not having the desired features	2	11	61	162	171	407
5	Cost of using it is more than expected benefits	0	10	41	222	134	407
6	Does not have sufficient exposure	5	6	43	193	160	407
7	Not offered by my banker	6	181	152	57	11	407
8	Insufficient exposure of market instrument	4	4	46	211	142	407
9	Does not want to disclose much about Forex risk exposure of business	2	9	166	224	6	407
10	Not liquid enough	304	16	44	43	0	407
11	Too Risky	5	8	207	181	6	407
12	Other (Please Specify)	356	3	19	27	2	407

Source: Calculations Done by Researcher

Table 69 has discussed the average maturity period opted by SMEs and unlisted non-financial firms for different hedging instruments. The average maturity period of hedging instruments is analyzed on the basis of usage of hedging instruments. As discussed in previous section, all types of hedging instruments are not used each of the SMEs and unlisted non-financial firm, therefore, the total of last column of Table 69 is not same in all cases. As shown in Table 69, an average period of 91-180 days (most preferred) is considered by sample units for different types of hedging instruments, to be more specific, in case of Futures (109), Forwards (123), Options (102), OTC forwards (154), and OTC options (70), the firms are hedging their forex risk exposure for an average period of 91-180 days followed by an average maturity period of 0-90 days and 180-360 days. The second last column of Table 69, means the firms are not considering the given standard options of average maturity period to hedge their forex risk and due to lack of a specified forex risk management policy, these firms were not giving due importance to thinking more meticulously about the specific maturity period for a hedging strategy.

Table 69

Average Maturity Period of Hedging Instruments

S. No	Statements	0-90 days	91-180 days	180-360 days	360-days to 2 years	Over 2 years	Not used	Total
1	Futures	88	109	73	49	51	37	407
2	Forwards	89	123	69	51	36	39	407
3	Options	80	102	85	68	59	13	407
4	Swaps	37	40	41	37	16	9	179
5	OTC Forwards	53	154	49	29	26	16	327
6	OTC Options	33	70	37	30	18	13	203
7	Structured Derivatives	28	25	30	28	25	24	160
8	Hybrid Debts	32	37	27	36	32	26	191
9	Other (Please Specify)	6	5	6	6	6	5	33

Source: Calculations Done by Researcher

Table 70 has exhibited the use of different hedging instruments for partial, full or dynamic hedge. As mentioned in Table 70, almost all types of hedging instruments were used for partial, full and dynamic hedging. But the use of various hedging instruments for partial and full hedge was found comparatively more than their use for dynamic hedge. As stated in Table 70, in case of Futures, out of 407 firms, 140 said that they use it for partial hedge and 145 firms said that they are using Futures instrument for full hedging. Similarly, in case of Forwards (164), Options (151), Swaps (71), Hybrid Debts (101) and Others (16), the firms were using more of these instruments for partial hedging rather than using them for full or dynamic hedging. The detailed figures related to full hedging and dynamic hedging can be observed with the figures given in Table 70.

Table 70

Usage of Different Hedging Instruments/Techniques

S. No	Statements	Partial Hedge	Full Hedge	Dynamic Hedge	Total
1	Futures	140	145	122	407
2	Forwards	164	123	120	407
3	Options	151	147	109	407
4	Swaps	71	55	54	179
5	OTC Forwards	130	174	23	327
6	OTC Options	76	84	43	203
7	Structured Derivatives	66	77	17	160
8	Hybrid Debts	101	82	8	191
9	Other (Please Specify	16	15	2	33

Source: Calculations Done by Researcher

Table 71 has exhibited the results obtained for three types of exposure of SMEs and unlisted non-financial firms and matching of hedging. As depicted in Table 71, 172 firms having translation exposure said that they were hedging their forex risk exposure for a period shorter than the maturity of the exposure. 95 firms with translation exposure stated that they were exactly matching their hedging position with the maturity of forex risk exposure while 108 firms having translation exposure said that they were taking hedging position for forex risk exposure for a period longer than the maturity of such type of risk exposure. Similarly, 232 firms having transaction exposure said that they were hedging their forex risk for a period which is exactly matching with their risk exposure. While 146 firms having transaction exposure stated that they were hedging forex risk for a period shorter than the maturity of forex risk exposure and 124 such firms were hedging for a period longer than the maturity of their forex risk exposure. Third type of exposure, i.e., economic exposure has indicated slight dissimilar results when compared with translation and transaction exposure. 175 firms having economic exposure stated that they prefer to hedge such type of exposure for a period longer than the maturity of risk exposure. While 89 firms said that they were hedging for a period shorter than the maturity of their forex risk and 80 firms having economic exposure were saying that they were taking hedging position exactly matching with the maturity of forex risk.

Table 71

Matching of Translation, Transaction and Economic Exposurewith Hedging

S. No	Statements	Translation	Transaction	Economic	Total
1	Hedge shorter than the maturity of the exposure	172	146	89	407
2	Hedge the maturity of the exposure	95	232	80	407
3	Hedge longer than the maturity of exposure	108	124	175	407

Source: Calculations Done by Researcher

Next, Table 72 has stated the percentage of hedging of forex risk exposure done by SMEs and unlisted non-financial firms in India. As depicted in Table 72, 140 firms were doing 40-60% hedging of their forex risk exposure. Only 24 firms were doing 80-100% of hedging of their forex risk exposure. A large number of sample firms, i.e., 173 (84+89), were hedging less than or equal to 40% hedging of their total forex risk exposure which is actually not a suitable approach of managing the forex risk exposure.

Table 72

Percentage of Hedging of Forex Risk Exposure

		Frequency	Percent	Valid Percent	Cumulative Percent
Valid	0-20%	84	20.6	20.6	20.6
	20-40%	89	21.9	21.9	42.5
	40-60%	140	34.4	34.4	76.9
	60-80%	70	17.2	17.2	94.1
	80-100%	24	5.9	5.9	100
	Total	407	100	100	

Source: Calculations Done by Researcher

Table 73 has indicated the frequency of SMEs and unlisted non-financial firms to readjust their hedging position. Since, the forex rates may fluctuate every day, which can have an impact on the overall hedging position of the firms therefore, there may require readjustment in the hedging position taken by firms. As depicted in Table 73, 34 out of 407 firms mentioned that they readjust their hedging position on daily basis and 93 firms said that their prepare a weekly schedule to readjust their hedging position in forex risk management avenues. A large number, i.e., 183 (45%) firms readjust their hedging position on monthly basis. A small number (13) of firms readjust their hedging position on yearly basis. The purpose of readjustment in hedging position is to ensure that the exposure to forex risk is fully covered. The sample units considered in the study are not of similar nature in terms of their forex risk exposure, annual turnover, and frequency of foreign transactions etc. therefore, their schedule to readjust their hedging position may also vary but considering the nature of forex market, a readjustment schedule of monthly, quarterly, semi-annual or annual may cause increase in forex risk exposure of the firms.

Table 73

Frequency of Readjusting the Hedging Position

		Frequency	Percent	Valid Percent	Cumulative Percent
Valid	Daily	34	8.4	8.4	8.4
	Weekly	93	22.9	22.9	31.2
	Monthly	183	45.0	45.0	76.2
	Quarterly	62	15.2	15.2	91.4
	Semi-annually	22	5.4	5.4	96.8
	Yearly	13	3.2	3.2	100.0
	Total	407	100.0	100.0	

Source: Calculations Done by Researcher

The next question related to forex risk management was related to timeline in execution of a forex risk hedging strategies. The sample respondents were asked whether they follow a pre-specified timeline in execution of their forex risk hedging strategy. Out of 407 respondents, 177 firms said that they are not following any specific timeline in execution of hedging strategy while 126 respondents said that whenever they submit a bid or transaction is initiated then they execute their hedging strategy for forex risk exposure. While 57 firms said that whenever an order is received from a customer in foreign currency or an order is received which involves inflow of cash flows in foreign currency, that is the time they initiate the execution of their forex risk hedging strategy. And 47 firms said that they execute a hedging strategy at the time of realization of revenues in terms of foreign currency.

Table 74

Timeline in Execution of Hedging Strategy

		Frequency	Percent	Valid Percent	Cumulative Percent
Valid	There is nothing fixed timeline for execution strategy	177	43.5	43.5	43.5
	At the time of submitting bid	126	31	31	74.4
	At the time when an order is received from the customer	57	14	14	88.5

	At the time when revenue is realized from the customer	47	11.5	11.5	100
	Total	407	100	100	

Source: Calculations Done by Researcher

There are several benefits attached to Exchange Earners' Foreign Currency (EEFC) Account. A firm having EEFC accounts is presumed to be more aware regarding the forex risk exposure management. Therefore, the sample units were also asked about their EEFC Accounts. Out of 407 firms, 275 firms said that they have EECF Account to manage their earnings in foreign currencies. While 132 (32.4 percent) of the SMEs and Unlisted firms were not having EECF Account. (See Results in Table 75)

Table 75

Exchange Earners' Foreign Currency Account

		Frequency	Percent	Valid Percent	Cumulative Percent
	No	132	32.4	32.4	32.4
Valid	Yes	275	67.6	67.6	100
	Total	407	100	100	

Source: Calculations Done by Researcher

In continuation with the results of Table 75, the respondents were also asked their opinion regarding use of EEFC Account. 70.8% (288) firms said that they think that Exchange Earners' Foreign Currency (EEFC) Account can eliminate the forex risk exposure of their business while 29.2% (119) firms were not agreed to this.

Table 76

Role of Exchange Earners' Foreign Currency Account in Risk Elimination

		Frequency	Percent	Valid Percent	Cumulative Percent
	No	119	29.2	29.2	29.2
Valid	Yes	288	70.8	70.8	100
	Total	407	100	100	

Source: Calculations Done by Researcher

Both economic sector and turnover of the firms are two important demographic features that have earlier been used for cross tabulation analysis. Similarly, while studying the results for attainment of second objective, these two parameters were used to find out if some significant association exists between these two basic parameters and other relevant inputs. For this, cross tabulation results were obtained for 16 different types of possible associations. The results of cross tabulation of these results are given in Appendix I. But the results obtained to test the significance of association and strength of that association are mentioned below. As discussed earlier too that chi-square is good measure for assessing the significance of association between two variables, therefore, considering the results of chi-square test indicate that the association between all the variables studies on the basis of their belongingness to specific economic sector and on the basis of different categories of their annual turnover was found significant. The phi coefficient and Cramer's V coefficient was also found significant at 5% level of significance which further indicated the existence of relationship between variables mentioned in Table 77. Also the phi coefficients and Cramer's V coefficients were found less than 0.5 and positive in majority of the cases, which suggested a moderate to low degree of association between the variables. For a strong level of association, these coefficients should be near to 1.

Table 77

Study of Significance and Strength of Association

Sr. No.	Association Between Variables	Chi Square	Phi	Cramer's V
1	**Association Between Economic Sector and Awareness Regarding Forex Risk Management**	31.893*	.280*	.198*
2	**Association Between Sector wise and Existence of Forex Risk Management Policy**	30.495*	.274*	.194*
3	**Association Between Sector wise and Frequency of Measuring Forex Risk Exposure**	44.890*	.332*	.166*

4	Association Between Sector wise and Average Period of Hedging	72.432*	.422*	.244*
5	Association Between Sector wise Policy of Hedge Ratio	50.080*	.351*	.175*
6	Association Between Sector wise and Percentage Hedging of Forex Risk Exposure	57.087*	.375*	.187*
7	Association Between Sector wise Readjustment of Hedging Position	37.263*	.303*	.151*
8	Association Between Sector wise Execution of Forex Risk Hedging Strategy	29.575*	.270*	.156*
9	Association Between Turnover wise and Awareness Regarding Forex Risk Exposure Management	46.590*	.338*	.239*
10	Association Between Turnover and Existence of Forex Risk Management Policy	49.726*	.350*	.247*
11	Association Between Turnover wise and Frequency of Measuring Forex Risk Exposure	96.906*	.488*	.255*
12	Association Between Turnover wise and Average Period of Hedging	69.104*	.412*	.238*
13	Association Between Turnover wise Policy of Hedge Ratio	142.139*	.591*	.264*
14	Association Between Turnover wise and Percentage Hedging of Forex Risk Exposure	144.898*	.597*	.298*
15	Association Between Turnover wise Readjustment of Hedging Position	130.499*	.566*	.253*
16	Association Between Turnover wise Execution of Forex Risk Hedging Strategy	86.469*	.461*	.266*

*Significant at 5% level of significance.

Source: Calculations Done by Researcher

C. Determinants of Forex Risk Hedging Strategies

The following section discusses the results obtained in the context of objective three of the study, i.e. to identify the determinants of forex risk hedging strategy by SMEs and Unlisted non-financial firms in India. The results regarding this have been discussed under three heading

FOREX RISK EXPOSURE AWARENESS, MANAGEMENT AND DETERMINANTS

1. To identify the factors determining forex risk hedging strategy with the help of Exploratory factor Analysis.

2. To identify the factors which need to be improved for a better forex risk management by SMEs and unlisted non-financial firms in India with the help of Exploratory factor Analysis.

3. To prioritize the different criteria (obtained by EFA) of forex risk hedging strategy by using Analytic Hierarchy Process

Results of Exploratory factor Analysis

Exploratory factor analysis is a leading method of data reduction and it has various extraction processes for producing a solution. This method is used to investigate the data and ascertain the framework of factors that required to be analyzed. The reduction of number of variables is the only objective of employing factor analysis whereas; the extent of information should be maximized during the analysis (Tabachnick & Fidell, 2007; Steward, 1981). The technique of exploratory factor analysis (EFA) intended to determine total number of factors which demonstrated correlation among variables (Kinnear & Gray, 2010).

The items are decreased to meaningful and common interconnected dimensions accompanied with a loss of less amount of information (Hair et al., 2006).

The appropriateness of exploratory factor analysis (EFA) needs to be checked before proceeding for the extracting factors by applying appropriate test statistics. In order to determine whether data is appropriate for the factor analysis, two tests were conducted. The one is Kaiser-Meyer-Olkin (KMO) test, which was applied to evaluate the adequacy of sample and another one is the Bartlett's test of Sphericity, measured the hypothesis that the correlation matrix is identity matrix and suggests the unsuitability and unrelatedness for framework revelation (Singh &Nobi, 2015; Pallant, 2007).

Table 78

KMO and Bartlett's Test

Kaiser-Meyer-Olkin Measure of Sampling Adequacy.		0.864
Bartlett's Test of Sphericity	Approx. Chi-Square	4751.257
	df	496
	Sig.	0.000

Notes: The value of KMO regarded as adequate if it is greater than 0.6 (Kaiser & rice, 1947).
The factor analysis can be exercised if the p-value found to beless than 0.05.

Source: Calculations Done by Researcher

Table 78 reported the statistics of Kaiser-Meyer-Olkin (KMO) as 0.864, which falls

under the acceptable range, indicates that factor analysis could be employed for the available

set of data. In addition, the Bartlett's Test of Sphericity examined the significance of the

correlation matrix of the variables. It was suggested that correlation among statements were

adequately large for principal component analysis because the correlation matrix found to be

significant that is less than 0.05. Hence, the results indicated that the data is befitted for the

factor analysis.

Table 79

Communalities

Statements	Initial	Extraction
Q9	1.000	0.554
Q11	1.000	0.578
Q13	1.000	0.610
Q14	1.000	0.570
Q15	1.000	0.469
Q16	1.000	0.615
Q26	1.000	0.592
Q32	1.000	0.565
Q1	1.000	0.545
Q2	1.000	0.546
Q3	1.000	0.554
Q4	1.000	0.494
Q5	1.000	0.529
Q7	1.000	0.552
Q8	1.000	0.583
Q12	1.000	0.547

Q17	1.000	0.496
Q21	1.000	0.479
Q27	1.000	0.535
Q28	1.000	0.554
Q18	1.000	0.500
Q19	1.000	0.510
Q22	1.000	0.498
Q23	1.000	0.567
Q24	1.000	0.588
Q29	1.000	0.592
Q25	1.000	0.574
Q33	1.000	0.586
Q34	1.000	0.587
Q31	1.000	0.592
Q20	1.000	0.560
Q30	1.000	0.554
Extraction Method: Principal Component Analysis.		

Source: Calculations Done by Researcher

Table 79 reported the values of communalities for the 32 statements. It was observed that the values of communalities were found to be greater than 0.4, except three statements whose communalities were quite near to 0.4 which is marginally acceptable. This indicates that the set of data was desirable for the analysis.

Principal Component Analysis

The Principal Component Analysis is the most common technique of factor analysis regarded as extraction method (Kinnear &Gray, 2010; Cooper & Schindler, 2008). This method examine the correlation of distinct variables to uncover the association among them and then decrease the variables into a small number of factors under the common dimension by aggregating or summing up them empirically (Tabachnick & Fidell, 2007). The varimax rotation is the most common and simplified technique of factor rotation (Zikmund et al., 2010; Kinnear & Gray, 2010). It was supported because it reduces the correlation across factors and increases within the factors. This as a consequence leads us to obtain clear factors (Nunnally, 1978).

ble 80:

tal Variance Explained

Component	Initial Eigenvalues			Extraction Sums of Squared Loadings			Rotation Sums of Squared Loadings		
	Total	% of Variance	Cumulative %	Total	% of Variance	Cumulative %	Total	% of Variance	Cumulative %
1	5.248	16.401	16.401	5.248	16.401	16.401	5.181	16.192	16.192
2	3.603	11.258	27.659	3.603	11.258	27.659	3.545	11.077	27.269
3	3.259	10.185	37.843	3.259	10.185	37.843	3.286	10.268	37.537
4	2.922	9.132	46.975	2.922	9.132	46.975	2.874	8.981	46.519
5	2.643	8.261	55.236	2.643	8.261	55.236	2.790	8.717	55.236

traction Method: Principal Component Analysis

urce: Calculations Done by Researcher

Table 80 exhibited a principal component analysis that was carried on over 32 statements along with varimax rotation (orthogonal rotation). An initial analysis was conducted to get Eigenvalues for each component in the set of data. The statements were suppressed which found to be less than 0.4 factor loadings (Hair et al., 2005). As a result of this three statements were dropped from the analysis due to low factor loading (< 0.4). In order to measure the suitability of the data for conducting factor analysis, the communalities generalised from the exploratory factor analysis were reviewed. It was observed that five factors had eigenvalues over Kaiser's criterion 1 and unitedly explained 55.236 percent of total variance. Therefore, results in the table 81 had shown five factors which were extracted with *seven* statements in one factor followed by *nine* statements in another factor, *five* statements each in two factors and *six* statements in one factor by undertaking exploratory factor analysis in the present study.

Table 81

Rotated Component Matrix[a]

	Component				
	1	2	3	4	5
Nature of the business of Firm, i.e., how much business is dependent upon the export and import	0.736				
Clear Forex Risk Hedging guidelines issued by the firm, viz. use of specific hedging instrument, duration of hedging strategy and time horizon of forex hedging strategy etc	0.756				

Forex Risk Exposure of the Business in proportion to total Turnover,	0.780				
Past Experience of the firm in hedging Forex Risk	0.750				
Balance sheet and cash flow position of the firm	0.678				
Political conditions of the foreign country with whom trade has happened		0.703			
Economic condition of the foreign country with whom trade has happened, i.e., GDP, Inflation Rate, Money Supply, Capital Market Conditions, Balance of Trade Position etc.		0.686			
Interest Rate Fluctuations in the International Market		0.731			
Overall sentiments regarding Forex Market		0.742			
Forex Control Mechanism in the foreign country		0.693			
Fluctuations in Crude oil Prices as it affect the volatility in prices of all major currencies		0.706			
Speculation (Forex Market, Real Estate, Securities and Uncovered Interest Arbitrage)		0.693			
Political conditions of Domestic country			0.779		
Interest Rate Fluctuations in the Domestic Market			0.762		
Economic condition of the domestic country, i.e., GDP, Inflation Rate, Money Supply, Capital Market Conditions, Balance of Trade Position etc.			0.749		
Development of Banking system			0.733		
Discovery of New Resources			0.737		
Government regulations regarding Forex Market				0.751	
Intervention of Central Bank in Forex Market				0.766	
Volatility in the value of Domestic Currency				0.767	
Volatility in Foreign Currency in which payment has to be made or any other currency used for international settlement				0.749	
Future Expectations regarding movement in Foreign exchange rate				0.761	
Demand and Supply Conditions of domestic Currency				0.763	
Demand and Supply Conditions of Foreign Currency				0.765	
Convertibility of Indian rupee				0.743	
Fluctuations in US Dollar Prices				0.740	
Availability of Forex hedging instruments at Exchange and OTC market					0.741
Ease of using various forex risk hedging instruments like options, futures, synthetic derivatives etc.					0.702

Popularity of the forex risk hedging instrument				0.724
Experience of Forex Risk Manager in using Forex Risk Hedging Instruments				0.731
Perception of Forex Risk Manager regarding various hedging instruments				0.755
Option of Customization of Various Forex Risk Hedging Instruments				0.739

Extraction Method: Principal Component Analysis.
Rotation Method: Varimax with Kaiser Normalization.
a. Rotation converged in 6 iterations.
Source: Calculations Done by Researcher

Table 81 depicted the rotated component matrix that suggested factor one is the linear combination of variable number 3, 2, 4, 5 and 1 with the value of 5.248 eigenvalue. Similarly, factor two comprises of variable number 30, 20, 8, 9, 13, 25 and 11 with the value of 3.603 eigenvalue. Factor three consists of five statements numbered as 21, 17, 12, 27 and 28 with the value of 3.259 eigenvalue. Followed by factor four and five comprised of nine statements 23, 24, 22, 19, 32, 18, 31, 29&26 and six statements 7, 34, 33, 15, 14 &16 with the value of 2.922and 2.643eigen values, respectively.

Table 82

Showing Reliability Results of Exploratory Factor Analysis

Construct	Statements	Cronbach Alpha
FACTOR ONE **(Firm Specific Indicators)**	1. Nature of the business of Firm, i.e., how much business is dependent upon the export and import. 2. Clear Forex Risk Hedging guidelines issued by the firm, viz. use of specific hedging instrument, duration of hedging strategy and time horizon of forex hedging strategy etc 3. Forex Risk Exposure of the Business in proportion to total Turnover, 4. Past Experience of the firm in hedging Forex Risk	**0.796**

	5. Balance sheet and cash flow position of the firm	
FACTORTWO **(Foreign/Global Economy's Macro Indicators)**	1. Political conditions of the foreign country with whom trade has happened 2. Economic condition of the foreign country with whom trade has happened, i.e., GDP, Inflation Rate, Money Supply, Capital Market Conditions, Balance of Trade Position etc. 3. Interest Rate Fluctuations in the International Market 4. Overall sentiments regarding Forex Market 5. Forex Control Mechanism in the foreign country 6. Fluctuations in Crude oil Prices as it affect the volatility in prices of all major currencies 7. Speculation (Forex Market, Real Estate, Securities and Uncovered Interest Arbitrage)	**0.834**
FACTOR THREE **(Domestic Economy's Macro Indicators)**	1. Political conditions of Domestic country 2. Interest Rate Fluctuations in the Domestic Market 3. Economic condition of the domestic country, i.e., GDP, Inflation Rate, Money Supply, Capital Market Conditions, Balance of Trade Position etc. 4. Development of Banking system 5. Discovery of New Resources	**0.810**
FACTOR FOUR **(Forex Market Scenario)**	1. Government regulations regarding Forex Market 2. Intervention of Central Bank in Forex Market 3. Volatility in the value of Domestic Currency 4. Volatility in Foreign Currency in which payment has to be made or any other currency used for international settlement 5. Future Expectations regarding movement in	

	Foreign exchange rate 6. Demand and Supply Conditions of domestic Currency 7. Demand and Supply Conditions of Foreign Currency 8. Convertibility of Indian rupee 9. Fluctuations in US Dollar Prices	**0.907**
FACTOR FIVE **(Forex Risk Hedging Instruments)**	1. Availability of Forex hedging instruments at Exchange and OTC market 2. Ease of using various forex risk hedging instruments like options, futures, synthetic derivatives etc. and their **3.** Popularity of the forex risk hedging instrument 4. Experience of Forex Risk Manager in using Forex Risk Hedging Instruments 5. Perception of Forex Risk Manager regarding various hedging instruments 6. Option of Customization of Various Forex Risk Hedging Instruments	**0.829**

Source: Calculations Done by Researcher

Table 82 showed the results of the exploratory factor analysis depicted a good construct reliability as all the five construct's alpha value is more than 0.70 (Nunnaly, 1978).

EFA results of question 29 (Objective third)

Table 83

KMO and Bartlett's Test

Kaiser-Meyer-Olkin Measure of Sampling Adequacy.		0.879
Bartlett's Test of Sphericity	**Approx. Chi-Square**	3740.938
	Df	105
	Sig.	.000

Notes: The value of KMO regarded as adequate if it is greater than 0.6 (Kaiser & rice, 1947).
The factor analysis can be exercised if the p-value found to beless than 0.05.
Source: Calculations Done by Researcher

Table 83 reported the statistics of Kaiser-Meyer-Olkin (KMO) as 0.879, which falls under the acceptable range, indicates that factor analysis could be employed for the available set of data. In addition, the Bartlett's Test of Sphericity examined the significance of the correlation matrix of the variables. It was suggested that correlation among statements were adequately large for principal component analysis because the correlation matrix found to be significant that is less than 0.05. Hence, the results indicated that the data is befitted for the factor analysis.

Table 84

Communalities

	Initial	Extraction
Q1	1.000	0.728
Q2	1.000	0.717
Q3	1.000	0.697
Q4	1.000	0.730
Q5	1.000	0.753
Q6	1.000	0.673
Q7	1.000	0.680
Q8	1.000	0.636
Q9	1.000	0.759
Q10	1.000	0.800
Q11	1.000	0.726
Q12	1.000	0.780
Q13	1.000	0.727
Q14	1.000	0.762
Q15	1.000	0.692

Extraction Method: Principal Component Analysis.
Source: Calculations Done by Researcher

Table 84 reported the values of communalities for the 15 statements. It was observed that the values of communalities were found to be greater than 0.5. This indicates that the set of data was desirable for the analysis.

Table 85

Total Variance Explained

Component	Initial Eigenvalues			Extraction Sums of Squared Loadings			Rotation Sums of Squared Loadings		
	Total	% of Variance	Cumulative %	Total	% of Variance	Cumulative %	Total	% of Variance	Cumulative %
1	4.619	30.791	30.791	4.619	30.791	30.791	4.275	28.502	28.502
2	3.401	22.673	53.464	3.401	22.673	53.464	3.622	24.146	52.648
3	2.839	18.928	72.393	2.839	18.928	72.393	2.962	19.745	72.393

Source: Calculations Done by Researcher

Table 85 exhibited a principal component analysis that was carried on over 15 statements along with varimax rotation (orthogonal rotation). An initial analysis was conducted to get eigenvalues for each component in the set of data. The statements were suppressed which found to be less than 0.4 factor loadings (Hair et al., 2005). As a result of this no statement was dropped from the analysis as all the factor loadings of all the statements were more than 0.4. In order to measure the suitability of the data for conducting factor analysis, the communalities generalized from the exploratory factor analysis were reviewed.

It was observed that three factors had eigenvalues over Kaiser's criterion 1 and unitedly explained 72.393 percent of total variance. Therefore, results in the table 86 had shown three factors which were extracted with six statements in one factor followed by five statements in another factor and four statements in the last factor by undertaking exploratory factor analysis in the present study.

Table 86

Rotated Component Matrix[a]

	Component		
	1	2	3
The management of business should play more intense role in formation of a forex risk management policy	0.818		
The management shall motivate for risk management practices	0.815		

The top management or decision maker should gain more expertise in forex risk management	0.795		
Forex risk management policy must be made mandatory for all Small and Medium Enterprises	0.867		
The business associations should provide necessary assistance and support to their members in managing forex risk	0.894		
More trained people are required	0.850		
More Hedging instruments need to be introduced		0.850	
The cost of hedging devices should be less		0.841	
Hedging instruments shall be introduced with some tax benefit schemes		0.830	
More innovative, customized and low cost hedging instruments should be introduced by regulators		0.854	
Clear guidelines should be forwarded by RBI regarding usage of derivative products		0.867	
More awareness shall be done by RBI			0.882
More certification and educational programs			0.850
The bank should aware business whenever it approaches the bank for export-import financing			0.870
The RBI or Government shall make it mandatory to hedge the forex risk			0.827

Extraction Method: Principal Component Analysis.
Rotation Method: Varimax with Kaiser Normalization.
a. Rotation converged in 5 iterations.
Source: Calculations Done by Researcher

Table 86 depicted the rotated component matrix that suggested factor one is the linear combination of variable number 3, 5, 2, 4, 1 and 6 with the value of 4.619 eigenvalue. Similarly, factor second comprises of variable number 10, 8, 7, 9, 11 and 13 with the value of 3.401 eigenvalue. Factor third consists of five statements numbered as 13, 15, 14 and 12 with the value of 2.839 eigenvalue.

Table 87

Showing Reliability Results of Exploratory Factor Analysis

Construct	Statements	Cronbach Alpha
FACTOR ONE **(Internal Management's Approach for Forex Risk Hedging Management)**	1. The management of business should play more intense role in formation of a forex risk management policy 2. The management shall motivate for risk management practices 3. The top management or decision maker should gain more expertise in forex risk management 4. Forex risk management policy must be made mandatory for all Small and Medium Enterprises 5. The business associations should provide necessary assistance and support to their members in managing forex risk 6. More trained people are required	**0.918**
FACTORTWO **(Awareness Regarding Forex Risk Hedging Instruments and Forex Market Regulations)**	1. More Hedging instruments need to be introduced 2. The cost of hedging devices should be less 3. Hedging instruments shall be introduced with some tax benefit schemes 4. More innovative, customized and low cost hedging instruments should be introduced by regulators 5. Clear guidelines should be forwarded by RBI regarding usage of derivative products	**0.904**
FACTOR THREE **(Regulators' initiatives to increase Hedging Instruments' Literacy)**	1. More awareness shall be done by RBI 2. More certification and educational programs 3. The bank should aware business whenever it approaches the bank for export-import financing 4. The RBI or Government shall make it mandatory to hedge the forex risk	**0.882**

Source: Calculations Done by Researcher

Table 87 showed the results of the exploratory factor analysis depicted a good construct reliability as all the three construct's alpha value is more than 0.70 (Nunnaly, 1978).

Results of Analytic Hierarchy Process (AHP)

The five constructs or criterion recognized by the outcomes of Exploratory Factor Analysis (EFA) were used to develop paired comparison questionnaire to be sent to Experts. This effectual tool for decision makers which was introduced by Saaty (1980) has extensivelybeen used in every decision area related to finance. These decision areas comprise risk management, portfolio construction, forecasting, leasing, mergers and acquisition, supply chain risk management and project risk management etc. (Zopounidis & Doumpos, 2002, Stuer & Na, 2003, and Verbanao & Venturini, 2011). The financial decision makers are also involved in making comparisons among alternative criteria for systematic decision making process. Acharyya (2009) discussed the use of AHP in implementing the risk management policy. AHP is asignificant tool in the category of multi criteria decision making (MCDM).

Aremarkable study was contributed by Sipahi and Timor (2010) in which the researchers discusssed bibliographic presentation of research related to Analytic Hierarchy Process(AHP) and Analytic Network Process(ANP) in detail during the time span of 2005-2009. The authors considered 235 papers referring the use of AHP and ANP. Chalupkova and Franek (2014) applied AHP criterion for taking decisions related to leasing and loans. The main objective of their study was to develop optimal form of acquisition of asset in accordance with the selection criteria of the clients. The findings of the study indicated that the financial leasing having a high down payment was identified as best among various alternatives. Balubaid and Alamoudi (2015) used AHP model for selection of contractors.

The author made the comparisons by providing ranking on the basis of the aggregate score of each candidate by using different criterion specified by researcher. This study focused on the construction sector only and applied multi-criteria AHP technique. The AHP

tool is equally preferred by decision makers in other fileds like engineering, industry

education, political, social, sports, manufacturing, and management too (Vaidya and Kumar,

2006). The authros

FOREX RISK EXPOSURE AWARENESS, MANAGEMENT AND DETERMINANTS

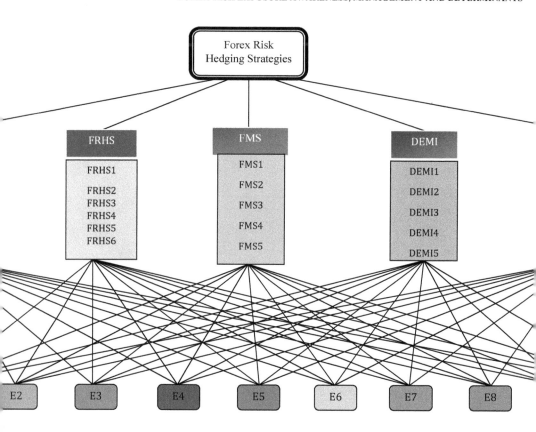

considered 150 papers in which AHP was used in all these desciplines. The authors
mentioned six types of decisions in an AHP approach. These are; selection of one alternative
among many, evaluation of these alternatives, doing cost-benefit analysis, allocating
resources as per cost-benefit analysis, and then prioritising and ranking. The current study
has used AHP to know the most preferred criterion while determining the hedging strategy.
The results of EFA has provided five important criteria which are considered while making a
forex risk hedging strategy.

Table 88

Showing the scale of measurement in pair-wise comparison

FSI	9	8	7	6	5	4	3	2	1	2	3	4	5	6	7	8	9	FRHS
FSI	9	8	7	6	5	4	3	2	1	2	3	4	5	6	7	8	9	FMS
FSI	9	8	7	6	5	4	3	2	1	2	3	4	5	6	7	8	9	DEMI
FSI	9	8	7	6	5	4	3	2	1	2	3	4	5	6	7	8	9	FGEMI
FRHS	9	8	7	6	5	4	3	2	1	2	3	4	5	6	7	8	9	FMS
FRHS	9	8	7	6	5	4	3	2	1	2	3	4	5	6	7	8	9	DEMI
FRHS	9	8	7	6	5	4	3	2	1	2	3	4	5	6	7	8	9	FGEMI
FMS	9	8	7	6	5	4	3	2	1	2	3	4	5	6	7	8	9	DEMI
FMS	9	8	7	6	5	4	3	2	1	2	3	4	5	6	7	8	9	FGEMI
DEMI	9	8	7	6	5	4	3	2	1	2	3	4	5	6	7	8	9	FGEMI

Note: Encircle to point out which of the two constructs is more important and explain how much more
important it is, with regards to the objective; 1 – equal importance, 3 –moderate, 5 – strong, 7 – very strong, 9 –
extreme importance; 2, 4, 6, 8 – for compromise between the above values

Source: Calculations Done by Researcher

Decision Making under AHP

The Analytic Hierarchy Process of AHP is used to know the most preferred criterion
for making the forex risk hedging strategy. For this, ten experts who are highly experienced
and involved in national level policy and guidelines formulation of hedging instruments and
strategies for the clients of all segments. The following five decision criteria were considered
by these experts from the hierarchy structure.

1. Firm Specific Indicators (FSI),

2. Foreign Risk Hedging Instruments (FRHS),

3. Foreign Market Scenario (FMS),

4. Domestic Market Macro Indicators(DMIC),

5. Foreign/Global Economy's Macro Indicators (FGEMI).

The survey was done on the basis of these five decision criterion for which paired comparision questionnaire was made and experts were interviewed through personal visits and on telephone both. The experts' priorities for various criteria were used and then reletive importance of each criteria is ascertained. While selecting the experts for the survey, it was ensured that the quality of survey is attained to a desired level while considering the limitations of budget and time-line.

Under each of these five decision criteria, the various alternatives or variables have been also coded. The following Table gives the description of criteria and alternatives of the AHP model.

Table 89

Codes of Crietria and sub-criteria for Paired Comparison Questionnaire

Codes↓	Expert Criteria
	Firm Specific Indicators (FSI)
FSI1	Nature of the business of Firm, i.e., how much business is dependent upon the export and import
FSI2	Clear Forex Risk Hedging guidelines issued by the firm, viz. use of specific hedging instrument, duration of hedging strategy and time horizon of forex hedging strategy etc
FSI3	Forex Risk Exposure of the Business in proportion to total Turnover,
FSI4	Past Experience of the firm in hedging Forex Risk
FSI5	Balance sheet and cash flow position of the firm
	Forex Risk Hedging Instruments (FRHS)

FRHS1	Availability of Forex hedging instruments at Exchange and OTC market
FRHS2	Ease of using various forex risk hedging instruments like options, futures, synthetic derivatives etc. and their
FRHS3	Popularity of the forex risk hedging instrument
FRHS4	Experience of Forex Risk Manager in using Forex Risk Hedging Instruments
FRHS5	Perception of Forex Risk Manager regarding various hedging instruments
FRHS6	Option of Customization of Various Forex Risk Hedging Instruments
	Forex Market Scenario (FMS)
FMS1	Government regulations regarding Forex Market
FMS2	Intervention of Central Bank in Forex Market
FMS3	Volatility in the value of Domestic Currency
FMS4	Volatility in Foreign Currency in which payment has to be made or any other currency used for international settlement
FMS5	Future Expectations regarding movement in Foreign exchange rate
FMS6	Demand and Supply Conditions of domestic Currency
FMS7	Demand and Supply Conditions of Foreign Currency
FMS8	Convertibility of Indian rupee
FMS9	Fluctuations in US Dollar Prices
	Domestic Economy's Macro Indicators (DEMI)
DEMI1	Political conditions of Domestic country
DEMI2	Interest Rate Fluctuations in the Domestic Market
DEMI3	Economic condition of the domestic country, i.e., GDP, Inflation Rate, Money Supply, Capital Market Conditions, Balance of Trade Position etc.
DEMI4	Development of Banking system
DEMI5	Discovery of New Resources
	Foreign/Global Economy's Macro Indicators (FGEMI)
FGEMI1	Political conditions of the foreign country with whom trade has happened
FGEMI2	Economic condition of the foreign country with whom trade has happened, i.e., GDP, Inflation Rate, Money Supply, Capital Market Conditions, Balance of Trade Position etc.
FGEMI3	Interest Rate Fluctuations in the International Market

FGEMI4	Overall sentiments regarding Forex Market
FGEMI5	Forex Control Mechanism in the foreign country
FGEMI6	Fluctuations in Crude oil Prices as it affect the volatility in prices of all major currencies
FGEMI7	Speculation (Forex Market, Real Estate, Securities and Uncovered Interest Arbitrage)

Source: Calculations Done by Researcher

(A) Results from Pair-wise Comparison Matrices

The following section discusses the results obtained through pair-wise comparison matrices for all constructs and sub-contructs. The pair-wise comparison metrices are based on geometric mean of each cell, i.e., response of each individual participated in the survey.

Table 90

Pair Wise Comparison Matrix of FSI Dimensions

	FSI1	FSI2	FSI3	FSI4	FSI5
FSI1	1.000	2.012	1.212	2.268	0.985
FSI2	0.497	1.000	0.488	0.736	0.579
FSI3	0.825	2.049	1.000	0.574	0.663
FSI4	0.441	1.358	1.741	1.000	0.637
FSI5	1.016	1.726	1.509	1.570	1.000
Sum	3.778	8.145	5.951	6.149	3.864

Source: Calculations Done by Researcher

Table 91

Pair Wise Comparison Matrix of FRHS Dimensions

	FRHS1	FRHS2	FRHS3	FRHS4	FRHS5	FRHS6
FRHS1	1.000	1.628	1.205	2.283	1.149	1.511
FRHS2	0.614	1.000	0.488	0.736	0.383	2.453
FRHS3	0.830	2.049	1.000	0.574	0.690	2.000
FRHS4	0.438	1.358	1.741	1.000	0.647	1.257
FRHS5	0.871	2.612	1.450	1.546	1.000	3.110
FRHS6	0.662	0.408	0.500	0.796	0.322	1.000
Sum	4.415	9.054	6.384	6.935	4.190	11.331

Source: Calculations Done by Researcher

Table 92

Pair Wise Comparison Matrix of FMS Dimensions

	FMS1	FMS2	FMS3	FMS4	FMS5	FMS6	FMS7	FMS8	FMS9
FMS1	1.000	1.628	1.205	2.283	1.149	0.812	2.130	4.536	1.511
FMS2	0.614	1.000	0.488	0.736	0.383	0.949	0.445	2.389	2.453
FMS3	0.830	2.049	1.000	0.574	0.690	2.381	3.482	4.260	2.000
FMS4	0.438	1.358	1.741	1.000	0.647	1.835	2.283	4.090	1.257
FMS5	0.871	2.612	1.450	1.546	1.000	2.272	3.732	4.586	3.110
FMS6	1.231	1.054	0.420	0.545	0.440	1.000	2.766	2.434	1.427
FMS7	0.470	2.246	0.287	0.438	0.268	0.361	1.000	2.429	0.848
FMS8	0.220	0.419	0.235	0.244	0.218	0.411	0.412	1.000	0.439
FMS9	0.662	0.408	0.500	0.796	0.322	0.701	1.180	2.279	1.000
Sum	6.336	12.772	7.326	8.163	5.116	10.722	17.43	28.00	14.045

Source: Calculations Done by Researcher

Table 93

Pair Wise Comparison Matrix of DEMI Dimensions

	DEMI1	DEMI2	DEMI3	DEMI4	DEMI5
DEMI1	1.0000	2.2072	1.3493	0.9391	1.0000
DEMI2	0.4531	1.0000	0.4881	0.9779	0.5020
DEMI3	0.7411	2.0486	1.0000	0.6598	0.9752
DEMI4	1.0649	1.0226	1.5157	1.0000	1.1262
DEMI5	1.0000	1.9921	1.0254	0.8880	1.0000
Sum	4.2591	8.2705	5.3786	4.4647	4.6033

Source: Calculations Done by Researcher

Table 94

Pair Wise Comparison Matrix of FGEMI Dimensions

	FGEMI1	FGEMI2	FGEMI3	FGEMI4	FGEMI5	FGEMI6	FGEMI7
FGEMI1	1.000	1.496	1.129	1.205	0.944	0.859	1.942
FGEMI2	0.669	1.000	0.488	0.736	0.383	0.949	0.580
FGEMI3	0.885	2.049	1.000	0.574	1.016	1.206	3.383
FGEMI4	0.830	1.358	1.741	1.000	0.647	1.182	1.987
FGEMI5	1.059	2.612	0.985	1.546	1.000	2.272	3.626
FGEMI6	1.164	1.054	0.829	0.846	0.440	1.000	2.107
FGEMI7	0.515	1.725	0.296	0.503	0.276	0.475	1.000
Sum	6.123	11.29	6.468	6.410	4.705	7.943	14.626

Source: Calculations Done by Researcher

(B) Normalized Weight Matrix, Priority Vector (PV) and Consistency Ratio (CR)

After completing all the pair-wise comparisons, the next task is to determine the consistency by using the Eigen value. To accomplish this, normalize the column of numbers by dividing each entry by the sum of all entries. Then sum each row of the normalized values and take the average to get the priority vector (PV).One of the important tasks of AHP is to calculate the consistency level of the estimated vector. Consistency ratio (CR) is used to measure the consistency in the pair-wise comparison. As mentioned in Table,1.....5, the consistency ratio for all decision criteria was found the standard ratio mentioned by Saaty (1994), i.e., 0.1. From the following tables, the Consistency Ratio (CR) for FSI, FRHS, FMS, DEMI, and FGEMI is 0.0322, 0.0454, 0.0472 , 0.0254 and 0.0337 respectively which is less than the standard of 10%, i.e., 0.1. The acceptance of these results indicates that there is consistency in the response of experts in the paired comparisons of decision criteria. The Consistency Index for FSI, FRHS, FMS, DEMI, and FGEMI is 0.0361, 0.0563, 0.0684, 0.0285 and 0.0445 respectively. And λmax = 5.144, 6.2813, 9.547, 5.114, and 7.267 respectively. The random consistency index for all decision criteria (FSI, FRHS, FMS, DEMI, and FGEMI) is as follows: RCI= 1.1200 for n=5, RCI= 1.2400 for n=6, RCI= 1.450, RCI=1.120 for n=5, RCI= 1.320 for n=7.

Table 95

Normalized Weight Matrix of FSI

	FSI1	FSI2	FSI3	FSI4	FSI5	Priority Vector (PV)
FSI1	0.2647	0.2471	0.2037	0.3688	0.2549	26.78%
FSI2	0.1315	0.1228	0.0820	0.1198	0.1500	12.12%
FSI3	0.2183	0.2515	0.1680	0.0934	0.1715	18.06%
FSI4	0.1167	0.1667	0.2926	0.1626	0.1648	18.07%
FSI5	0.2688	0.2119	0.2536	0.2553	0.2588	24.97%

CR= 0.0322; CI=0.0361; λmax = 5.144 ; RCI= 1.1200 for n=5

Source: Calculations Done by Researcher

Table 96

Normalized Weight Matrix of FRHS

	FRHS1	FRHS2	FRHS3	FRHS4	FRHS5	FRHS6	Priority Vector (PV)
FRHS1	0.2265	0.1798	0.1887	0.3291	0.2742	0.1333	22.19%
FRHS2	0.1391	0.1105	0.0765	0.1062	0.0914	0.2165	12.34%
FRHS3	0.1880	0.2263	0.1566	0.0828	0.1646	0.1765	16.58%
FRHS4	0.0992	0.1500	0.2727	0.1442	0.1544	0.1109	15.52%
FRHS5	0.1972	0.2885	0.2272	0.2229	0.2387	0.2745	24.15%
FRHS6	0.1499	0.0450	0.0783	0.1147	0.0767	0.0883	9.22%
CR=0.0454; CI=0.0563; λmax = 6.281; RCI= 1.2400 for n=6							

Source: Calculations Done by Researcher

Table 97

Normalized Weight Matrix of FMS

	FMS1	FMS2	FMS3	FMS4	FMS5	FMS6	FMS7	FMS8	FMS9	Priority Vector (PV)
FMS1	0.1578	0.1275	0.1644	0.2796	0.2245	0.0758	0.1222	0.1620	0.1076	15.79%
FMS2	0.0970	0.0783	0.0666	0.0902	0.0748	0.0885	0.0255	0.0853	0.1747	8.68%
FMS3	0.1310	0.1604	0.1365	0.0704	0.1348	0.2221	0.1998	0.1521	0.1424	14.99%
FMS4	0.0691	0.1063	0.2377	0.1225	0.1264	0.1711	0.1310	0.1461	0.0895	13.33%
FMS5	0.1374	0.2045	0.1980	0.1894	0.1955	0.2119	0.2141	0.1638	0.2214	19.29%
FMS6	0.1943	0.0825	0.0573	0.0668	0.0860	0.0933	0.1587	0.0869	0.1016	10.30%
FMS7	0.0741	0.1759	0.0392	0.0537	0.0524	0.0337	0.0574	0.0867	0.0604	7.04%
FMS8	0.0348	0.0328	0.0320	0.0300	0.0426	0.0383	0.0236	0.0357	0.0312	3.35%
FMS9	0.1045	0.0319	0.0683	0.0975	0.0629	0.0654	0.0677	0.0814	0.0712	7.23%
CR=0.0472; CI=0.0684; λmax = 9.547; RCI= 1.450 for n=9										

Source: Calculations Done by Researcher

Table 98

Normalized Weight Matrix of DEMI

	DEMI1	DEMI2	DEMI3	DEMI4	DEMI5	Priority Vector (PV)
DEMI1	0.2348	0.2669	0.2509	0.2103	0.2172	23.60%
DEMI2	0.1064	0.1209	0.0908	0.2190	0.1090	12.92%
DEMI3	0.1740	0.2477	0.1859	0.1478	0.2118	19.35%
DEMI4	0.2500	0.1236	0.2818	0.2240	0.2446	22.48%
DEMI5	0.2348	0.2409	0.1907	0.1989	0.2172	21.65%
CR=0.0254; CI=0.0285; λmax =5.114 ; RCI=1.120 for n=5						

Source: Calculations Done by Researcher

Table 99

Normalized Weight Matrix of FGEMI

	FGEMI 1	FGEMI 2	FGEMI 3	FGEMI 4	FGEMI 5	FGEMI 6	FGEMI 7	Priority Vector (PV)
FGEMI1	0.1633	0.1324	0.1746	0.1879	0.2006	0.1082	0.1328	15.71%
FGEMI2	0.1092	0.0886	0.0755	0.1149	0.0814	0.1195	0.0396	8.98%
FGEMI3	0.1446	0.1814	0.1546	0.0896	0.2158	0.1518	0.2313	16.70%
FGEMI4	0.1356	0.1203	0.2692	0.1560	0.1375	0.1488	0.1359	15.76%
FGEMI5	0.1730	0.2313	0.1522	0.2412	0.2125	0.2860	0.2479	22.06%
FGEMI6	0.1901	0.0933	0.1282	0.1320	0.0935	0.1259	0.1441	12.96%
FGEMI7	0.0841	0.1528	0.0457	0.0785	0.0586	0.0597	0.0684	7.83%
CR=0.0337; CI=0.0445; λmax = 7.267 ; RCI= 1.320 for n=7								

Source: Calculations Done by Researcher

(iii) Synthesis-finding solution to the problem

After calculating the normalized weight, consistency ratio the next step is to synthesize the solution for prioritization of factors. The local priority weights of factors, sub-factors are combined together with respect to all successive hierarchical levels to obtain the global composite priority weight of all the sub-factors. Table 100 given below has given local weights and global weights of five decision criteria and sub-criteria. As depicted in the Table 100, the domestic economy's macro indicators (DEMI) scored the highest global weight, i.e., 22.54% followed by firm specific indicators (22.13%) and foreign and global economy's macro indicators (21.74%). It indicates that for a decision maker of hedging strategies, the domestic economy's macro indicators are considered as foremost important decision criteria. Among the sub-criteria for firm specific indicators (FSI), nature of business (5.93%) and balance sheet and cash flow position (5.53%) are found with highest global weights , in case of decision criterion on forex risk hedging instruments (FRHS), the perception of forex risk manager regarding various hedging instruments is found most important sub-criterion as its global weight is highest (3.14%) among all other sub-criteria, i.e., FRHSI (2.89%), FRHS2(1.61%), FRHS3 (2.15%), FRHS4 (2.02%), FRHS6 (1.2%). The availability of forex hedging instruments at exchange and OTC market and popularity of the forex risk hedging instrument are other two important sub-criterions under forex risk hedging instruments decision criterion. Next decision criterion is fore market scenario (FMS). Under this decision criterion, the global weight for future expectations regarding movement in foreign exchange rate(FMS5) is highest, i.e., 3.97% followed by followed by government regulations regarding forex market(FMS1 with 3.25% as global weight) and volatility in the value of domestic currency (FMS# with 3.08% as global weight) as next two important sub-criterion. Further, political condition of domestic country (DEMI1) and development of banking system (DEMI4) scored highest weight, i.e., 5.32% and 5.07% respectively as sub-criterion of domestic economy's macro indicators (DEMI). The most important determinant of foreign/global economy's macro indicators (FGEMI) is forex control mechanism in the foreign country with highest global weight of 4.80% followed by interest rate fluctuations in the international market (FGEMI with global weight of 3.63%). The priority order according to local weights is also similar to the results of global weights indicating the importance of various sub-criteria in determining the major criterion respectively.

Table 100

Local and Global Weight for the Factors and sub Factors

Codes for Factors/Sub-factors	Factors/Sub-factors	Local Weights	Global Weights
	Firm Specific Indicators (FSI)	**22.1295%**	**22.1295%**
FSI1	Nature of the business of Firm, i.e., how much business is dependent upon the export and import	**26.78%**	**5.93%**
FSI2	Clear Forex Risk Hedging guidelines issued by the firm, viz. use of specific hedging instrument, duration of hedging strategy and time horizon of forex hedging strategy etc	**12.12%**	**2.68%**
FSI3	Forex Risk Exposure of the Business in proportion to total Turnover,	**18.06%**	**4.00%**
FSI4	Past Experience of the firm in hedging Forex Risk	**18.07%**	**4.00%**
FSI5	Balance sheet and cash flow position of the firm	**24.97%**	**5.53%**
	Forex Risk Hedging Instruments (FRHS)	**13.0232%**	**13.0232%**
FRHS1	Availability of Forex hedging instruments at Exchange and OTC market	**22.19%**	**2.89%**
FRHS2	Ease of using various forex risk hedging instruments like options, futures, synthetic derivatives etc. and their	**12.34%**	**1.61%**
FRHS3	Popularity of the forex risk hedging instrument	**16.58%**	**2.16%**
FRHS4	Experience of Forex Risk Manager in using Forex Risk Hedging Instruments	**15.52%**	**2.02%**
FRHS5	Perception of Forex Risk Manager regarding	**24.15%**	**3.14%**

	various hedging instruments		
FRHS6	Option of Customization of Various Forex Risk Hedging Instruments	9.22%	1.20%
	Forex Market Scenario (FMS)	**20.5676%**	**20.5676%**
FMS1	Government regulations regarding Forex Market	15.79%	3.25%
FMS2	Intervention of Central Bank in Forex Market	8.68%	1.78%
FMS3	Volatility in the value of Domestic Currency	14.99%	3.08%
FMS4	Volatility in Foreign Currency in which payment has to be made or any other currency used for international settlement	13.33%	2.74%
FMS5	Future Expectations regarding movement in Foreign exchange rate	19.29%	3.97%
FMS6	Demand and Supply Conditions of domestic Currency	10.30%	2.12%
FMS7	Demand and Supply Conditions of Foreign Currency	7.04%	1.45%
FMS8	Convertibility of Indian rupee	3.35%	0.69%
FMS9	Fluctuations in US Dollar Prices	7.23%	1.49%
	Domestic Economy's Macro Indicators (DEMI)	**22.5416%**	**22.5416%**
DEMI1	Political conditions of Domestic country	23.60%	5.32%
DEMI2	Interest Rate Fluctuations in the Domestic Market	21.65%	4.88%
DEMI3	Economic condition of the domestic country, i.e., GDP, Inflation Rate, Money Supply, Capital Market Conditions, Balance of Trade Position etc.	19.35%	4.36%
DEMI4	Development of Banking system	22.48%	5.07%
DEMI5	Discovery of New Resources	12.92%	2.91%
	Foreign/Global Economy's Macro Indicators	**21.7381%**	**21.7381%**

	(FGEMI)		
FGEMI1	Political conditions of the foreign country with whom trade has happened	15.71%	3.42%
FGEMI2	Economic condition of the foreign country with whom trade has happened, i.e., GDP, Inflation Rate, Money Supply, Capital Market Conditions, Balance of Trade Position etc.	8.98%	1.95%
FGEMI3	Interest Rate Fluctuations in the International Market	16.70%	3.63%
FGEMI4	Overall sentiments regarding Forex Market	15.76%	3.43%
FGEMI5	Forex Control Mechanism in the foreign country	22.06%	4.80%
FGEMI6	Fluctuations in Crude oil Prices as it affect the volatility in prices of all major currencies	12.96%	2.82%
FGEMI7	Speculation (Forex Market, Real Estate, Securities and Uncovered Interest Arbitrage)	7.83%	1.70%

Source: Calculations Done by Researcher

So, above are the overall results obtained after doing thorough analysis of the data obtained through survey. The next chapter has concluded the findings and has also mentioned the implications of the study. The last chapter of the study also explain the theoretical and practical contribution of the whole research.

Chapter 5

Conclusion, Recommendations and Policy Implications

The present chapter draws the conclusion of all previous chapters and discusses the implications of the whole research and its contribution to existing literature and theory. Before giving closing statements, let's have a recapitulate of the objectives of the study so that the whole discussion could be synchronized with these objectives.

As stated earlier too, the following are the objectives of the study for which various research activities were performed during the study period.

1. To study the Forex Risk Exposure of SMEs and Unlisted Non-Financial Firms in India.

2. To study the Forex Risk Exposure Management by SMEs and Unlisted Non-Financial Firms in India.

3. To study the determinants of Forex Risk Hedging Strategies by SMEs and Unlisted Non-Financial Firms in India.

In lieu of above objectives, the following are the major findings of the study.

Objective One

The first objective of the study was to know the awareness level of SMEs and unlisted non-financial firms regarding forex risk exposure measurement. The management of forex risk exposure is possible only when firms are giving due importance to its measurement. Although companies in international operations found to be fully aware regarding foreign exchange risk management based on different sector but overall results depicted that maximum number of companies were partially aware. Section "B" of survey instrument focused on Forex risk exposure of sample units and four questions were asked in order to measure the awareness level regarding forex risk exposure among the respondents. These questions were related to knowing the level of cost, revenues and assets expressed in terms of foreign currency, in which foreign currency they trade more, are these firm measuring their forex risk exposure and what type of forex risk exposure is more in these firms.

❖ It was observed that 30.8 percent firms in the construction sector had less than 10 percent of total cost and 15.4 percent firms had 80 to 90 percent of their total cost in terms of foreign currency. Followed by the manufacturing sector, which reported 7.2 percent, firms having less than 10 percent of their total cost and 5.9 percent firms were incurring 90 to 100 percent of their total cost in terms of foreign currency. Similarly, 12.5 percent firms in service sector were having less than 10 percent of their total cost and 9.4 percent firms were having 90 to 100 percent of their total cost in terms of foreign currency. The firms belonged to Trading sector demonstrated that 15.1 percent firms were having less than 10 percent of their total cost and only 3.8 percent of firms in 90-100 percent cost. In the same manner, 50 percent firms from other sectors reported less than 10 percent of their total cost and 50 percent firms in 80 to 90 percent cost in terms of foreign currency.

❖ Further, it was observed that 30.8 percent firms in the construction sector had reported their revenues in foreign currency in the ranges of 30 to 40 percent and 80-90 percent each. Next, in case of manufacturing sector, which showed 2.3 percent firms having less than 10 percent of their revenues in foreign currency and 15.1 percent firms were having their revenue in foreign currency in the range of 90 to 100 percent. Similarly, 6.2 percent firms in service sector received the revenue less than 10 percent on the other hand, 6.2 percent firms got the revenue between 90 to 100 percent. Trading sector indicated7.5

percent firms came under less than 10 percent revenue however, 11.3 percent firms in 90 to 100 percent revenue. In the similar manner, 50 percent firms from other sectors reported 10 to 20 percent of their revenues in foreign currency and 50 percent firms were ranging in 80 to 90 percent. Hence, it can be determined that firms in manufacturing sector earned more revenue on the contrary, construction and other sector exhibited less revenue in terms of foreign currency.

❖ It was also noticed that in case of firms in Construction sector, 15.4 percent SMEs and unlisted non-financial firms belonged to construction sector were having less than 10 percent of their assets in foreign currency and 30.8 percent firms were rested in 80 to 90 percent category. Further, in case of manufacturing sector, 6.9 percent firms were holding less than 10 percent of their assets and 12.1 percent sampled firms were having 90 to 100 percent of their assets in foreign currency. Likewise, 12.5 percent firms in service sector were holding assets less than 10 percent and 18.8 percent firms were holding 90 to 100 percent of their assets in foreign currency. Trading sector revealed26.4 percent firms comes under less than 10 percent assets however, 3.8 percent firms in 90 to 100 percent assets. Likewise, 50 percent of firms from other sectors reported less than 10 percent of their assets in foreign currency and 50 percent of firms were holding 80 to 90 percent of their assets in foreign currency. In view of this, it can be established that firms in service sector possessed more assets on the other hand, manufacturing sector exhibited less assets in terms of foreign currency.

❖ Next, it was observed that 15.4 percent firms in the construction sector had less than 10 percent debt and 30.8 percent firms were having 80 to 90 percent of their debt in foreign currency. The manufacturing sector has reported 9.5 percent firms having less than 10 percent debt and 6.6 percent SMEs and Unlisted non-financial firms were having debt between 90 to 100 percent of their total debt. Alike, 28.1 percent firms under service sector were having 50-60 percent and 21.9 percent firms were having 40 to 50 percent of their total debt in foreign currency. Next, firms under Trading sector confirmed 26.4 percent were having less than 10 percent debt however and 17 percent of firms were having 30-40 percent their total debt in foreign currency. In the same manner, 50 percent firms from other sector reported less than 10 percent debt and 50 percent firms in 70 to 80 percent debt in terms of foreign currency.

❖ When an analysis based on annual turnover and the percentage of total cost incurred by the SMEs and unlisted non-financial firms in terms of foreign currency was made then it was observed that 31.2 percent of firms with an annual turnover of less than five crore, were having less than 10 percent of their total cost and 9.4 percent firms were having 90 to 100 percent of their total cost in terms of foreign currency. Next, firms having 5 to 10 crore annual turnover, reported 9.4 percent of firms in this category were having less than 10 percent cost. Similarly, firms with the annual turnover between 10 to 15 crore, 7.3 percent of these firms were having less than 10 percent of their total cost in terms of foreign currency. On the other hand, firms having annual turnover between 15 to 20 crore, 17.2 percent of such SMEs and unlisted non-financial firms showed 90 to 100 percent of their total cost in terms of foreign currency. Further, firms with the annual turnover between 20 to 25 crore reported that 62.5 percent of these firms were having 50 to 60 percent of their total cost in foreign currency. Further, 35.5 percent firms with the annual turnover between 25 to 30crore showed 70 to 80 percent cost. It was found that SMEs and unlisted non-financial firms with annual turnover between 30 to 35 crore, 35 to 40 crore, 40 to 45 crore and 45 to 50 crore were having more than 20 percent of their total cost in terms of foreign currencyunder different classification. In addition to this 11.1 percent firms with the annual turnover of 50 to 100 crore reported less than 10 percent of their total cost and 90 to 100 percent of their cost in foreign currency. Whereas, 15.2 percent firms with the annual turnover above 100 crore depicted less than 10 percent of their total cost and 5.7 percent firms showed 90 to 100 percent of their total cost in terms of foreign currency. So, it can be determined that firms with annual turnover between 45 to 50 crore were incurring more cost and firms with the less than 5 crore annual turnover were incurring less cost in terms of foreign currency.

❖ Similarly, if an analysis is made on the basis of annual turnover of the SMEs and unlisted non-financial firms and the percentage of their total revenue received in terms of foreign currency then the results indicated that 12.5 percent firms with the annual turnover less than five crore had less than 10 percent revenue and 21.9 percent firms received 70 to 80 percent revenue in terms of foreign currency. Next, firms with 5 to 10 crore annual turnover have reported that 18.9 percent firms observed to have 90 to 100 percent revenue. Similarly, firms having their annual turnover in 10-15 crore, 26.8 percent of such firms were having their annual turnover between 80 to 90 percent in terms of foreign currency. Further, firms with annual turnover between 15 to 20 crore demonstrated less that 31 percent of such firms were having 90 to 100 percent of their total revenues in terms of foreign currency. In the same manner, firms with the annual turnover between 20 to 25 crore, reported that their proportion of total revenue was lying in two categories, i.e., 30-40 percent or 90 to 100 percent which was in foreign currency. Added to this, firms with annual turnover in the remaining categories 25 to 30, 30 to 35, 35 to 40, 40 to 45, 45 to 50 and 50 to100 crore have shown more than 30 percent of their total revenues in terms of foreign currency. Whereas, 3.8 percent firms with the annual turnover above 100 crore depicted that less than 10 percent of their total revenues and 10.5 percent firms indicated that 90 to 100 percent of their total revenues was in foreign currency. Therefore, it can be identified that firms within the annual turnover of 20 to 25 crore were having comparatively more revenues in foreign currency in comparison to firms having their annual turnover more than 100 crore.

❖ Further, when annual turnover of the sampled firms was studied with the percentage of their total assets in terms of foreign currency then the results stated that firms having less than 5 crore as annual turnover, 37.5% fall under the category of less than 10 percent of their total assets followed by 18.8 percent firms falling in the category of 50-60 percent of their total assets in foreign currency. In case of firms having annual turnover between 5-10 crore, maximum (20.8 percent) were having 60-70 percent of their total assets in foreign currency followed by 15.1 percent firms having 40-50 percent of their assets in foreign currency. Likewise, firms having annual turnover between 10-15 crore were having maximum (26.8 percent) 90-100 percent of their total assets in foreign currency. In case of firms with 15-20 crore annual turnover 31 percent (maximum) firms were having 90-100 percent of their total assets, firms with 20-25 crore annual turnover 37.5 percent (maximum) firms were having 60-70 percent and 70-80 percent of their total assets, firms with 25-30 crore annual turnover 29 percent (maximum) firms were having 20-30 percent of their total assets, firms with 30-35 crore annual turnover 50 percent (maximum) firms were having 40-50 percent of their total assets, and firms with 35-40 crore annual turnover 33.3 percent (maximum) firms were having 60-70 percent, 70-80 percent and 90-100 percent of their total assets in each of these three categories in terms of foreign currency.

❖ Next, the smaller the size of the firm, lesser is the exposure of firm/firm for foreign debt. More than 40% of the firms have less than 10% foreign debt in case of firms having turnover lesser than five crore. The firms, having annual turnover more than 100 crore, have shown that their foreign debt is more than 50% of their annual turnover. The larger the size of firm in terms of annual turnover, the higher is the possibility of high amount of foreign debt and hence more exposure to forex risk. This association between more annual turnover of the firm and more is the possibility of high amount of foreign debt has been tested through various tests of association too.

❖ Also it was revealed that majority of the firms/firms, that is, 281 out of 407 (69%) of the firms or firms is not involved in the management of forex risk exposure. It means that only 126 firms or firms are managing their forex risk exposure. In other words, out of our sample size only 30.96% of firms or firms are managing their forex risk exposure. Further, out of this 126 firms/firms, majority of the firms falls under either the category of high of medium level of management in respect of forex risk. So, we can conclude that not very much firms in India is inclined towards the management of forex risk exposure.

❖ Supplementary, when the firms were asked regarding management of translation, transaction and economic exposure, then the results obtained showed that firms whose annual turnover in term of Indian rupees falls under the category of 35-40 Crore, often manage translation exposure (accounting translation into base currency) followed by firms/firms whose annual turnover in term of Indian rupees falls under the range of 20-25, 15-20, above 100, 25-3030-35, 5-10, and 10-15 crore respectively. Overall, 47.9% of the firms/firms sometimes manage for translation exposure (accounting translation into base currency). On the other hand, only 15% of the firms in the sample do not manage for translation exposure (accounting translation into base currency) in the present study which showed that most of the firms either go for often or sometimes options for managing translation exposure (accounting translation into base currency). Regarding management of transaction exposure, the firms who often go for managing the transaction exposure (Foreign receivable and payable currency), two third of these firms were those firms whose annual turnover in Indian rupees is more than 100 crore. The firms whose annual turnover is 40-45 crore, these firms mostly (75.0%) go for some time management of transaction exposure (Foreign receivable and payable currency). Same patter was observed in the firms whose annual turnover falls under the range of less than 5 crore, 5-10, 10-15, 15-20, 25-30, 45-50 and 50-100 crore. That is, all the firms under this range of turnover in Indian rupees mostly go for some times management of transaction exposure (Foreign receivable and payable currency). Another observation from the analysis is that there are very few firms who never go for managing the transaction exposure (Foreign receivable and payable currency). And regarding management of economic exposure, the results also showed that firms whose annual turnover fall under the range of 20-25 crore, they mostly manage economic exposure (future expected cash flow and competitive position). The firms having annual turnover was in the range of 5-10 and 25-30 crore, stated that they were not managing economic exposure (future expected cash flow and competitive position). Further, firms whose annual turnover falls under the range of 35-40crore, they have equal proportion for managing economic exposure (future expected cash flow and competitive position). Also firms whose annual turnover falls under the range of 10-15, 30-35, 40-45 and above 100 crore they mostly manage economic exposure (future expected cash flow and competitive position).

Objective Two

As stated above, objective two was intended to study the forex risk exposure management by SMEs and unlisted non-financial firms in India. The following are the major findings of the study for objective two.

❖ The results attained for this objective stated that that only 15% of the sampled units were fully aware about the forex risk management and 55% of the sampled units were partially aware about forex risk management. A large number, i.e., 122 out of 407 (30%) of the firms were not at all aware regarding the forex risk management. And out of 407 firms, only 74 firms were having a specified policy on forex risk management. More than 70 (73.7%) percent of SMEs and unlisted non-financial firms said they were not having any policy document for forex risk exposure management while 7.9% firms admitted that they are in the process of framing such a policy.

❖ Further, various parties can define forex risk management policy in the business. Also, different persons working in the firms can do the implementation of forex risk management. The results indicated that 155 out of 407 firms, the management team of the business collectively designs the forex risk management policy followed by Board of Directors and CEOs of the firms. Finance controller and Accountants were also designing the forex risk management policy of their businesses but the number of such firms was very less. Likewise, the management team of the business, CEOs, and Board of Directors were taking the responsibility of effective implementation of the forex risk management policy of SMEs and unlisted non-financial firms in India.

❖ Next significant question asked was related to the purpose of hedging the forex risk. There can be several purposes of hedging the forex risk by a firm. It can increase the profitability, reducing the volatility in cash flows or speculation etc. It was found that speculation was also a major reason for hedging the forex risk. Although, the technical meaning of the term hedging risk itself indicates a specific meaning but finding speculation (330 out of 407) as a purpose of taking opposite positions in a hedging instrument is an fascinating outcome of the analysis. In addition to speculation, SMEs and unlisted non-financial firms also informed that hedging forex risk is essential for the sustainability of their businesses. 323 out of 407 firms admitted that hedging is indispensible for survival of their businesses. 326 firms said that they were doing hedging to improve the financial performance of their businesses, 285 firms said that it reduces the volatility in the earnings of their business, and 256 firms said that it reduces the volatility in their cash flows etc. The other purposes of hedging forex risk were related to controlling the risk of fluctuations in foreign currencies, to increase the market value of firm and to increase the profitability of the business.

❖ In addition to above, SMEs and unlisted non-financial firms were using multiple methods to measure their forex risk exposure. Among these most popular methods, estimation of cash flows was used most frequently to measure forex risk exposure. The sampled firms were also using rough estimates to forecast their forex risk exposure. Value at Risk, Scenario Analysis and Matching approach were also among other methods adopted by firms to measure forex risk exposure. Although, 78 respondents said that they were not using any kind of methods for this purpose.

❖ When the tendency or frequency of managing the forex risk exposure by the firms was studied then 15.2% of firms said that they always manage their forex risk exposure. It means, whenever there is an exposure of forex risk due to any business transaction, these firms were taking a hedging strategy to manage the forex exposure risk. While 26.3% of the firms said that they often take hedging position for their forex risk exposure. 11.3% and 10.6%of the firms said never or rarely meaning thereby, these firms were not taking any concrete action to manage their forex risk exposure.

❖ Some of the SMEs and unlisted non-financial firms mentioned that they were never managing their forex risk exposure even though they were aware about the risk. As mentioned in previous section, 11.3% of SMEs and unlisted non-financial firms said that they never manage their forex risk exposure then these firms were asked to state the reasons for such type of behavior. The results obtained in this context indicated that lack of awareness about measuring forex risk and cost convoluted in hedging the forex risk were two major reasons for never managing the forex risk exposure. In addition to this, possibility of insufficient loss due to no-management, less quantum of forex exposure and availability of natural hedge were among the other reasons mentioned by these firms.

❖ The sampled firms were also asked about their strategy regarding average period of hedging the forex risk exposure. The results directed that 45.7 % (186) of SMEs and unlisted non-financial firms were taking their hedging position for an average period of 90 days. And 98 firms out of 407 forms were taking hedging positions for an average period of 180 days. Only 7 firms were doing hedging for a complete year, i.e., 360 days. The variation in hedging period can be because of the quantum of forex risk exposure of the respective firms too. But, it is good if the firms having forex risk exposure are having hedging for a period matching with their risk exposure.

❖ An appropriate hedge ratio is a significant criterion to manage the forex risk. Hedge ratio is an important aspect of determining the forex risk exposure management. The results found in this direction have revealed that 49.9% of the firms (203) were following no specific hedge ratio for the management of forex risk exposure whereas, 88 (21.6%) firms (highest) were using 41-60% as hedge ratio to manage their forex risk exposure management. Further, 14 % (57) firms were having 21-40% as hedge ratio for the purpose of managing forex risk exposure. Out of 407, 37 firms were having a practice of 1-20% ratio as their hedge ratio policy to manage forex risk exposure. Finally, there were only 7 (1.7%) firms who were having highest hedge ratio, i.e., 81-100% to manage forex risk exposure. The findings have indicated that majority of the SMEs and unlisted non-financial firms in the study were having moderate hedge ratio as a policy to manage forex risk exposure.

❖ There are various instruments provided by financial institutions, which are used for hedging the forex risk. In addition to these instruments, the practitioners also use various techniques like cash flow matching and asset-liability management etc. to hedge the forex risk. The cash flow matching technique has been preferred than asset liability management for hedging forex risk. Out of 407 firms, 87 firms said that they always use cash flow matching, and 74 firms said that they often use cash flow matching technique to hedge forex risk. More than 100 firms said that they use asset-liability management to hedge forex risk. Structured derivatives is the least used instrument by various firms (247) followed by Hybrid Debt in order to hedge forex risk exposure followed by exchange traded options, swaps, hybrid debts, asset liability management and OTC options respectively. Exchange Traded Futures, OTC traded Options and Exchange Traded Options were also found comparatively popular instruments of hedging forex risk by SMEs and unlisted non-financial firms in India.

❖ There are multiple options available in selecting the instrument or technique to hedge the forex risk. But the SMEs and unlisted firms were not using all such instruments and techniques with same frequency. When they were asked that why they were not considering any specific instrument or technique for the purpose of hedging forex risk then there these firms stated many reasons for not using or rarely using specified type of instrument or technique. These reasons can be that the instrument or technique is too complex, causing problem in accounting treatment, not allowed in some markets, high cost involved or too complex etc. There were 285 firms (70%) who were either agreed or strongly agreed that complexities involved in the hedging instrument was the major reason for not considering a specific instrument for hedging purpose. The next prominent reason was related to accounting problems (364), followed by higher cost than expected benefits (356), insufficient exposure (353), not having the desired features (333), not having sufficient exposure of market instruments (253), and lack of willingness to disclose much about forex risk exposure of business (230) respectively. The least important reason that was affecting the firms' decision regarding not choosing of a specific hedging instrument or technique "Not liquid enough" (304). Whereas 207 respondents believed that these hedging instruments are too risky to use for managing forex risk exposure. In nutshell, there are many reasons, which are causing firms' decision to not to use various instruments and techniques of hedging the forex risk exposure.

❖ The average maturity period of hedging instruments is analyzed on the basis of usage of hedging instruments. As discussed in previous section, all types of hedging instruments are not used each of the SMEs and unlisted non-financial firm, therefore, the total of last column of Table 13 is not same in all cases. As shown in Table 13, an average period of 91-180 days (most preferred) is considered by sample units for different types of hedging instruments, to be more specific, in case of Futures (109), Forwards (123), Options (102), OTC forwards (154), and OTC options (70), the firms are hedging their forex risk exposure for an average period of 91-180 days followed by an average maturity period of 0-90 days and 180-360 days. Almost all types of hedging instruments were used for partial, full and dynamic hedging. But the use of various hedging instruments for partial and full hedge was found comparatively more than their use for dynamic hedge. In case of Futures, out of 407 firms, 140 said that they use it for partial hedge and 145 firms said that they are using Futures instrument for full hedging. Similarly, in case of Forwards (164), Options (151), Swaps (71), Hybrid Debts (101) and Others (16), the firms were using more of these instruments for partial hedging rather than using them for full or dynamic hedging.

❖ As we know that there are three types of forex risk exposures faced by SMEs and unlisted non-financial firms and the firms can have a hedging position shorter than or longer than the duration of forex risk exposure. In some cases, firms can have an exact matching of hedging with the forex risk exposure. The results attained in this direction showed that 172 firms having translation exposure said that they were hedging their forex risk exposure for a period shorter than the maturity of the exposure. 95 firms with translation exposure stated that they were exactly matching their hedging position with the maturity of forex risk exposure while 108 firms having translation exposure said that they were taking hedging position for forex risk exposure for a period longer than the maturity of such type of risk exposure. Similarly, 232 firms having transaction exposure said that they were hedging their forex risk for a period which is exactly matching with their risk exposure. While 146 firms having transaction exposure stated that they were hedging forex risk for a period shorter than the maturity of forex risk exposure and 124 such firms were hedging for a period longer than the maturity of their forex risk exposure. Third type of exposure, i.e., economic exposure has indicated slight dissimilar results when compared with translation and transaction exposure. 175 firms having economic exposure stated that they prefer to hedge such type of exposure for a period longer than the maturity of risk exposure. While 89 firms said that they were hedging for a period shorter than the maturity of their forex risk and 80 firms having economic exposure were saying that they were taking hedging position exactly matching with the maturity of forex risk. Supplement to this, 140 firms were doing 40-60% hedging of their forex risk exposure. Only 24 firms were doing 80-100% of hedging of their forex risk exposure. A large number of sample firms, i.e., 173 (84+89), were hedging less than or equal to 40% hedging of their total forex risk exposure which is actually not a suitable approach of managing the forex risk exposure.

❖ In a volatile market scenario, readjustment of hedging position is equally important. Therefore, the survey instrument of the study also asked about the frequency of readjustment in the forex risk management hedging strategy. Out of 407 firms, 34 firms mentioned that they readjust their hedging position on daily basis and 93 firms said that they prepare a weekly schedule to readjust their hedging position in forex risk management avenues. A large number, i.e., 183 (45%) firms readjust their hedging position on monthly basis. A small number (13) of firms readjust their hedging position on yearly basis. The purpose of readjustment in hedging position is to ensure that the exposure to forex risk is fully covered. The sample units considered in the study are not of similar nature in terms of their forex risk exposure, annual turnover, and frequency of foreign transactions etc. therefore, their schedule to readjust their hedging position may also vary but considering the nature of forex market, a readjustment schedule of monthly, quarterly, semi-annual or annual may cause increase in forex risk exposure of the firms.

❖ The execution of forex risk management policy also play imperative role in apposite management of forex risk. Out of 407 respondents, 177 firms said that they are not following any specific timeline in execution of hedging strategy while 126 respondents said that whenever they submit a bid or transaction is initiated then they execute their hedging strategy for forex risk exposure. While 57 firms said that whenever an order is received from a customer in foreign currency or an order is received which involves inflow of cash flows in foreign currency, that is the time they initiate the execution of their forex risk hedging strategy. And 47 firms said that they execute a hedging strategy at the time of realization of revenues in terms of foreign currency.

❖ There are several benefits attached to Exchange Earners' Foreign Currency (EEFC) Account. A firm having EEFC accounts is presumed to be more aware regarding the forex risk exposure management. Therefore, the sample units were also asked about their EEFC Accounts. Out of 407 firms, 275 firms said that they have EEFC Account to manage their earnings in foreign currencies. While 132 (32.4 percent) of the SMEs and Unlisted firms were not having EEFC Account.

❖ Both economic sector and turnover of the firms are two important demographic features that have earlier been used for cross tabulation analysis. Similarly, while studying the results for attainment of second objective, these two parameters were used to find out if some significant association exists between these two basic parameters and other relevant inputs. For this, cross tabulation results were obtained for 16 different types of possible associations. The results of cross tabulation of these results are given in Appendix A. But the results obtained to test the significance of association and strength of that association are mentioned below. As discussed earlier too that chi-square is good measure for assessing the significance of association between two variables, therefore, considering the results of chi-square test indicate that the association between all the variables studies on the basis of their belongingness to specific economic sector and on the basis of different categories of their annual turnover was found significant. The phi coefficient and Cramer's V coefficient was also found significant at 5% level of significance which further indicated the existence of relationship between variables. Also the phi coefficients and Cramer's V coefficients were found less than 0.5 and positive in majority of the cases, which suggested a moderate to low degree of association between the variables.

Objective Three

The third objective was to identify the determinants of forex risk hedging strategies considered by SMEs and unlisted non-financial firms. As already revealed in chapter three that to attain this objective, an exploratory factor analysis was applied to know the major determinants or factors or latent variables or constructs to recognize the major factors which are considered by the SMEs and unlisted non-financial firms in India. These factors are further prioritized on the basis of experts' opinion by using AHP (Analytic Hierarchy Process). The SMEs and unlisted non-financial firms were also asked that how forex risk management strategy of a firm could be improvised. The overall results attained to achieve objective three can be concluded as under.

❖ The results of exploratory factor analysis designated that 32 variables examined for determining the forex risk hedging strategy can be categorized into five main determinants. These variables are given in Table 101 below along with the variables defining them.

Table 101

Determinants/Factors of Forex Risk Hedging Strategy

Determinants/Factors	Variables
FACTOR ONE **(Firm Specific Indicators)**	1. Nature of the business of Firm, i.e., how much business is dependent upon the export and import. 2. Clear Forex Risk Hedging guidelines issued by the firm, viz. use of specific hedging instrument, duration of hedging strategy and time horizon of forex hedging strategy etc 3. Forex Risk Exposure of the Business in proportion to total Turnover, 4. Past Experience of the firm in hedging Forex Risk 5. Balance sheet and cash flow position of the firm
FACTOR TWO **(Foreign/Global Economy's Macro Indicators)**	1. Political conditions of the foreign country with whom trade has happened 2. Economic condition of the foreign country with whom trade has happened, i.e., GDP, Inflation Rate, Money Supply, Capital Market Conditions, Balance of Trade Position etc. 3. Interest Rate Fluctuations in the International Market 4. Overall sentiments regarding Forex Market 5. Forex Control Mechanism in the foreign country 6. Fluctuations in Crude oil Prices as it affect the volatility in prices of all major currencies 7. Speculation (Forex Market, Real Estate, Securities and Uncovered Interest Arbitrage)
FACTOR THREE **(Domestic Economy's Macro Indicators)**	1. Political conditions of Domestic country 2. Interest Rate Fluctuations in the Domestic Market 3. Economic condition of the domestic country, i.e., GDP, Inflation Rate, Money Supply, Capital Market Conditions, Balance of Trade Position etc. 4. Development of Banking system

	5. Discovery of New Resources
FACTOR FOUR **(Forex Market Scenario)**	1. Government regulations regarding Forex Market 2. Intervention of Central Bank in Forex Market 3. Volatility in the value of Domestic Currency 4. Volatility in Foreign Currency in which payment has to be made or any other currency used for international settlement 5. Future Expectations regarding movement in Foreign exchange rate 6. Demand and Supply Conditions of domestic Currency 7. Demand and Supply Conditions of Foreign Currency 8. Convertibility of Indian rupee 9. Fluctuations in US Dollar Prices
FACTOR FIVE **(Forex Risk Hedging Instruments)**	1. Availability of Forex hedging instruments at Exchange and OTC market 2. Ease of using various forex risk hedging instruments like options, futures, synthetic derivatives etc. and their 3. Popularity of the forex risk hedging instrument 4. Experience of Forex Risk Manager in using Forex Risk Hedging Instruments 5. Perception of Forex Risk Manager regarding various hedging instruments 6. Option of Customization of Various Forex Risk Hedging Instruments

Source: Calculations Done by Researcher

❖ Next, the important factors, which are requisite to be upgraded for a superior forex risk hedging strategy, were also obtained by using the exploratory factor analysis. Table 102 given below has given the list of factors along with their observed variables which were submitted by SMEs and unlisted non-financial firms to improve forex risk hedging strategies by them.

Table 102

Determinants/Factors to Improve Forex Risk Hedging Strategy

Determinants/Factors	Statements
FACTOR ONE (Internal Management's Approach for Forex Risk Hedging Management)	1. The management of business should play more intense role in formation of a forex risk management policy 2. The management shall motivate for risk management practices 3. The top management or decision maker should gain more expertise in forex risk management 4. Forex risk management policy must be made mandatory for all Small and Medium Enterprises 5. The business associations should provide necessary assistance and support to their members in managing forex risk 6. More trained people are required
FACTOR TWO (Awareness Regarding Forex Risk Hedging Instruments and Forex Market Regulations)	1. More Hedging instruments need to be introduced 2. The cost of hedging devices should be less 3. Hedging instruments shall be introduced with some tax benefit schemes 4. More innovative, customized and low cost hedging instruments should be introduced by regulators 5. Clear guidelines should be forwarded by RBI regarding usage of derivative products
FACTOR THREE (Regulators' initiatives to increase Hedging Instruments' Literacy)	1. More awareness shall be done by RBI 2. More certification and educational programs 3. The bank should aware business whenever it approaches the bank for export-import financing 4. The RBI or Government shall make it mandatory to hedge the forex risk

Source: Calculations Done by Researcher

❖ The five constructs or criterion recognized by the outcomes of Exploratory Factor Analysis (EFA) were used to develop paired comparison questionnaire to be sent to Experts. This effectual tool for decision makers which was introduced by Saaty (1980) has extensively been used in every decision area related to finance. The experts' priorities for various criteria were used and then reletive importance of each criteria is ascertained. While selecting the experts for the survey, it was ensured that the quality of survey is attained to a desired level while considering the limitations of budget and time-line. The local priority weights of factors, sub-factors are combined together with respect to all successive hierarchical levels to obtain the global composite priority weight of all the sub-factors. (Detailed calculations are already mentioned in Chapter IV). The domestic economy's macro indicators (DEMI) scored the highest global weight, i.e., 22.54% followed by firm specific indicators (22.13%) and foreign and global economy's macro indicators (21.74%). It indicates that for a decision maker of hedging strategies, the domestic economy's macro indicators are considered as foremost important decision criteria. Among the sub-criteria for firm specific indicators (FSI), nature of business (5.93%) and balance sheet and cash flow position (5.53%) are found with highest global weights, in case of decision criterion on forex risk hedging instruments (FRHS), the perception of forex risk manager regarding various hedging instruments is found most important sub-criterion as its global weight is highest (3.14%) among all other sub-criteria, i.e., FRHSI (2.89%), FRHS2(1.61%), FRHS3 (2.15%), FRHS4 (2.02%), FRHS6 (1.2%). The availability of forex hedging instruments at exchange and OTC market and popularity of the forex risk hedging instrument are other two important sub-criterions under forex risk hedging instruments decision criterion. Next decision criterion is fore market scenario (FMS). Under this decision criterion, the global weight for future expectations regarding movement in foreign exchange rate(FMS5) is highest, i.e., 3.97% followed by followed by government regulations regarding forex market(FMS1 with 3.25% as global weight) and volatility in the value of domestic currency (FMS3 with 3.08% as global weight) as next two important sub-criterion. Further, political condition of domestic country (DEMI1) and development of banking system (DEMI4) scored highest weight, i.e., 5.32% and 5.07% respectively as sub-criterion of domestic economy's macro indicators (DEMI). The most important determinant of foreign/global economy's macro indicators (FGEMI) is forex control mechanism in the foreign country with highest global weight of 4.80% followed by interest rate fluctuations in the international market (FGEMI with global weight of 3.63%). The priority order according to local weights is also similar to the results of global weights indicating the importance of various sub-criteria in determining the major criterion respectively. The summarized results are given in Table 103 below.

Table 103

Local and Global Weight for the Factors and sub Factors

Codes for Factors/Sub-factors	Factors/Sub-factors	Local Weights	Global Weights
	Firm Specific Indicators (FSI)	22.1295%	22.1295%
FSI1	Nature of the business of Firm, i.e., how much business is dependent upon the export and import	26.78%	5.93%
FSI2	Clear Forex Risk Hedging guidelines issued by the firm, viz. use of specific hedging instrument, duration of hedging strategy and time horizon of forex hedging strategy etc.	12.12%	2.68%

FSI3	Forex Risk Exposure of the Business in proportion to total Turnover,	18.06%	4.00%
FSI4	Past Experience of the firm in hedging Forex Risk	18.07%	4.00%
FSI5	Balance sheet and cash flow position of the firm	24.97%	5.53%
	Forex Risk Hedging Instruments (FRHS)	13.0232%	13.0232%
FRHS1	Availability of Forex hedging instruments at Exchange and OTC market	22.19%	2.89%
FRHS2	Ease of using various forex risk hedging instruments like options, futures, synthetic derivatives etc. and their	12.34%	1.61%
FRHS3	Popularity of the forex risk hedging instrument	16.58%	2.16%
FRHS4	Experience of Forex Risk Manager in using Forex Risk Hedging Instruments	15.52%	2.02%
FRHS5	Perception of Forex Risk Manager regarding various hedging instruments	24.15%	3.14%
FRHS6	Option of Customization of Various Forex Risk Hedging Instruments	9.22%	1.20%
	Forex Market Scenario (FMS)	20.5676%	20.5676%
FMS1	Government regulations regarding Forex Market	15.79%	3.25%
FMS2	Intervention of Central Bank in Forex Market	8.68%	1.78%
FMS3	Volatility in the value of Domestic Currency	14.99%	3.08%
FMS4	Volatility in Foreign Currency in which payment has to be made or any other currency used for international settlement	13.33%	2.74%
FMS5	Future Expectations regarding movement in Foreign exchange rate	19.29%	3.97%
FMS6	Demand and Supply Conditions of domestic Currency	10.30%	2.12%

FMS7	Demand and Supply Conditions of Foreign Currency	7.04%	1.45%
FMS8	Convertibility of Indian rupee	3.35%	0.69%
FMS9	Fluctuations in US Dollar Prices	7.23%	1.49%
	Domestic Economy's Macro Indicators (DEMI)	**22.5416%**	**22.5416%**
DEMI1	Political conditions of Domestic country	23.60%	5.32%
DEMI2	Interest Rate Fluctuations in the Domestic Market	21.65%	4.88%
DEMI3	Economic condition of the domestic country, i.e., GDP, Inflation Rate, Money Supply, Capital Market Conditions, Balance of Trade Position etc.	19.35%	4.36%
DEMI4	Development of Banking system	22.48%	5.07%
DEMI5	Discovery of New Resources	12.92%	2.91%
	Foreign/Global Economy's Macro Indicators (FGEMI)	**21.7381%**	**21.7381%**
FGEMI1	Political conditions of the foreign country with whom trade has happened	15.71%	3.42%
FGEMI2	Economic condition of the foreign country with whom trade has happened, i.e., GDP, Inflation Rate, Money Supply, Capital Market Conditions, Balance of Trade Position etc.	8.98%	1.95%
FGEMI3	Interest Rate Fluctuations in the International Market	16.70%	3.63%
FGEMI4	Overall sentiments regarding Forex Market	15.76%	3.43%
FGEMI5	Forex Control Mechanism in the foreign country	22.06%	4.80%
FGEMI6	Fluctuations in Crude oil Prices as it affect the volatility in prices of all major currencies	12.96%	2.82%
FGEMI7	Speculation (Forex Market, Real Estate, Securities and Uncovered Interest Arbitrage)	7.83%	1.70%

Source: Calculations Done by Researcher

Recommendations/Implications for Various Stakeholders

- **Recommendations/Implications for SMEs and Unlisted non-financial Firms:** The SMEs and unlisted firms need to improve the awareness level regarding forex risk hedging instruments among the people involved in financial decision-making. Further, these firms need to have clear guidelines for forex risk management. The findings of the study recommends that SMEs and unlisted non-financial firms should use full hedging strategies in place of partial hedging to reduce the forex risk. Also, these firms need to devise methods to train the concerned person regarding all types of hedging instruments and techniques. It will provide them more choices to frame strategies to hedge their forex risk exposure.The SMEs and unlisted firms can also consider the determinants recommended by present study to devise their hedging strategies and which factors these firms should focus to contrive their hedging strategies.

- **Recommendations/Implicationsfor Forex Risk Managers/Advisors/Professionals:** The forex risk managers should consider various determinants for forex risk hedging while determining a hedging strategy. Moreover, these practitioners can design training programs or capacity building programs for SMEs and unlisted non-financial firms so that the gap in their understanding for various hedging instruments and techniques can be filled to reduce forex risk.

- **Recommendations/Implicationsfor Government/Regulators:** The empirical evidences of the study have revealed lack of awareness regarding forex risk exposure and its management. As a regulator, Government should take initiatives to increase the awareness level among SMEs and unlisted non-financial firms. The government and regulators need to createseveral platforms for SMEs and unlisted non-financial firms where forex risk exposure management, forex risk hedging instrument and other related matters can be undertaken.

- **Recommendations/Implications for Academia:** The less awareness regarding forex risk, forex risk hedging instruments, and determinants of forex risk hedging strategies etc. signifies that such an fundamental subject should be a part of most of the finance/SMEs related programs in different universities and institutions. The elements covered in the study can provide broader guidelines to develop curriculum related to Forex Risk Awareness among SMEs and Unlisted Firms, and Forex Risk Management by SMEs and Unlisted Firms etc.

- **Recommendations/Implications for Researchers:** The study under consideration stipulates valuable comprehensions to the researchers on the related field. It will benefit the researchers to cognize this field in an enrichedmanner to conduct research related to forex risk management, determinationof hedging strategies and exploring various types of relation between demographic features and forex risk exposure and its management related variables for SMEs and unlisted firms in India and worldwide.

Contribution to Existing Literature and Theory

The empirical evidences obtained from the present study will postulate further insight into the forex risk management and hedging practices by SMEs and unlisted non-financial firms in an emerging economy like India. The findings of the study complement to the existing literature related to forex risk exposure, forex risk management practices and forex risk hedging strategies. The main contribution to existing theory will be in the form of determinants of forex risk hedging strategy, determinants of improvement in forex risk hedging strategy and hierarchy of decision criteria in determining forex risk hedging strategy. The existing theories and literature (as discussed in introduction and review of literature) addresstheissues linked to impact of hedging on cash flows of the business, relevance of hedging, use of derivatives to hedge forex risk etc.

But the determinants of forex risk hedging strategy, determinants to improve forex risk hedging strategy and Hierarchy of Decision Criteria for forex risk hedging strategy by experts involved in framing policy guidelines regarding forex risk hedging are the threeoriginal contributions to the existing theory on forex risk management and hedging practices by firms in general and by SMEs and unlisted non-financial firms in specific. These three inputs are cited below in exhibit I, II and exhibit III respectively.

Exhibit I

Determinants of Forex Risk Hedging Strategy by SMEs and unlisted Non-financial Firms

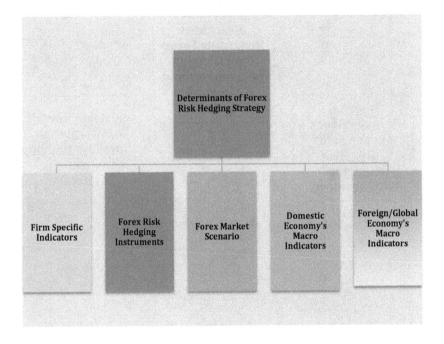

Exhibit II

Determinants to Improve Forex Risk Hedging Strategy by SMEs and unlisted Non-financial Firms

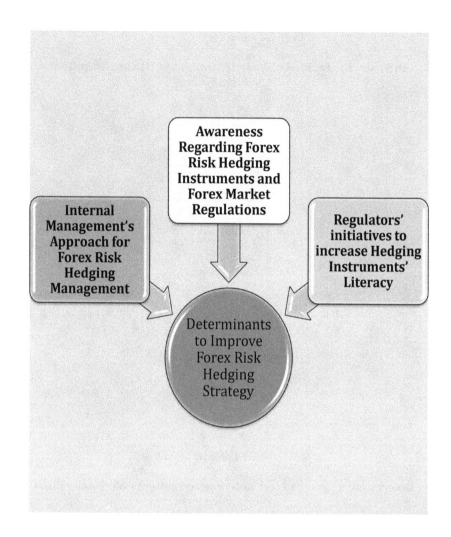

Exhibit III

Hierarchy of Decision Criteria for Forex Risk Hedging by Experts

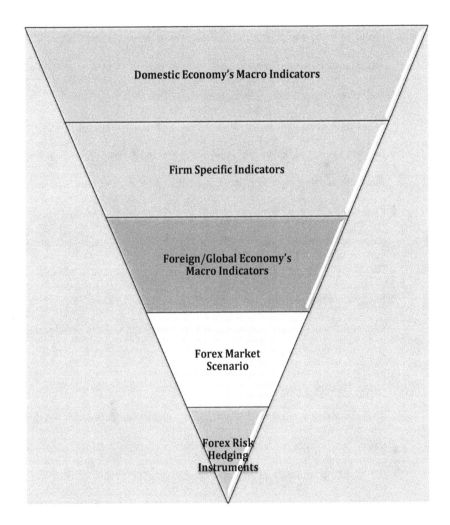

Scope for Future Research

❖ The current research provides a list of various determinants for hedging strategies with the help of exploratory factor analysis. The determinants identified in the current study can be re-investigated or validated with a fresh survey to confirm the factors. Such type of research will require in-depth analysis using confirmatory factor analysis.

❖ The evidences of the study have shown strong indication of association between the demographic profile of the SMEs and unlisted firms with their forex risk hedging awareness and management policies. The future studies in the related field can be narrowed down on the basis of individual specific demographic features based classification of SMEs and unlisted non-financial. For example, sector wise, turnover wise, size of the firm, and turnover in foreign currency wise etc. can be the criteria to study the forex risk exposure awareness, management and determinants of SMEs and unlisted non-financial firms.

❖ There is good scope for investigating causal studies on the basis of determinants and effectiveness of hedging strategy as dependent variable. Such type of studies can be based on application of regression analysis or tools like structural equation modeling. The demographic profile of SMEs and unlisted non-financial firms can be considered to examine the mediation effect.

❖ The research areas suggested above have scope to be extended to international markets too as there is dearth of empirical studies on the related field in India and worldwide too.

APPENDIX I

Table A1

Crosstab Sector wise and Awareness Regarding Forex Risk Management

Sector			Yes, Fully Aware	Yes, but Partially aware	Not aware about the concept of forex risk management	Total
Economic Sector	Construction	Count	8	5	0	13
		% within Economic Sector	61.5	38.5	0	100
		% within Aware	13.1	2.2	0	3.2
		% of Total	2.0	1.2	0	3.2
	Manufacturing	Count	42	166	97	305
		% within Economic Sector	13.8	54.4	31.8	100
		% within Aware	68.9	74.1	79.5	74.9
		% of Total	10.3	40.8	23.8	74.9
	Services	Count	3	23	6	32
		% within Economic Sector	9.4	71.9	18.8	100
		% within Aware	4.9	10.3	4.9	7.9
		% of Total	0.7	5.7	1.5	7.9
	Trading	Count	8	26	19	53
		% within Economic Sector	15.1	49.1	35.8	100
		% within Aware	13.1	11.6	15.6	13
		% of Total	2	6.4	4.7	13
	Any Other	Count	0	4	0	4
		% within Economic Sector	0	100.0	0.0	100.0
		% within Aware	0	1.8	0	1
		% of Total	0	1.0	0	1
Total		Count	61	224	122	407
		% within Economic Sector	15	55.0	30	100
		% within Aware	100	100	100	100
		% of Total	15	55	30	100

Source: Calculations Done by Researcher

Table A2

Crosstab Analysis of Sector wise and Existence of Forex Risk Management Policy

Economic Sector		Yes	No	No, but currently it is under consideration and soon will be in place	Total
Construction	Count	8	3	2	13
	% within Economic Sector	61.5	23.1	15.4	100
	% within Policy	10.7	1.0	6.3	3.2
	% of Total	2.0	0.7	0.5	3.2
Manufacturing	Count	51	234	20	305
	% within Economic Sector	16.7	76.7	6.6	100
	% within Policy	68.	78	62.5	74.9
	% of Total	12.5	57.5	4.9	74.9
Services	Count	7	24	1	32
	% within Economic Sector	21.9	75	3.1	100
	% within Policy	9.3	8.0	3.1	7.9
	% of Total	1.7	5.9	0.2	7.9
Trading	Count	7	37	9	53
	% within Economic Sector	13.2	69.8	17	100
	% within Policy	9.3	12.3	28.1	13
	% of Total	1.7	9.1	2.2	13
Any Other	Count	2	2	0	4
	% within Economic Sector	50	50	0	100
	% within Policy	2.7	0.7	0	1
	% of Total	0.5	0.5	0	1
Total	Count	75	300	32	407
	% within Economic Sector	18.4	73.7	7.9	100
	% within Policy	100	100	100	100
	% of Total	18.4	73.7	7.9	100.0

Source: Calculations Done by Researcher

Table A3

Crosstab Analysis of Sector wise and Frequency of Measuring Forex Risk Exposure

Economic Sectors		Always	Often	Sometimes	Rarely	Never	Total
Construction	Count	7	6	0	0	0	13

	% within Economic Sector	53.8	46.2	0	0	0	100
	% within How frequently the forex risk exposure is	11.3	5.6	0	0	0	3.2
	% of Total	1.7	1.5	0	0	0	3.2
Manufacturing	Count	39	85	109	37	35	305
	% within Economic Sector	12.8	27.9	35.7	12.1	11.5	100
	% within How frequently the forex risk exposure is	62.9	79.4	73.2	86.	76.1	74.9
	% of Total	9.6	20.9	26.8	9.1	8.6	74.9
Services	Count	8	7	12	0	5	32
	% within Economic Sector	25	21.9	37.5	0	15.6	100
	% within How frequently the forex risk exposure is	12.9	6.5	8.1	0	10.9	7.9
	% of Total	2	1.7	2.9	0	1.2	7.9
Trading	Count	6	7	28	6	6	53
	% within Economic Sector	11.3	13.2	52.8	11.3	11.3	100
	% within How frequently the forex risk exposure is	9.7	6.5	18.8	14	13	13
	% of Total	1.5	1.7	6.9	1.5	1.5	13
Any Other	Count	2	2	0	0	0	4
	% within Economic Sector	50	50	0	0	0	100
	% within How frequently the forex risk exposure is	3.2	1.9	0	0	0	1
	% of Total	0.5	0.5	0	0	0	1
	Count	62	107	149	43	46	407
	% within Economic Sector	15.2	26.3	36.6	10.6	11.3	100
	% within How frequently the forex risk exposure is	100	100	100	100	100	100
	% of Total	15.2	26.3	36.6	10.6	11.3	100

Source: Calculations Done by Researcher

Table A 4

Crosstab Analysis of Sector wise and Average Period of Hedging

Economic Sector		Less than 90 Days	90 Days	180 Days	360 Days	Total
Construction	Count	4	6	3	0	13
	% within Economic Sector	30.8	46.2	23.1	0	100
	% within Average period the company is hedging	3.4	3.2	3.1	0	3.2

	% of Total	1	1.5	0	0	3.2
Manufacturing	Count	**74**	**150**	**76**	**5**	**305**
	% within Economic Sector	24.3	49.2	24.9	1.6	100
	% within Average period the company is hedging	63.8	80.6	77.6	71.4	74.9
	% of Total	18.2	36.9	18.7	1.2	74.9
Services	Count	**16**	**8**	**8**	**0**	**32**
	% within Economic Sector	50	25	25	0	100
	% within Average period the company is hedging	13.8	4.3	8.2	0	7.9
	% of Total	3.9	2	2	0	7.9
Trading	Count	**20**	**22**	**11**	**0**	**53**
	% within Economic Sector	37.7	41.5	20.8	0	100
	% within Average period the company is hedging	17.2	11.8	11.2	0	13
	% of Total	4.9	5.4	2.7	0	13
Any Other	Count	**2**	**0**	**0**	**2**	**4**
	% within Economic Sector	50	0	0	50	100
	% within Average period the company is hedging	1.7	0	0	28.6	1
	% of Total	0.5	0	0	0.5	1
Total	Count	**116**	**186**	**98**	**7**	**407**
	% within Economic Sector	28.5	45.7	24.1	1.7	100
	% within Average period the company is hedging	100	100	100	100	100
	% of Total	28.5	45.7	24.1	1.7	100

Source: Calculations Done by Researcher

Table A5

Crosstab Analysis of Sector wise Policy of Hedge Ratio

Economic Sectors		Not specific ratio	1-20%	21-40%	41-60%	61-80%	81-100%	Total
Construction	Count	7	4	2	0	0	0	13
	% within Economic Sector	53.8	30.8	15.4	0	0	0	100
	% within Policy of the business regarding hedge ratio in case of forex risk management	3.4	10.8	3.5	0	0	0	3.2
	% of Total	1.7	1	0.5	0	0	0	3.2
Manufacturing	Count	145	24	44	74	13	5	305
	% within Economic Sector	47.5	7.9	14.4	24.3	4.3	1.6	100

	% within Policy of the business regarding hedge ratio in case of forex risk management	71.4	64.9	77.2	84.1	86.7	71.4	74.9
	% of Total	35.6	5.9	10.8	18.2	3.2	1.2	74.9
Services	Count	18	5	3	4	0	2	32
	% within Economic Sector	56.3	15.6	9.4	12.5	0	6.3	100
	% within Policy of the business regarding hedge ratio in case of forex risk management	8.9	13.5	5.3	4.5	0	28.6	7.9
	% of Total	4.4	1.2	0.7	1	0	0.5	7.9
Trading	Count	31	4	8	10	0	0	53
	% within Economic Sector	58.5	7.5	15.1	18.9	0	0	100
	% within Policy of the business regarding hedge ratio in case of forex risk management	15.3	10.8	14	11.4	0	0	13
	% of Total	7.6	1	2	2.5	0	0	13
Any Other	Count	2	0	0	0	2	0	4
	% within Economic Sector	50	0	0	0	50	0	100
	% within Policy of the business regarding hedge ratio in case of forex risk management	1	0	0	0	13.3	0	1
	% of Total	0.5	0	0	0	0.5	0	1
Total	Count	203	37	57	88	15	7	407
	% within Economic Sector	49.9	9.1	14	21.6	3.7	1.7	100
	% within Policy of the business regarding hedge ratio in case of forex risk management	100	100	100	100	100	100	100
	% of Total	49.9	9.1	14	21.6	3.7	1.7	100

Source: Calculations Done by Researcher

Table A6

Crosstab Analysis of Sector wise and Percentage Hedging of Forex Risk Exposure

Economic Sector		0-20%	20-40%	40-60%	60-80%	80-100%	Total
Construction	Count	2	8	2	1	0	13
	% within Economic Sector	15.4	61.5	15.4	7.7	0	100

	% within What Percentage of the exchange rate exposure is Hedged	2.4	9	1.4	1.4	0	3.2
	% of Total	0.5	2	0.5	0.2	0	3.2
Manufacturing	Count	53	58	122	51	21	305
	% within Economic Sector	17.4	19	40.0	16.7	6.9	100
	% within What Percentage of the exchange rate exposure is Hedged	63.1	65.2	87.1	72.9	87.5	74.9
	% of Total	13	14.3	30	12.5	5.2	74.9
Services	Count	12	5	8	6	1	32
	% within Economic Sector	37.5	15.6	25	18.8	3.1	100
	% within What Percentage of the exchange rate exposure is Hedged	14.3	5.6	5.7	8.6	4.2	7.9
	% of Total	2.9	1.2	2	1.5	0.2	7.9
Trading	Count	17	18	8	8	2	53
	% within Economic Sector	32.1	34.	15.1	15.1	3.8	100.
	% within What Percentage of the exchange rate exposure is Hedged	20.2	20.2	5.7	11.4	8.3	13
	% of Total	4.2	4.4	2.	2	0.5	13
Any Other	Count	0	0	0	4	0	4
	% within Economic Sector	0	0	0	100	0	100
	% within What Percentage of the exchange rate exposure is Hedged	0	0	0	5.7	0	1
	% of Total	0	0	0	1	0	1
	Count	84	89	140	70	24	407
	% within Economic Sector	20.6	21.9	34.4	17.2	5.9	100
	% within What Percentage of the exchange rate exposure is Hedged	100	100	100	100	100	100
	% of Total	20.6	21.9	34.4	17.2	5.9	100

Source: Calculations Done by Researcher

Table A7

Crosstab Analysis of Sector wise Readjustment of Hedging Position

Economic Sectors		Daily	Weekly	Monthly	Quarterly	Semi-annually	Yearly	Total
Construction	Count	1	2	4	2	2	2	13
	% within Economic Sector	7.7	15.4	30.8	15.4	15.4	15.4	100
	% within How often do you readjust the hedge	2.9	2.2	2.2	3.2	9.1	15.4	3.2
	% of Total	0.2	0.5	1	0.5	0.5	0.5	3.2
Manufacturing	Count	26	69	139	44	16	11	305

	% within Economic Sector	8.5	22.6	45.6	14.4	5.2	3.6	100
	% within How often do you readjust the hedge	76.5	74.2	76	71	72.7	84.6	74.9
	% of Total	6.4	17	34.2	10.8	3.9	2.7	74.9
Services	Count	4	9	13	4	2	0	32
	% within Economic Sector	12.5	28.1	40.6	12.5	6.3	0	100
	% within How often do you readjust the hedge	11.8	9.7	7.1	6.5	9.1	0	7.9
	% of Total	1	2.2	3.2	1	0.5	0	7.9
Trading	Count	3	13	27	8	2	0	53
	% within Economic Sector	5.7	24.5	50.9	15.1	3.8	0	100
	% within How often do you readjust the hedge	8.8	14	14.8	12.9	9.1	0	13
	% of Total	0.7	3.2	6.6	2	0.5	0	13
Any Other	Count	0	0	0	4	0	0	4
	% within Economic Sector	0	0	0	100.0	0	0	100
	% within How often do you readjust the hedge	0	0	0	6.5	0	0	1
	% of Total	0	0	0	1	0	0	1
Total	Count	34	93	183	62	22	13	407
	% within Economic Sector	8.4	22.9	45	15.2	5.4	3.2	100
	% within How often do you readjust the hedge	100	100	100	100	100	100	100
	% of Total	8.4	22.9	45	15.2	5.4	3.2	100

Source: Calculations Done by Researcher

Table A8

Crosstab Sector wise Execution of Forex Risk Hedging Strategy

Economic Sectors		There is nothing fixed timeline for execution strategy	At the time of submitting bid	At the time when an order is received from the customer	At the time when revenue is realized from the customer	Total
Construction	Count	4	9	0	0	13
	% within Economic Sector	30.8	69.2	0.0	0.0	100

	% within Hedging execution strategy	2.3	7.1	0.0	0.0	3.2
	% of Total	1.	2.2	0.0	0.0	3.2
Manufacturing	Count	138	80	49	38	305
	% within Economic Sector	45.2	26.2	16.1	12.5	100
	% within Hedging execution strategy	78	63.5	86	80.9	74.9
	% of Total	33.9	19.7	12	9.3	74.9
Services	Count	10	18	2	2	32
	% within Economic Sector	31.3	56.3	6.3	6.3	100
	% within Hedging execution strategy	5.6	14.3	3.5	4.3	7.9
	% of Total	2.5	4.4	0.5	0.5	7.9
Trading	Count	21	19	6	7	53
	% within Economic Sector	39.6	35.8	11.3	13.2	100
	% within Hedging execution strategy	11.9	15.1	10.5	14.9	13
	% of Total	5.2	4.7	1.5	1.7	13
Any Other	Count	4	0	0	0	4
	% within Economic Sector	100	0	0.0	0.0	100
	% within Hedging execution strategy	2.3	0	0.0	0.0	1
	% of Total	1	0	0.0	0.0	1
Total	Count	177	126	57	47	407
	% within Economic Sector	43.5	31	14	11.5	100.0
	% within Hedging execution strategy	100	100	100	100	100
	% of Total	43.5	31	14	11.5	100

Source: Calculations Done by Researcher

Table A9

Crosstab Analysis of Turnover wise and Awareness Regarding Forex Risk Exposure Management

Annual Turnover (in terms of Indian Rupee)		Yes, Fully Aware	Yes, but Partially aware	Not aware about the concept of forex risk management	Total
Less Than 5 Crore	Count	6	17	9	32
	% within Annual Turnover (in terms of Indian Rupee)	18.8	53.1	28.1	100

	% within Aware	9.8	7.6	7.4	7.9
	% of Total	1.5	4.2	2.2	7.9
5-10	Count	10	33	10	53
	% within Annual Turnover (in terms of Indian Rupee)	18.9	62.3	18.9	100
	% within Aware	16.4	14.7	8.2	13
	% of Total	2.5	8.1	2.5	13
10-15	Count	6	26	9	41
	% within Annual Turnover (in terms of Indian Rupee)	14.6	63.4	22	100
	% within Aware	9.8	11.6	7.4	10.1
	% of Total	1.5	6.4	2.2	10.1
15-20	Count	2	23	4	29
	% within Annual Turnover (in terms of Indian Rupee)	6.9	79.3	13.8	100
	% within Aware	3.3	10.3	3.3	7.1
	% of Total	0.5	5.7	1	7.1
20-25	Count	5	3	0	8
	% within Annual Turnover (in terms of Indian Rupee)	62.5	37.5	0	100
	% within Aware	8.2	1.3	0	2
	% of Total	1.2	0.7	0	2
25-30	Count	3	16	12	31
	% within Annual Turnover (in terms of Indian Rupee)	9.7	51.6	38.7	100
	% within Aware	4.9	7.1	9.8	7.6
	% of Total	0.7	3.9	2.9	7.6
30-35	Count	3	5	10	18
	% within Annual Turnover (in terms of Indian Rupee)	16.7	27.8	55.6	100
	% within Aware	4.9	2.2	8.2	4.4
	% of Total	0.7	1.2	2.5	4.4
35-40	Count	1	3	5	9
	% within Annual Turnover (in terms of Indian Rupee)	11.1	33.3	55.6	100
	% within Aware	1.6	1.3	4.1	2.2
	% of Total	0.2	0.7	1.2	2.2
40-45	Count	3	4	5	12
	% within Annual Turnover (in terms of Indian Rupee)	25	33.3	41.7	100
	% within Aware	4.9	1.8	4.1	2.9
	% of Total	0.7	1	1.2	2.9

45-50	Count	1	6	8	15
	% within Annual Turnover (in terms of Indian Rupee)	6.7	40	53.3	100
	% within Aware	1.6	2.7	6.6	3.7
	% of Total	0.2	1.5	2	3.7
50-100	Count	4	31	19	54
	% within Annual Turnover (in terms of Indian Rupee)	7.4	57.4	35.2	100
	% within Aware	6.6	13.8	15.6	13.3
	% of Total	1	7.6	4.7	13.3
Above 100	Count	17	57	31	105
	% within Annual Turnover (in terms of Indian Rupee)	16.2	54.3	29.5	100
	% within Aware	27.9	25.4	25.4	25.8
	% of Total	4.2	14	7.6	25.8
Total	Count	61	224	122	407
	% within Annual Turnover (in terms of Indian Rupee)	15	55	30	100
	% within Aware	100	100	100	100
	% of Total	15	55.0	30	100

Source: Calculations Done by Researcher

Table A10

Crosstab Analysis of Turnover and Existence of Forex Risk Management Policy

Annual Turnover (in terms of Indian Rupee)		Yes	No	No, but currently it is under consideration and soon will be in place	Total
Less Than 5 Crore	Count	6	20	6	32
	% within Annual Turnover (in terms of Indian Rupee)	18.8	62.5	18.8	100
	% within Policy	8	6.7	18.8	7.9
	% of Total	1.5	4.9	1.5	7.9
5-10	Count	12	33	8	53
	% within Annual Turnover (in terms of Indian Rupee)	22.6	62.3	15.1	100
	% within Policy	16	11	25	13
	% of Total	2.9	8.1	2	13
10-15	Count	10	29	2	41

	% within Annual Turnover (in terms of Indian Rupee)	24.4	70.7	4.9	100
	% within Policy	13.3	9.7	6.3	10.1
	% of Total	2.5	7.1	0.5	10.1
15-20	Count	13	15	1	29
	% within Annual Turnover (in terms of Indian Rupee)	44.8	51.7	3.4	100
	% within Policy	17.3	5	3.1	7.1
	% of Total	3.2	3.7	0.2	7.1
20-25	Count	0	6	2	8
	% within Annual Turnover (in terms of Indian Rupee)	0	75	25	100
	% within Policy	0	2	6.3	2
	% of Total	0	1.5	0.5	2
25-30	Count	3	24	4	31
	% within Annual Turnover (in terms of Indian Rupee)	9.7	77.4	12.9	100
	% within Policy	4	8	12.5	7.6
	% of Total	0.7	5.9	1	7.6
30-35	Count	0	18	0	18
	% within Annual Turnover (in terms of Indian Rupee)	0	100	0	100
	% within Policy	0	6	0	4.4
	% of Total	0	4.4	0	4.4
35-40	Count	1	8	0	9
	% within Annual Turnover (in terms of Indian Rupee)	11.1	88.9	0	100
	% within Policy	1.3	2.7	0	2.2
	% of Total	0.2	2.0	0	2.2
40-45	Count	1	9	2	12
	% within Annual Turnover (in terms of Indian Rupee)	8.3	75	16.7	100
	% within Policy	1.3	3	6.3	2.9
	% of Total	0.2	2.2	0.5	2.9
45-50	Count	1	14	0	15
	% within Annual Turnover (in terms of Indian Rupee)	6.7	93.3	0	100
	% within Policy	1.3	4.7	0	3.7
	% of Total	0.2	3.4	0	3.7
50-100	Count	10	44	0	54
	% within Annual Turnover (in terms of Indian Rupee)	18.5	81.5	0	100
	% within Policy	13.3	14.7	0	13.3

		2.5	10.8	0	13.3
	% of Total	2.5	10.8	0	13.3
	Count	**18**	**80**	**7**	**105**
Above 100	% within Annual Turnover (in terms of Indian Rupee)	17.1	76.2	6.7	100.
	% within Policy	24.0	26.7	21.9	25.8
	% of Total	4.4	19.7	1.7	25.8
	Count	**75**	**300**	**32**	**407**
Total	% within Annual Turnover (in terms of Indian Rupee)	18.4	73.7	7.9	100
	% within Policy	100	100	100	100
	% of Total	18.4	73.7	7.9	100

Source: Calculations Done by Researcher

Table A11

Crosstab Analysis of Turnover wise and Frequency of Measuring Forex Risk Exposure

			Always	Often	Sometimes	Rarely	Never	Total
Less Than 5 Crore		Count	3	6	15	2	6	32
		% within Annual Turnover (in terms of Indian Rupee)	9.4	18.8	46.9	6.3	18.8	100
		% within How frequently the forex risk exposure is	4.8	5.6	10.1	4.7	13	7.9
		% of Total	0.7	1.5	3.7	0.5	1.5	7.9
5-10		Count	7	11	23	9	3	53
		% within Annual Turnover (in terms of Indian Rupee)	13.2	20.8	43.4	17	5.7	100
		% within How frequently the forex risk exposure is	11.3	10.3	15.4	20.9	6.5	13
		% of Total	1.7	2.7	5.7	2.2	0.7	13
10-15		Count	2	8	20	2	9	41
		% within Annual Turnover (in terms of Indian Rupee)	4.9	19.5	48.8	4.9	22	100
		% within How frequently the forex risk exposure is	3.2	7.5	13.4	4.7	19.6	10.1
		% of Total	0.5	2.0	4.9	0.5	2.2	10.1
15-20		Count	1	8	12	1	7	29
		% within Annual Turnover (in terms of Indian Rupee)	3.4	27.6	41.4	3.4	24.1	100
		% within How frequently the	1.6%	7.5%	8.1%	2.3%	15.2%	7.1%

			Less than 90 Days	90 Days	180 Days	360 Days	Total
Annual Turnover (in terms of Indian Rupee)	Less Than 5 Crore	Count	19	7	6	0	32
		% within Annual Turnover (in terms of Indian Rupee)	59.4	21.9	18.8	0	100
		% within Average period the company is hedging	16.4	3.8	6.1	0.	7.9
		% of Total	4.7	1.7	1.5	0	7.9
	5-10	Count	22	20	11	0	53
		% within Annual Turnover (in terms of Indian Rupee)	41.5	37.7	20.8	0	100
		% within Average period the company is hedging	19	10.8	11.2	0	13
		% of Total	5.4	4.9	2.7	0	13
	10-15	Count	10	21	9	1	41
		% within Annual Turnover (in terms of Indian Rupee)	24.4	51.2	22	2.4	100
		% within Average period the company is hedging	8.6	11.3	9.2	14.3	10.1
		% of Total	2.5	5.2	2.2	0.2	10.1
	15-20	Count	14	12	3	0	29
		% within Annual Turnover (in terms of Indian Rupee)	48.3	41.4	10.3	0	100
		% within Average period the company is hedging	12.1	6.5	3.1	0	7.1
		% of Total	3.4	2.9	0.7	0.	7.1
	20-25	Count	2	3	3	0	8
		% within Annual Turnover (in terms of Indian Rupee)	25.	37.5	37.5	0	100

		% within Average period the company is hedging	1.7	1.6	3.1	0.0	2
		% of Total	0.5	0.7	0	0	2
	25-30	Count	**8**	**19**	**2**	**2**	**31**
		% within Annual Turnover (in terms of Indian Rupee)	25.8	61.3	6.5	6.5	100
		% within Average period the company is hedging	6.9	10.2	2	28.6	7.6
		% of Total	2.	4.7	0.5	0.5	7.6
	30-35	Count	**1**	**12**	**5**	**0**	**18**
		% within Annual Turnover (in terms of Indian Rupee)	5.6	66.7	27.8	0	100
		% within Average period the company is hedging	0.9	6.5	5.1	0	4.4
		% of Total	0.2	2.9	1.2	0	4.4
	35-40	Count	**4**	**5**	**0**	**0**	**9**
		% within Annual Turnover (in terms of Indian Rupee)	44.4	55.6	0	0	100
		% within Average period the company is hedging	3.4	2.7	0	0	2.2
		% of Total	1	1.2	0	0	2.2
	40-45	Count	**3**	**5**	**4**	**0**	**12**
		% within Annual Turnover (in terms of Indian Rupee)	25	41.7	33.3	0	100
		% within Average period the company is hedging	2.6	2.7	4.1	0.0	2.9
		% of Total	0.7	1.2	1.0	0.0	2.9
	45-50	Count	**6**	**7**	**2**	**0**	**15**

		% within Annual Turnover (in terms of Indian Rupee)	40	46.7	13.3	0	100
		% within Average period the company is hedging	5.2	3.8	2	0	3.7
		% of Total	1.5	1.7	0.5	0	3.7
	50-100	Count	9	30	15	0	54
		% within Annual Turnover (in terms of Indian Rupee)	16.7	55.6	27.8	0	100
		% within Average period the company is hedging	7.8	16.1	15.3	0	13.3
		% of Total	2.2	7.4	3.7	0	13.3
	Above 100	Count	18	45	38	4	105
		% within Annual Turnover (in terms of Indian Rupee)	17.1	42.9	36.2	3.8	100
		% within Average period the company is hedging	15.5	24.2	38.8	57.1	25.8
		% of Total	4.4	11.1	9.3	1	25.8
Total		Count	116	186	98	7	407
		% within Annual Turnover (in terms of Indian Rupee)	28.5	45.7	24.1	1.7	100
		% within Average period the company is hedging	100	100	100	100	100
		% of Total	28.5	45.7	24.1	1.7	100

Source: Calculations Done by Researcher

Table A12

Crosstab Analysis of Turnover wise Policy of Hedge Ratio

Annual Turnover (in terms of Indian Rupee)	Turnover	f forex risk management						Total
		Not specific ratio	1-20%	21-40%	41-60%	61-80%	81-100%	
Less Than 5 Crore	Count	21	6	2	3	0	0	32
	% within Annual Turnover (in terms of Indian Rupee)	65.6	18.8	6.3	9.4	0	0	100
	% within Policy of the business regarding hedge ratio in case of forex risk management	10.3	16.2	3.5	3.4	0	0	7.9
	% of Total	5.2	1.5	0.5	0.7	0	0	7.9
5-10	Count	33	7	11	2	0	0	53
	% within Annual Turnover (in terms of Indian Rupee)	62.3	13.2	20.8	3.8	0	0	100
	% within Policy of the business regarding hedge ratio in case of forex risk management	16.3	18.9	19.3	2.3	0	0	13
	% of Total	8.1	1.7	2.7	0.5	0	0	13
10-15	Count	26	7	6	2	0	0	41
	% within Annual Turnover (in terms of Indian Rupee)	63.4	17.1	14.6	4.9	0	0	100
	% within Policy of the business regarding hedge ratio in case of forex risk management	12.8	18.9	10.5	2.3	0	0	10.1
	% of Total	6.4	1.7	1.5	0.5	0	0	10.1
15-20	Count	25	1	1	2	0	0	29
	% within Annual Turnover (in terms of Indian Rupee)	86.2	3.4	3.4	6.9	0	0	100
	% within Policy of the business regarding hedge ratio in case of forex risk management	12.3	2.7	1.8	2.3	0	0	7.1
	% of Total	6.1	0.2	0.2	0.5	0	0	7.1
20-25	Count	7	0	0	1	0	0	8

	% within Annual Turnover (in terms of Indian Rupee)	87.5	0	0	12.5	0	0	100
	% within Policy of the business regarding hedge ratio in case of forex risk management	3.4	0	0	1.1	0	0	2
	% of Total	1.7	0	0	0.2	0	0	2
25-30	Count	15	2	9	4	1	0	31
	% within Annual Turnover (in terms of Indian Rupee)	48.4	6.5	29	12.9	3.2	0	100
	% within Policy of the business regarding hedge ratio in case of forex risk management	7.4	5.4	15.8	4.5	6.7	0	7.6
	% of Total	3.7	0.5	2.2	1	0.2	0	7.6
30-35	Count	9	3	2	4	0	0	18
	% within Annual Turnover (in terms of Indian Rupee)	50	16.7	11.1	22.2	0	0	100
	% within Policy of the business regarding hedge ratio in case of forex risk management	4.4	8.1	3.5	4.5	0	0	4.4
	% of Total	2.2	0.7	0.5	1	0	0	4.4
35-40	Count	8	0	0	1	0	0	9
	% within Annual Turnover (in terms of Indian Rupee)	88.9	0	0	11.1	0	0	100
	% within Policy of the business regarding hedge ratio in case of forex risk management	3.9	0	0	1.1	0	0	2.2
	% of Total	2	0	0	0.2	0.	0	2.2
40-45	Count	4	3	2	3	0	0	12
	% within Annual Turnover (in terms of Indian Rupee)	33.3	25	16.7	25	0	0	100
	% within Policy of the business regarding hedge ratio in case of forex risk management	2	8.1	3.5	3.4	0	0	2.9
	% of Total	1	0.7	0.5	0.7	0	0	2.9
45-50	Count	8	0	0	7	0	0	15
	% within Annual Turnover (in terms of Indian Rupee)	53.3	0	0	46.7	0	0	100

% within Policy of the business regarding hedge ratio in case of forex risk management	3.9	0	0	8	0	0	3.7
% of Total	2	0	0	1.7	0	0	3.7
50-100 Count	**16**	**3**	**9**	**19**	**6**	**1**	**54**
% within Annual Turnover (in terms of Indian Rupee)	29.6	5.6	16.7	35.2	11.1	1.9	100
% within Policy of the business regarding hedge ratio in case of forex risk management	7.9	8.1	15.8	21.6	40	14.3	13.3
% of Total	3.9	0.7	2.2	4.7	1.5	0.2	13.3
Above 100 Count	**31**	**5**	**15**	**40**	**8**	**6**	**105**
% within Annual Turnover (in terms of Indian Rupee)	29.5	4.8	14.3	38.1	7.6	5.7	100
% within Policy of the business regarding hedge ratio in case of forex risk management	15.3	13.5	26.3	45.5	53.3	85.7	25.8
% of Total	7.6	1.2	3.7	9.8	2	1.5	25.8
Count	**203**	**37**	**57**	**88**	**15**	**7**	**407**
% within Annual Turnover (in terms of Indian Rupee)	49.9	9.1	14	21.6	3.7	1.7	100
% within Policy of the business regarding hedge ratio in case of forex risk management	100	100	100	100	100	100	100
% of Total	49.9	9.1	14.0	21.6	3.7	1.7	100

Table A13

Crosstab Analysis of Turnover wise and Percentage Hedging of Forex Risk Exposure

Annual Turnover (in terms of Indian Rupee)		0-20%	20-40%	40-60%	60-80%	80-100%	Total
Less Than 5 Crore	Count	16	9	6	1	0	32
	% within Annual Turnover (in terms of Indian Rupee)	50.	28.1	18.8	3.1	0	100

	% within What Percentage of the exchange rate exposure is Hedged	19	10.1	4.3	1.4	0	7.9
	% of Total	3.9	2.2	1.5	0.2	0.0	7.9
5-10	Count	**17**	**18**	**14**	**4**	**0**	**53**
	% within Annual Turnover (in terms of Indian Rupee)	32.1	34	26.4	7.5	0	100
	% within What Percentage of the exchange rate exposure is Hedged	20.2	20.2	10	5.7	0	13
	% of Total	4.2	4.4	3.4	1	0	13
10-15	Count	**13**	**9**	**13**	**5**	**1**	**41**
	% within Annual Turnover (in terms of Indian Rupee)	31.7	22	31.7	12.2	2.4	100
	% within What Percentage of the exchange rate exposure is Hedged	15.5	10.1	9.3	7.1	4.2	10.1
	% of Total	3.2	2.2	3.2	1.2	0.2	10.1
15-20	Count	8	13	5	1	2	29
	% within Annual Turnover (in terms of Indian Rupee)	27.6	44.8	17.2	3.4	6.9	100
	% within What Percentage of the exchange rate exposure is Hedged	9.5	14.6	3.6	1.4	8.3	7.1
	% of Total	2	3.2	1.2	0.2	0.5	7.1
20-25	Count	**0**	**3**	**5**	**0**	**0**	**8**
	% within Annual Turnover (in terms of Indian Rupee)	0	37.5	62.5	0	0	100
	% within What Percentage of the exchange rate exposure is Hedged	0	3.4	3.6	0	0	2
	% of Total	0.0	0.7	1.2	0	0	2
25-30	Count	**10**	**10**	**7**	**2**	**2**	**31**
	% within Annual Turnover (in terms of Indian Rupee)	32.3	32.3	22.6	6.5	6.5	100
	% within What Percentage of the exchange rate exposure is Hedged	11.9	11.2	5.0	2.9	8.3	7.6
	% of Total	2.5	2.5	1.7	0.5	0.5	7.6
30-35	Count	**4**	**3**	**8**	**2**	**1**	**18**
	% within Annual Turnover (in terms of Indian Rupee)	22.2	16.7	44.4	11.1	5.6	100
	% within What Percentage of the exchange rate exposure is Hedged	4.8	3.4	5.7	2.9	4.2	4.4
	% of Total	1	0.7	2	0.5	0.2	4.4
35-40	Count	**0**	**1**	**6**	**2**	**0**	**9**
	% within Annual Turnover (in terms of Indian Rupee)	0	11.1	66.7	22.2	0	100

	% within What Percentage of the exchange rate exposure is Hedged	0	1.1	4.3	2.9	0	2.2
	% of Total	0	0.2	1.5	0.5	0	2.2
40-45	Count	2	3	1	2	4	12
	% within Annual Turnover (in terms of Indian Rupee)	16.7	25	8.3	16.7	33.3	100
	% within What Percentage of the exchange rate exposure is Hedged	2.4	3.4	0.7	2.9	16.7	2.9
	% of Total	0.5	0.7	0.2	0.5	1	2.9
45-50	Count	2	1	8	3	1	15
	% within Annual Turnover (in terms of Indian Rupee)	13.3	6.7	53.3	20	6.7	100
	% within What Percentage of the exchange rate exposure is Hedged	2.4	1.1	5.7	4.3	4.2	3.7
	% of Total	0.5	0.2	2	0.7	0.2	3.7
50-100	Count	3	3	31	15	2	54
	% within Annual Turnover (in terms of Indian Rupee)	5.6	5.6	57.4	27.8	3.7	100
	% within What Percentage of the exchange rate exposure is Hedged	3.6	3.4	22.1	21.4	8.3	13.3
	% of Total	0.7	0.7	7.6	3.7	0.5	13.3
Above 100	Count	9	16	36	33	11	105
	% within Annual Turnover (in terms of Indian Rupee)	8.6	15.2	34.3	31.4	10.5	100
	% within What Percentage of the exchange rate exposure is Hedged	10.7	18	25.7	47.1	45.8	25.8
	% of Total	2.2	3.9	8.8	8.1	2.7	25.8
Total	Count	84	89	140	70	24	407
	% within Annual Turnover (in terms of Indian Rupee)	20.6	21.9	34.4	17.2	5.9	100
	% within What Percentage of the exchange rate exposure is Hedged	100	100	100	100	100	100
	% of Total	20.6	21.9	34.4	17.2	5.9	100

Source: Calculations Done by Researcher

Table A14

Crosstab Analysis of Turnover wise Readjustment of Hedging Position

Annual Turnover (in terms of Indian Rupee)		Readjust the hedge						Total
		Daily	Weekly	Monthly	Quarterly	Semi-annually	Yearly	
Less Than 5	Count	7	7	10	4	2	2	32

Crore	% within Annual Turnover (in terms of Indian Rupee)	21.9	21.9	31.3	12.5	6.3	6.3	100
	% within How often do you readjust the hedge	20.6	7.5	5.5	6.5	9.1	15.4	7.9
	% of Total	1.7	1.7	2.5	1	0.5	0.5	7.9
5-10	Count	3	11	23	10	4	2	53
	% within Annual Turnover (in terms of Indian Rupee)	5.7	20.8	43.4	18.9	7.5	3.8	100
	% within How often do you readjust the hedge	8.8	11.8	12.6	16.1	18.2	15.4	13
	% of Total	0.7	2.7	5.7	2.5	1.	0.5	13
10-15	Count	0	10	25	2	2	2	41
	% within Annual Turnover (in terms of Indian Rupee)	0	24.4	61	4.9	4.9	4.9	100
	% within How often do you readjust the hedge	0	10.8	13.7	3.2	9.1	15.4	10.1
	% of Total	0	2.5	6.1	0.5	0.5	0.5	10.1
15-20	Count	1	3	17	7	0	1	29
	% within Annual Turnover (in terms of Indian Rupee)	3.4	10.3	58.6	24.1	0	3.4	100
	% within How often do you readjust the hedge	2.9	3.2	9.3	11.3	0	7.7	7.1
	% of Total	0.2	0.7	4.2	1.7	0	0.2	7.1
20-25	Count	0	2	2	2	0	2	8
	% within Annual Turnover (in terms of Indian Rupee)	0	25	25	25	0	25	100
	% within How often do you readjust the hedge	0	2.2	1.1	3.2	0	15.4	2
	% of Total	0	0.5	0.5	0.5	0	0.5	2
25-30	Count	4	14	10	2	1	0	31
	% within Annual Turnover (in terms of Indian Rupee)	12.9	45.2	32.3	6.5	3.2	0	100
	% within How often do you readjust the hedge	11.8	15.1	5.5	3.2	4.5	0	7.6
	% of Total	1	3.4	2.5	0.5	0.2	0	7.6
30-35	Count	8	0	4	2	3	1	18

	% within Annual Turnover (in terms of Indian Rupee)	44.4	0	22.2	11.1	16.7	5.6	100
	% within How often do you readjust the hedge	23.5	0	2.2	3.2	13.6	7.7	4.4
	% of Total	2	0	1	0	0.7	0.2	4.4
35-40	Count	0	1	5	3	0	0	9
	% within Annual Turnover (in terms of Indian Rupee)	0	11.1	55.6	33.3	0	0	100
	% within How often do you readjust the hedge	0	1.1	2.7	4.8	0	0	2.2
	% of Total	0	0.2	1.2	0.7	0	0	2.2
40-45	Count	2	2	5	0	1	2	12
	% within Annual Turnover (in terms of Indian Rupee)	16.7	16.7	41.7	0	8.3	16.7	100
	% within How often do you readjust the hedge	5.9	2.2	2.7	0	4.5	15.4	2.9
	% of Total	0.5	0.5	1.2	0	0.2	0.5	2.9
45-50	Count	1	4	4	2	4	0	15
	% within Annual Turnover (in terms of Indian Rupee)	6.7	26.7	26.7	13.3	26.7	0	100
	% within How often do you readjust the hedge	2.9	4.3	2.2	3.2	18.2	0.0	3.7
	% of Total	0.2	1	1	0.5	1	0	3.7
50-100	Count	4	11	28	10	1	0	54
	% within Annual Turnover (in terms of Indian Rupee)	7.4	20.4	51.9	18.5	1.9	0	100
	% within How often do you readjust the hedge	11.8	11.8	15.3	16.1	4.5	0	13.3
	% of Total	1	2.7	6.9	2.5	0.2	0	13.3
Above 100	Count	4	28	50	18	4	1	105
	% within Annual Turnover (in terms of Indian Rupee)	3.8	26.7	47.6	17.1	3.8	1	100
	% within How often do you readjust the hedge	11.8	30.1	27.3	29	18.2	7.7	25.8
	% of Total	1	6.9	12.3	4.4	1	0.2	25.8
Total	Count	34	93	183	62	22	13	407

		8.4	22.9	45	15.2	5.4	3.2	100
	% within Annual Turnover (in terms of Indian Rupee)	8.4	22.9	45	15.2	5.4	3.2	100
	% within How often do you readjust the hedge	100	100	100	100	100	100	100
	% of Total	8.4	22.9	45	15.2	5.4	3.2	100

Source: Calculations Done by Researcher

Table A15

Crosstab Analysis of Turnover wise Execution of Forex Risk Hedging Strategy

Annual Turnover (in terms of Indian Rupee)		Strategy				Total
		There is nothing fixed timeline for execution strategy	At the time of submitting bid	At the time when an order is received from the customer	At the time when revenue is realized from the customer	
Less Than 5 Crore	Count	9	15	4	4	32
	% within Annual Turnover (in terms of Indian Rupee)	28.1	46.9	12.5	12.5	100
	% within Hedging execution strategy	5.1	11.9	7	8.5	7.9
	% of Total	2.2	3.7	1	1	7.9
5-10	Count	16	27	5	5	53
	% within Annual Turnover (in terms of Indian Rupee)	30.2	50.9	9.4	9.4	100
	% within Hedging execution strategy	9.0	21.4	8.8	10.6	13
	% of Total	3.9	6.6	1.2	1.2	13
10-15	Count	12	14	10	5	41
	% within Annual Turnover (in terms of Indian Rupee)	29.3	34.1	24.4	12.2	100
	% within Hedging execution strategy	6.8	11.1	17.5	10.6	10.1
	% of Total	2.9	3.4	2.5	1.2	10.1
15-20	Count	3	18	6	2	29
	% within Annual Turnover (in terms of Indian Rupee)	10.3	62.1	20.7	6.9	100
	% within Hedging execution strategy	1.7	14.3	10.5	4.3	7.1
	% of Total	0.7	4.4	1.5	0.5	7.1
20-25	Count	7	1	0	0	8

	% within Annual Turnover (in terms of Indian Rupee)	87.5	12.5	0	0	100
	% within Hedging execution strategy	4.0	0.8	0	0	2
	% of Total	1.7	0.2	0	0	2
25-30	Count	**15**	**3**	**3**	**10**	**31**
	% within Annual Turnover (in terms of Indian Rupee)	48.4	9.7	9.7	32.3	100
	% within Hedging execution strategy	8.5	2.4	5.3	21.3	7.6
	% of Total	3.7	0.7	0.7	2.5	7.6
30-35	Count	**11**	**3**	**2**	**2**	**18**
	% within Annual Turnover (in terms of Indian Rupee)	61.1	16.7	11.1	11.1	100
	% within Hedging execution strategy	6.2	2.4	3.5	4.3	4.4
	% of Total	2.7	0.7	0.5	0.5	4.4
35-40	Count	**6**	**1**	**2**	**0**	**9**
	% within Annual Turnover (in terms of Indian Rupee)	66.7	11.1	22.2	0	100
	% within Hedging execution strategy	3.4	0.8	3.5	0	2.2
	% of Total	1.5	0.2	0.5	0	2.2
40-45	Count	**6**	**3**	**2**	**1**	**12**
	% within Annual Turnover (in terms of Indian Rupee)	50	25	16.7	8.3	100
	% within Hedging execution strategy	3.4	2.4	3.5	2.1	2.9
	% of Total	1.5	0.7	0.5	0.2	2.9
45-50	Count	11	4	0	0	15
	% within Annual Turnover (in terms of Indian Rupee)	73.3	26.7	0	0.0	100
	% within Hedging execution strategy	6.2	3.2	0	0	3.7
	% of Total	2.7	1	0	0	3.7
50-100	Count	**32**	**11**	**3**	**8**	**54**
	% within Annual Turnover (in terms of Indian Rupee)	59.3	20.4	5.6	14.8	100
	% within Hedging execution strategy	18.1	8.7	5.3	17	13.3
	% of Total	7.9	2.7	0.7	2.0	13.3
Above 100	Count	**49**	**26**	**20**	**10**	**105**

% within Annual Turnover (in terms of Indian Rupee)	46.7	24.8	19.0	9.5	100
% within Hedging execution strategy	27.7	20.6	35.1	21.3	25.8
% of Total	12.0	6.4	4.9	2.5	25.8
Count	**177**	**126**	**57**	**47**	**407**
% within Annual Turnover (in terms of Indian Rupee)	43.5	31	14	11.5	100
% within Hedging execution strategy	100	100	100	100	100
% of Total	43.5	31	14	11.5	100

Source: Calculations Done by Researcher

Appendix II

Details of Research Papers Published and Presented

Papers Published in Journals

1. Chugh Aman, Mehta Kiran and Sharma Renuka, "Management of Forex Risk Exposure: A Study of SMEs and Unlisted Non-Financial Firms in India", *International Journal of Applied Business and Economic Research* **(SCOPUS)**, 15 (9), 2017, 43-54

2. Chugh Aman, Mehta Kiran and Sharma Renuka, "Forex Risk Management by SMEs and Unlisted Non- nancial Firms: A Literature Survey," *Journal of Technology Management for Growing Economies*, 8(2):9, October, 2017, 7-39

Papers Accepted for Publication

3. Chugh Aman, Mehta Kiran and Sharma Renuka, "Managing Forex Risk Exposure: A Study of SMEs and Unlisted Non-Financial Firms in India", *International Journal of Applied Business and Economic Research* (2018) **(SCOPUS).**

Papers Presented in Conferences

4. Chugh Aman, Mehta Kiran and Sharma Renuka, "Managing Forex Risk Exposure: A Study on SMEs and Unlisted Non-financial firms in India" CUDC-Chitkara University Doctoral Consortium (13th May 2017)

5. Chugh Aman, Mehta Kiran and Sharma Renuka, "Management of Forex Risk Exposure by SMEs and Unlisted Non-Financial Firms in India" 20th International Conference on "Sustainable Growth, Innovation & Revolution in the New Millennium" (IC-SGIRNM) at JAIPUR (Rajasthan), India during March 25-26, 2017.

6. Chugh Aman, Mehta Kiran and Sharma Renuka, "Management of Forex Risk Exposure: A Study of SMEs and Unlisted Non-Financial Firms in India", ICBF International Conference on Banking & Finance (ICBF)-2016, 10th and 11th December 2016

REFERENCES

Aabo, T., Høg, E., & Kuhn, J. (2010). Integrated foreign exchange risk management: the role of import in medium-sized, manufacturing firms. *Journal of Multinational Financial Management, 20*(4-5), 235-250. DOI: 10.1016/j.mulfin.2010.08.002

Aabo, Tom, Jochen Kuhn, Giovanna Zanotti, (2011). Founder family influence and foreign exchange risk management. *International Journal of Managerial Finance,* 7(1), 38-67. doi: 10.1108/17439131111108991.

Abor, J. (2005). Managing foreign exchange risk among Ghanaian firms. *The Journal of Risk Finance,* 6(4), 306-318.

Adler, M., & Dumas, B. (1984). Exposure to Currency Risk: Definition and Measurement. *Financial Management, 13*(2), 41-50.

Akshatha, B. G. (2013). Financial Derivatives: An Innovative Financial Instrument to Hedge Risk. *International Journal of Applied Financial Management Perspectives,* 2(1), 294.

Alkebäck, P. and Hagelin, N., 'Derivatives usage by non-financial firms in Sweden with an international comparison', *Journal of International Financial Management and Accounting* 10(2), 1999, 105–20.

Allayannis, G., and Weston, J.P., (2001). The use of foreign currency derivatives and firm market value, *The Review of Financial Studies,* 14, 1, 243-276.

Allayannis, G., &Ofek, E. (2001). Exchange Rate Exposure, Hedging, and the use of Foreign Currency Derivatives. *Journal of International Money and Finance, a20,* 273-296.

Allayannis, G., and Ofek, E., (2001). Exchange rate exposure, Hedging and the use of currency derivatives.*Journal of International Money and Finance,* March, 20, 2, 273-96.

Allayannis, G., and Weston, J.P., (2001). The use of foreign currency derivatives and firm market value, *The Review of Financial Studies,* 14, 1, 243-276.

Allayannis, G., Ihrig, J., and Weston, J.P., (2001). Exchange rate hedging: Financial versus operational strategies, American Economic Review Papers and Proceedings, 91, 2, 391-395.

Apte, P. G. (2006). *International Financial Management,* Tata McGraw-Hill Publishing Company Limited, New Delhi, (2006).

Bartram, S. M. (2008). What lies beneath: Foreign exchange rate exposure, hedging and cash flows. *Journal of Banking & Finance, 32,* 1508–1521.

Bartram, S. M., & Karolyi, G. A. (2006). The impact of the introduction of the Euro on foreign exchange rate risk exposures. *Journal of Empirical Finance, 13,* 519–549.

Bartram, S., Brown, G., & Conrad, J. (2011).The Effects of Derivatives on Firm Risk and Value. *Journal of Financial and Quantitative Analysis, 46*(4), 967-999. doi:10.1017/S0022109011000275.

Bartram, Söhnke M. and Dufey, Gunter and Frenkel, Michael, A Primer on the Exposure of Nonfinancial Corporations to Foreign Exchange Rate Risk .*Journal of Multinational Financial Management*, 15(4/5), 394-413, October/December 2005.

Batten, J., & Mellor, R. (1993). Foreign Exchange Risk Management Practices and Products Used by Australian Firms. *Journal of International Business Studies, 24*(3), 557-573.

Belk, P. A., & Glaum, M. (1990). The management of foreign exchange risk in UK multinationals: an empirical investigation. *Accounting and Business Research*, 21(81), 3-13.

Berkman, H., Bradbury, M. E., & Magan, S. (1997). An international comparison of derivatives use. Financial Management, 69-73.

Bligh, C. (2012). Foreign currency hedging. Financial Management, 39. http://connection.ebscohost.com/c/articles/74023001/foreign-currency-hedging

Block, S. B. and Gallagher, T. J., 'An empirical study of the utilization of futures and options by corporate management', *Financial Review*, 21(3), 1986, 73–8.

Bodnar, G. M., & Gebhardt, G. (1999). Derivatives Usage in Risk Management by US and German Non-Financial Firms: A Comparative Survey. *Journal of International Financial Management & Accounting*, 10(3), 153-187.

Bodnar, G. M., Consolandi, C., Gabbi, G., &Jaiswal-Dale, A. (2013). Risk Management for Italian Non-Financial Firms: Currency and Interest Rate Exposure. *European Financial Management, 19*(5), 887-910.

Bodnar, G. M., Hayt, G. S., Marston, R. C., & Smithson, C. W. (1995). Wharton survey of derivatives usage by US non-financial firms. *Financial management*, 24(2), 104-114.

Bodnar, G. M., Hayt, G. S. and Marston, R. C., '1998 Wharton survey of financial risk management by U.S. non-financial firms', *Financial Management*, 27(4), 1998, 70–91.

Bradley, K., & Moles, P. (2002). Managing strategic exchange rate exposures: evidence from UK firms. *Managerial Finance*, 28(11), 28-42.

Bris, A., Koskinen, Y., & Nilsson, M. (2006). The Real Effects of the Euro: Evidence from Corporate Investments. *Review of Finance, 10,* 1–37.

Bris, A., Koskinen, Y., & Nilsson, M.(2003). The Euro and Corporate Valuations. Yale School of Management Working Paper.

Brown, G. W. (2001). Managing Foreign Exchange Risk with Derivatives. *Journal of Financial Economics, 60,* 401-448.

Budheshwar Prasad Singhraul , GnyanaRanjanBal (2014) "Hedging of Currency exposure by Indian corporate: evidence from select Indian IT companies" *Indian Streams Research Journal*, 4:4, May, 1-9.

Carter D., Rogers D., and Simkins B., 2006, "Does Hedging Affect Firm Value? Evidence from the US Airline Industry." *Financial Management* 35:1, 53-86

Ceuster, M.J.K., De Durinck, E., Laveren, E., Lodewyckx, J., 2000. A survey into the use of derivatives by large non-financial firms operating in Belgium. *European Financial Management* 6, 301–318.

Carter, D.A., Pantzalis, C., &Simkins, B.J.(2001). Firm wide Risk management of Foreign Exchange Exposure by U.S. Multinational Corporations. SSRN Working paper.

Chan, K. F., Gan, C., & McGraw, P. A. (2003). A Hedging Strategy for New Zealand's Exporters in Transaction Exposure to Currency Risk. *Multinational Finance Journal*, 7(1&2), 25-54.

Choi, J. J., & Prasad, A. M. (1995). Exchange Risk Sensitivity and Its Determinants: A Firm and Industry Analysis of U.S. Multinationals. *Financial Management, 24* (3), 77-88.

Chong, L. L., Chang, X. J., & Tan, S. H. (2014). Determinants of corporate foreign exchange risk hedging. *Managerial Finance*, 40(2), 176-188.

Chow, E. H., & Chen, H. L. (1998). The determinants of foreign exchange rate exposure: Evidence on Japanese firms. *Pacific-Basin Finance Journal, 6,* 153–174.

Churchill Jr., Gilbert A. (2001). Marketing Research, Orlando: The Dryden Press.

Clark, E., & Judge, A. (2008). The Determinants of Foreign Currency Hedging: Does Foreign Currency Debt Induce a Bias? *European Financial Management, 14* (3), 445–469.

Clark, E., & Judge, A. (2009). Foreign Currency Derivatives versus Foreign Currency Debt and the Hedging Premium. . *European Financial Management, 15* (3), 606–642.

Coad, A., & Tamvada, J. P. (2012). Firm growth and barriers to growth among small firms in India. *Small Business Economics*, 39(2), 383-400.

Collier, P., & Davis, E. W. (1985). The management of currency transaction risk by UK multi-national companies. *Accounting and business research*, 15(60), 327-334.

Collier, P., Davis, E. W., Coates, J. B., &Longden, S. G. (1990). The management of currency risk: case studies of US and UK multinationals. *Accounting and Business Research*, 20(79), 206-210.

Crabb, P. R. (2003). Multinational corporations and hedging exchange rate exposure. *International Review of Economics and Finance, 11,* 299–314.

Dangayach, G. S., & Deshmukh, S. G. (2005). Advanced manufacturing technology implementation: evidence from Indian small and medium enterprises (SMEs). *Journal of Manufacturing Technology Management*, 16(5), 483-496.

Das, K., & Pradhan, J. P. (2010). Externally-oriented small and medium enterprises in India: predicament and possibilities. *Economics, Management and Financial Markets, 5*(3), 194-206.

Dash, M., Kodagi, M., &Babu, N. (2008). An Empirical Study of FOREX Risk Management Strategies.

DeMarzo, P. M., and D. Duffie. "Corporate Incentives for Hedging and Hedge Accounting." *Review of Financial Studies*, 8 (1995), 743–771.

Doidge, C., J. M. Griffin, and R. Williamson, 2002, Does exchange rate exposure matter?, working paper, Ohio State University, Arizona State University, and Georgetown University.

Dolde, W., 'The trajectory of corporate financial risk management', *Journal of Applied Corporate Finance*, 6(3), 1993, pp. 33–41.

Du, D., Ng, P., & Zhao, X. (2013). Measuring currency exposure with quantile regression. *Review of Quantitative Finance and Accounting*, 41(3), 549-566. Etteman, Stonehill and Moffett (2004).

Elliott, C. M., & Vaughan, E. J. (1972). *Fundamentals of risk and insurance, 5*: Wiley.

Etteman, D.K. Stonehill, A.I. &Moffet, M.H., 2004. *Multinational Business Finance*, 10th ed., Pearson Education, Inc (Pearson Addison Wesley).

Eng, M.V., Lees, F.A., and Mauer, L.J., 1998, Global Finance, 2nd edition.

Finger. Christopher (1999), "Conditional Approaches for CreditMetrics _ Portfolio Distributions", CreditMetrics_ Monitor. April.

Fraser, S. P., &Pantzalis, C. (2004).Foreign exchange rate exposure of US multinational corporations: a firm-specific approach. *Journal of Multinational Financial Management, 14,* 261-281.

Froot, K. A., Scharfstein, D. S. and Stein, J. C., 'Risk management: coordinating corporate investment and financing policies', *The Journal of Finance*, 48(5), 1993, 1629–58.

Goetz, S. J., & Hu, D. (1996). Economic growth and human capital accumulation: Simultaneity and expanded convergence tests. *Economics Letters, 51*(3), 355-362.

González, L. O., Búa, M. V., Lopez, S. F., &Sandías, A. R. (2007). Why Spanish Firms Hedge with Derivatives: An Examination of Transaction Exposure. *SSRN eLibrary.*

Graham, J.R., and Rogers, D.A., (2002). Do Firms Hedge in Response to Tax Incentives? *Journal of Finance*, 57, 2, 815-839.

Graham, J.R., and Rogers, D.A., (2000). Is Corporate Hedging Consistent with Value-Maximization? An Empirical Analysis. Working paper, Fuqua School of Business, Duke University, January 2000.

Grant, K., & Marshall, A. P. (1997). Large UK companies and derivatives. *European Financial Management*, 3(2), 191-208.

Guay, W., & Kothari, S.P. (2003). How much do firms hedge with derivatives? *Journal of Financial Economics, 70,* 423–461.

Hagelin, N., &Pramborg, B. (2004). Hedging Foreign Exchange Exposure: Risk Reduction from Transaction and Translation Hedging. *Journal of International Financial Management and Accounting, 15* (1), 1-20.

Hakkarainen, A., Kasanen, E. and Puttonen, V., 'Interest rate risk management in major Finnish firms', *European Financial Management*, 3(3), 1997, pp. 255–68.

He, J., & Ng, L. K. (1998). The foreign exchange exposure of Japanese multinational corporations. *The Journal of Finance*, 53(2), 733-753.

Helliar, C. (2004). An analysis of the reasons why UK companies use interest rate and currency swaps. *Journal of applied accounting research, 7*(1), 1-45.

Henderson, C. A. L. L. U. M. (2002). Editorial: Hedging emerging market currency risk. Derivatives Use, Trading & Regulation, 8(1).

Homaifar, G., 2004, *Managing Global Financial and Foreign Exchange Rate Risk*, Wiley Finance, USA

Howton, S. D., & Perfect, S. B. (1998). Currency and interest-rate derivatives use in US firms. *Financial Management*, 111-121.

Hrubošová, E., &Kameníková, B. (2013). Foreign Exchange Risk Management in SME in the Czech Republic. *Advances in Finance and Accounting*, 110-115.

Hu, C., & Wang, P. (2005). The determinants of foreign currency hedging–evidence from Hong Kong non-financial firms. *Asia-Pacific Financial Markets, 12*(1), 91-107. Hughes & MacDonald, 2002;

IlaPatnaik, Ajay Shah, Nirvikar Singh (2016). Foreign Currency Borrowing by Indian Firms: Towards a New Policy Framework, No. 167 05-Apr-16 , NIPF working paper series.

Jalilvand, A. and Switzer, J., 'A global perspective on the use of derivatives for corporate risk management decisions', *Managerial Finance*, 6(3), 2000, 29–38.

International banking : text and cases, Boston, MA : Addison Wesley, ©2002

Hallwood, P. MacDonald, R. and Marsh, I (2000a), "An Assessment of the Causes of the Abandonment of the Gold Standard by the USA in 1933", *Southern Economic Journal*, 67 (2), October, 448-459

Hallwood, P., MacDonald, R. and Marsh, I. (2000b) "Realignment Expectations and the US Dollar: Was there a Peso Problem?", *Journal of Monetary Economics*, 46, 605-620.

Hansen, M. A. (2009). An empirical study of strategic approaches to foreign exchange risk management used by Danish medium-sized non-financial companies. Unpublished Master of Science Thesis. Aarhus School of Business, University of Aarhus.

Jain, P. K., Yadav, S. S., &Rastogi, A. K. (2009). Risk Management Practices of Corporate Firms in India: A Comparative Study of Public Sector, Private Sector Business Houses and Foreign Controlled Firms. Decision (0304-0941), 36(2), 73-97.

Joseph, N. L. (2000). The choice of hedging techniques and the characteristics of UK industrial firms.*Journal of Multinational Financial Management,* 10(2), 161-184.

Judge, A. (2006). The Determinants of Foreign Currency Hedging by U.K. Non-Financial Firms. *Multinational Finance Journal, 10* (1/2), 1–41.

Judge, A. (2015). The determinants of foreign currency hedging by UK non-financial firms. *Multinational Finance Journal,* 10(1/2), 1-41.

Kallman, J. (2005). What is risk? Risk Management Magazine, 52(10).

Kim, W., & Sung, T. (2005). What makes firms manage FX risk? *Emerging Markets Review, 6,* 263– 288.

Kim, Y. S., Mathur, I., & Nam, J. (2006). Is operational hedging a substitute for or a Complement to financial hedging? *Journal of Corporate Finance, 12,* 834– 853.

Kula, V. (2005).Foreign exchange exposure perception and management of Turkish SMEs. *Journal of Small Business and Entrepreneurship,* 18(4), 416-437.

Kumar, B. S., &Malyadri, G. (2013). A STUDY ON CURRENCY FUTURES. International *Journal of Applied Financial Management Perspectives,* 2(3), 548.

Leland, H., 1998, "Agency costs, risk management, and capital structure", *Journal of Finance* 53, 1213-1243

Leland, Hayne E., (1998), Agency Costs, Risk Management, and Capital Structure, *Journal of Finance,* 53 (4), 1213-1243.

Leland, L. J. (1960). The Theory of Hedging and Speculation in Commodity Futures. The Review of Economic Studies, 27(3), 139-151.

Liriano Frank Migues (2016), Eighth IFC Conference on *"Statistical implications of the new financial landscape"* Basel, 8–9 September 2016 ,"The use of Foreign Exchange Derivatives by Exporters and Importers: the Chilean Experience"

Loderer, C., &Pichler, K. (2000). Firms, do you know your currency risk exposure? Survey results. *Journal of Empirical Finance, 7,* 317–344.

Madura, J. (2010). International Financial Management, 10th Edition, South-Western College Publishing.

Makar, S. D., & Huffman, S. P. (2011). Foreign currency risk management practices in US multinationals. *Journal of Applied Business Research* (JABR), 13(2), 73-86.

Malhotra, N. L. (2004). Marketing Research: An Applied Orientation. New Delhi: Pearson Education.

Mallin, C., Ow-Yong, K. and Reynolds, M., 'Derivatives usage in UK non-financial listed companies', *The European Journal of Finance*, 7, 2001, 63–91.

Marshall, A. P. (2000). Foreign exchange risk management in UK, USA and Asia Pacific multinational companies. *Journal of Multinational Financial Management, 10,* 185–211.

Marston, R., 'The effects of industry structure on economic exposure', *Journal of International Money and Finance*, 20, 2001, 149–64.

Mihaljek, D. and Packer, F. (2010), "Derivatives in emerging markets", Bank of International Settlement Quarterly Review, December, 43-58.

McMenamin, J. (2009). Financial Management: an introduction, London: Routledge

McNamee, D. (1997). Risk Management Today and Tomorrow. Management Control Concepts. California, USA.

Modigliani, M. and Miller, M. (1958), "The cost of capital, corporate finance and theory of investment", The American Economic Review, 48(3), 261-297.

Moffett, M.H., Stonehill, A. I., and Eiteman, D.K., 2006, Fundamentals of Multinational Finance, 2nd Edition, Addison Wesley, United States of America.

Moosa, I. A. (2004), *International Finance: An Analytical Approach*, 2 edn, McGraw-Hill, Sydney

Muller, A., &Verschoor, W. F. C. (2006). Asymmetric Foreign Exchange Risk Exposure: Evidence from U.S. Multinational Firms. *Journal of Empirical Finance, 13,* 495–518.

Muller, A., &Verschoor, W. F. C. (2006). Foreign Exchange Risk Exposure: Survey and Suggestions. *Journal of Multinational Financial Management, 16,* 385-410.

Muller, A., &Verschoor, W. F. C. (2007). Asian Foreign Exchange Risk Exposure. *Journal of the Japanese and International Economies, 21,* 16-37.

Mun, K. C., & Morgan, G. E. (1997). Cross-hedging foreign exchange rate risks: The case of deposit money banks in emerging Asian countries. *Pacific-Basin Finance Journal,* 5,215-230.

Myers, 1977; Myers, S. C. (1977). Determinants of corporate borrowing. *Journal of Financial*, Economics, 5(2), 147-175.

Nance, D.R., Smith Jr., C.W., & Smithson, C.W.(1993). On the determinants of corporate hedging. *Journal of Finance 48,* 267– 284.

Nargundkar, R. (2003). Marketing Research. New Delhi: Tata McGraw-Hill.

Nguyen, H., & Faff, R. (2003).Can the Use of Foreign Currency Derivatives Explain Variations in Foreign Exchange Exposure? Evidence from Australian Companies. *Journal of Multinational Financial Management, 13*,193-215.

Nunnally, J. (1978). Psychometric theory. New York: Mc Graw-Hill

Pantzalis, C., Simkins, B.J., & Laux, P. (2001). Operational hedges and the foreign exchange exposure of U.S. multinational corporations. *Journal of International Business Studie, 32*, 793– 812.

Papaioannou, M. G. (2006). Exchange Rate Risk Measurement and Management: Issues and Approaches for Firms. SSRN eLibrary.

P. BalaBhaskaran and P. K. Priyan (2015). Strategies of Indian Firms in Coping with Forex Risk Management: An Inquiry through Case- Research Method by, SDMIMD *Journal of management*, 6(1), March, 13-23.

Pramborg, B. (2005). Foreign exchange risk management by Swedish and Korean nonfinancial firms: A comparative survey. *Pacific-Basin Finance Journal, 13*, 343– 366.

Prasad K, Suprabha KR (2016). Exchange Rate Exposure of Indian Firms Using Capital Market Approach. *Journal of Accounting and Marketing* 5:165. doi:10.4172/2168-9601.1000165

Raghavendra, R. H., &Velmurugan, P. S. (2014). The Determinants of Currency Hedging in Indian IT Firms. *Journal of Business and Financial Affairs*, 3(125), 1-7.

Rajendran, M. (2007). Derivative Use by Banks in INDIA. *Academy of Banking Studies Journal*, 6(1/2), 27-37.

Saito, R., &Schiozer, R. F. (2005). Derivatives Usage and Risk Management by Non-Financial Firms: A Comparison between Brazilian and International Evidence.

Saunders and Cornett (2007) "Financial Markets and Institutions: An Introduction to the Risk management Approach", McGraw Hill Pub. 2007.

Savchenko, O., &Makar, S. (2010). Derivatives Use in the Partial Hedging of Currency Risk: A Firm-Specific Approach to Understanding the Exchange Rate Exposure Puzzle. *Journal of Applied Business Research* (JABR), 26(1), 109-120.

Schiozer, R. F., & Saito, R. (2009). The determinants of currency risk management in Latin American nonfinancial firms. *Emerging Markets Finance and Trade, 45*(1), 49-71.

Shapiro, A. C. (2003). Multinational financial Management,7th ed. New York: Wiley.

Shin, H. H., &Soenen, L. (1999). Exposure to Currency Risk by US Multinational Corporations. *Journal of Multinational Financial Management, 9*, 195–207.

Sivakumar, A., & Sarkar, R. (2008). Corporate hedging for foreign exchange risk in India. In 11th Annual Convention of the Strategic Management Forum, Indian Institute of

Technology, Kanpur, May.

Smith, C. W., &Stulz, R. M. (1985). The Determinants of Firms' Hedging Policies. *The Journal of Financial and Quantitative Analysis, 20*(4), 391-405.

Solnik, Bruno J, 1974, An equilibrium model of the international capital market, *Journal of Economic Theory* 8.4, 500-524.

Solnik, Bruno J, and Dennis McLeavey, International investments, 2004, Pearson

Sonali Madhusmita Mohapatra and Badri Narayan Rath (2017). Exchange Rate Exposure and its Determinants: Evidence from Indian Firms, *The International Trade Journal*, 31(2), 2017.

Stulz, R. M. "Optimal Hedging Policies." *Journal of Financial and Quantitative Analysis*, 19 (1984), 127–140.

Todd, P. R., & Javalgi, R. R. G. (2007). Internationalization of SMEs in India: Fostering entrepreneurship by leveraging information technology. *International Journal of Emerging Markets*, 2(2), 166-180.

TuranErol, AyhanAlgüner, GürayKüçükkocaoğlu. Exchange Rate Exposure of Real Sector Firms in an Emerging Economy. *Journal of Finance and Accounting*. 2013; 1(1):1-12. doi: 10.12691/jfa-1-1-1.

Vasumathy S. (2015). Currency Risk Management Practices of Indian Export SMEs: A Descriptive Study, *Indian Journal of Finance*, 9(8), August 2015

Vaughan, E. J., & Vaughan, T. (2007). Fundamentals of risk and insurance: John Wiley & Sons.

Wang, Z. (2008). Industry hedging level and firm risk management (Doctoral dissertation, Concordia University).

Warwick, D. T.; Lininger, C. A. (1975), The Sample Survey: Theory and Practice, New York: McGraw-Hill.

Worasinchai, L. (2013). What is the Management Attitude of Leading Thai Organizations towards Currency Hedging Strategy in Today's Dynamic Environment?. Management, Leadership and Governance, 340.

Yadav S.S. and Jain P.K. (2000). Corporate practices of risk management in international business operations in India. *South Asian Journal of Management (SAJM)*, 7(1-2),1-14

YEO, K.T., Lai, W.C. (2004). Risk Management Strategies for SME Investing in China: a Singaporean Perspective. IEMC2004, International Engineering Management Conference.

Zikmund, W. (2003). Business research methods 7th ed., Thomson/South-Western: Appendices.

CPSIA information can be obtained
at www.ICGtesting.com
Printed in the USA
BVHW051331180423
662564BV00013B/906